PRODUCTIVITY IN PUBLIC
AND NONPROFIT
ORGANIZATIONS

Strategies and Techniques

Evan M. Berman

SAGE Publications
International Educational and Professional Publisher
Thousand Oaks London New Delhi

For information:

SAGE Publications, Inc.
2455 Teller Road
Thousand Oaks, California 91320
E-mail: order@sagepub.com

SAGE Publications Ltd.
6 Bonhill Street
London EC2A 4PU
United Kingdom

SAGE Publications India Pvt. Ltd.
M-32 Market
Greater Kailash I
New Delhi 110 048 India

Printed in the United States of America

Library of Congress Cataloging-in-Publication Data

Berman, Evan M.
    Productivity in public and nonprofit organizations: Strategies and techniques / by Evan M. Berman.
        p. cm.
    Includes bibliographical references and index.
    ISBN 0-7619-1030-1 (acid-free paper). — ISBN 0-7619-1031-X (pbk. : acid-free paper)
    1. Government productivity. 2. Nonprofit organizations—Labor productivity. I. Title.
    JF1525.P67B47 1998
    352.3'75—dc21   97-33869

98 99 00 01 02 03   10 9 8 7 6 5 4 3 2 1

Acquiring Editor:	Catherine Rossbach
Editorial Assistant:	Kathleen Derby
Production Editor:	Michele Lingre
Production Assistant:	Denise Santoyo
Typesetter/Designer:	Danielle Dillahunt
Indexer:	Molly Hall
Cover Designer:	Ravi Balasuriya

Contents

PART II. FOUNDATIONS

PART III. STRATEGIES

Preface

Public and nonprofit organizations are finding new ways to increase their productivity and responsiveness. The result is that citizens and clients are now able to have more input into decisions about which services are provided and how they are delivered. Citizens and clients now routinely take advantage of improved services in emergency care, public health inspections, and road construction and other functions, as well as comprehensive services provided through partnerships between public and private organizations, one-stop shopping opportunities, and outcome-oriented (rather than rules-driven) organizations. The productivity goals of public and nonprofit organizations are very similar: to be more responsive to citizens and clients, to be more effective and efficient in their service delivery, and to be more timely and cost-effective too. These goals are being followed by city hall, law enforcement agencies, the Internal Revenue Service, nationally acclaimed museums, social service agencies, and other public and nonprofit organizations.

This book examines how managers in public and nonprofit organizations are revitalizing their organizations. It discusses strategies used by senior, midlevel, and supervisory managers to improve productivity. New and enduring strategies are discussed. Analytic techniques are provided with applications as well.

In addition, this book provides new results from a systematic survey among city managers and directors of museums and social service organizations about the use of productivity improvement strategies in these public and nonprofit organizations.

Concern with increasing productivity is not new: Conscientious, professional managers have often sought to improve their services. Yet four trends greatly increase the salience of productivity improvement efforts in recent years. First, and perhaps foremost, is the growing need to regain stakeholder trust in public and nonprofit organizations. Stakeholders are citizens, clients, elected officials, employees, and others who have interests in these organizations. Public trust in the federal government is at a historic low, although trust is somewhat higher in local government and nonprofit organizations. In part distrust is caused by inadequate responsiveness. Second, federal funding has greatly decreased for many programs. This causes many organizations to review their old missions and adopt innovative forms of service delivery and funding, for example, by using partnering and privatization. Third, society is increasingly impatient with lingering problems such as crime, education, environment, and family breakup. These complex problems require new responses: Public and nonprofit organizations experience increasing pressures to formulate more effective responses. Fourth, new tools and strategies have become available such as community-based strategic planning, Total Quality Management, and benchmarking. (New implementation strategies exist as well.) Public and nonprofit organizations expect their managers to be familiar with these strategies.

To suggest that public and nonprofit organizations can be made more effective is not to suggest that they are ineffective, as is sometimes ideologically stated about organizations in the public sector. There are many outstanding public and nonprofit organizations, some of which are described in this book. However, organizations do not always use productivity improvement efforts that might help, and strategies that are used sometimes have mixed success. Productivity improvement can be a learning experience. This book also helps productivity improvement efforts by identifying potential barriers and providing step-by-step guidance as well as by suggesting solutions for frequently encountered situations.

Some scholars and practitioners might question whether a book on productivity improvement is needed that is explicitly tailored to public and nonprofit organizations. How are these organizations different? Why can't business techniques be applied to them in the same manner as in business? The reason is that productivity tools are greatly influenced by the goals of public and nonprofit organizations. Productivity strategies must be adapted to the purposes and contexts of the public and nonprofit sectors, and infused with values from these sectors as well. For example, strategic planning becomes community-based strategic planning, and customer satisfaction becomes client, citizen, taxpayer, and business satisfaction in the public sector. Public and nonprofit organizations seek public rather than private goals, measure success by multiple rather than single standards (effectiveness, efficiency, fairness, and inclusiveness rather than profitability), and are subject to different constraints (for example, dealing with elected officials). Managers and business consultants who fail to appreciate such sectoral differences often fail, exasperated. It should be noted that differences exist between the public and nonprofit sectors as well. For example, nonprofit organizations often have less restrictive human resource policies and are governed by a board of directors rather than elected officials. This book is mindful of differences that exist between the sectors and it also acknowledges differences among organizations within these sectors. There is a lot of variation among public and nonprofit organizations.

The following developments and considerations shape this book. First, the field of productivity is fast paced and ever changing. During the last two decades, productivity has shifted away from earlier emphases on project management and the analytical techniques appropriate for project management. Today, productivity emphasizes strategic leadership, commitment, and innovation as well as analytical tools. As a result, a balance is required among strategic, analytical, and interpersonal skills for productivity improvement. For example, analytical techniques must serve strategic ends and be used in ways that are mindful of garnering support and commitment. Second, this book reflects a change in professional practice: Professionals and students increasingly pursue careers in both public and nonprofit organizations. This book contains applications from each sector, and shows how they are relevant to both sectors. Third, knowledge about productivity improvement efforts has greatly increased during the last two decades as a result of better and more systematic research. This book reports research findings including research conducted by the author. Some research findings, have not been reported previously. This book also draws on nearly a decade of research and teaching in the areas of management and productivity as well as comments made by colleagues, students, and anonymous reviewers. Fourth, this book aims to be comprehensive, but not exhaustive. The sucess of productivity strategies depends on the knowledge of key objectives, principles, and implementation steps. The examples in this book illustrate outcomes, strategies, assessments, and techniques, and suggestions are made for further applications. References follow each chapter, providing additional readings.

Overview of Chapters

This book is written for managers and scholars who are interested in improving productivity in public and nonprofit organizations. Part I contains an introduction to productivity. Chapter 1 discusses the need for productivity, definition, trends, and use of productivity improvement, and a strategic perspective on using productivity. Part II lays the foundation for productivity improvement. Chapter 2 describes productivity problems that often arise in public and nonprofit organizations. It includes a brief treatment of problem diagnosis. Chapter 3 discusses performance measurement and the need for analytical techniques in general. It discusses methods for measuring effectiveness and efficiency as well as the use of survey research for measuring stakeholder satisfaction. Chapter 4 discusses the important problem of obtaining commitment for productivity and provides strategies for doing so. It also deals with overcoming resistance to productivity improvement. Together, Chapters 2 through 4 provide a foundation of problem identification, intervention, and assessment of productivity improvement efforts.

Productivity improvement goes down many different roads. Part III discusses specific productivity improvement efforts, including specific applications in public and nonprofit organizations. Chapter 5 examines strategies for identifying, and building commitment for, new goals. It discusses the use of strategic planning for building communitywide consensus as well as the traditional application to processes of "internal" strategic planning. Chapter 6 examines productivity improvement through organization. It focuses on strategies for partnering. It also discusses organizational restructuring and the use of contracting. Chapter 7 examines the "quality" paradigm. It discusses Total Quality Management (TQM) as a full-fledged management philosophy, as well as specific quality strategies and reengineering. This chapter also notes that, despite some rollbacks, customer responsiveness and error-free services are increasingly emphasized in public and nonprofit organizations. Chapter 8 provides a potpourri of "traditional" productivity improvement strategies, updated to reflect current concerns. Among other issues, it discusses the use of volunteers in providing services. Chapter 9 examines the use of information technology in organizations. Such efforts are relatively recent, and this chapter discusses strategies for increasing the productivity of information technology. Chapter 10 is titled "Productivity Through People" and discusses modern supervisory techniques for training, empowerment, motivation, and team-building. Chapter 11 examines the future outlook of productivity, including an assessment of the impact of productivity improvement strategies on the careers of managers. It also discusses the role of ethics in productivity improvement.

Most of the chapters stand on their own, although the first chapters do provide the context for those that follow. This approach allows managers to be flexible in using this book as they seek productivity improvements in their organizations.

Acknowledgments

I thank many people for the support, insight, and encouragement they have provided me. Above all, I thank my wife in more ways than can be enumerated here. I thank my present employer, the University of Central Florida, and past employers (especially the University of Miami and the National Science Foundation) for the resources that enabled me to learn and grow. I am very grateful for the comments and encouragement of my editor at Sage, Catherine Rossbach. Among my many colleagues, I especially thank Jonathan West, William (Bill) Werther, Arthur Levine, Maurice Richter, and Jay Jurie for their comments and support. True friends are a source of joy and inspiration. I also thank Norton Berman and Thomas Rinsma for their insights over many years. My professional frame of reference remains my many friends and acquaintances at the American Society for Public Administration. I also acknowledge my clients for the opportunities to learn through their travails, especially Dean Sprague and Stephen Bonczell. Special thanks are due to about two dozen students who over many years provided research assistance (especially Rocio Diaz, John Griffin, Lorraine Roy, and Glenn McGee).

PART

I

Introduction

1

The Productivity Challenge

Productivity is not an option.

The Need for Productivity

Can public and nonprofit organizations be improved? If so, how and in which ways? Such questions are often raised by citizens, clients, and board members concerned about the performance of public and nonprofit organizations in such areas as public safety, transportation, parks and recreation, education, housing, public health, social services, and museums. They want to ensure that, for example, public and nonprofit organizations are effective, not wasteful, and as good as other organizations providing similar services. Specific concerns often focus on the *effectiveness* of policies and programs—such as what students learn in school, whether teen counseling services really prevent suicide and pregnancy, the recidivism rate of inmate programs, and the impact of AIDS awareness programs. Additional issues concern the level of services—for example, ensuring an adequate number of schools in a community—and the efficiency of services—for example, the cost of educational services per student. Widespread concern about these issues is often regarded as a sign that public trust in public and nonprofit organizations is waning: Productivity helps restore public trust by connecting organizations with the concerns of their stakeholders (including

3

clients, citizens, and employees), by prioritizing objectives, by improving effectiveness and efficiency, and by providing accountability for results (Herzlinger, 1996; Holzer & Callahan).

Productivity addresses other issues as well. In recent years, federal cutbacks have caused many organizations to rethink their missions. Organizations are challenged when funding priorities change or even disappear. Dealing with unexpected shortfalls causes a scramble for alternative funding sources and a reassessment of existing priorities. Organizations must look for more cost-effective ways of accomplishing their missions. Again, productivity helps. Through productivity, managers reorganize work so that organizations can accomplish more with less, build consensus for new priorities, and work collaboratively with other organizations. Productivity helps address myriad pressures that organizations experience including those arising from client complaints and funding agencies that demand evidence of increased effectiveness and efficiency.

Productivity is important in keeping organizations up to date, vibrant, and relevant to society. Although the pressures of responsiveness and budgets have been significant in recent years, other reasons for productivity vary among organizations and within units. Some of these are stated in Table 1.1. They include reducing overhead costs, making employees more efficient, increasing accountability, reducing costly errors, minimizing customer complaints, increasing the skills of employees, improving the internal climate of trust, increasing citizens' familiarity with agency services, improving the effectiveness and management of partnerships, reducing training time for volunteers, and improving the targeting of marketing efforts. Many of these concerns stem from specific concerns about units or projects in organizations. In these instances, the driving forces behind these efforts are managers rather than clients or citizens.

The need for productivity is not based solely on stakeholder pressures, however. It also arises from managerial cultures and shared beliefs about the performance of organizations. Well-defined, shared beliefs and cultures are valuable to productivity because they often lead to proactive and committed actions—more so than when they are based solely on stakeholder pressures. For example, managers who feel that stakeholders are inadequately served are more likely to react to the first complaint than managers who do not share these values. Other managers might opt to wait until stakeholder pressures threaten to have consequences. Another value is avoiding waste of resources. When organizations are found to be wanting in this regard, managers may feel prompted to action. Such standards about what is right and wrong are part of the culture of organizations. They are reinforced by directors, other senior managers, reward

TABLE 1.1 Selected Reasons for Productivity Improvement

External Relations:
- Increasing trust with external stakeholders
- Getting organizations to be more responsive to clients
- Improving communications with citizens and elected officials
- Increasing the ability to partner effectively with other organizations

Management:
- Increasing efficiency of routine tasks
- Increasing effectiveness of services
- Reducing administrative overhead costs
- Decreasing error rates and litigation
- Improving accountability
- Improving employee motivation and commitment
- Increasing advantages from information technology
- Getting employees to take responsibility for skill upgrading
- Making work teams more productive
- Improving the climate of trust in organizations

Marketing and Fund-Raising:
- Increasing awareness of potential clients
- Increasing yields from fund-raising efforts
- Identifying new client groups for services
- Improving the effectiveness of marketing efforts
- Improving the yield from grant proposals

Volunteerism:
- Reducing training time for volunteers
- Reducing turnover among volunteers
- Identifying new groups of volunteers
- Reducing complaints from supervisors and volunteers

systems, prior experience, and education. Organizational culture matters, as do stakeholder pressures, in productivity improvement.

Defining Productivity

This book defines *productivity* as *the effective and efficient use of resources to achieve outcomes. Effectiveness* is defined as the *level of outcomes,* for example, the number of arrests made by police officers, the number of welfare clients who find employment after being counseled by caseworkers, or the amount of money raised through fund-raisers. Outcomes are accomplishments. Many citizens and clients care greatly about service effectiveness, and measures of effectiveness are significant in dealing with their concerns about responsiveness. For example, increasing the mathematics and reading abilities of children is a greatly valued measure of school effectiveness. In addition, some authors also distinguish between *outputs* and *outcomes;* outputs are *immediate* consequences of activities and outcomes are related to *long-term* goals (Rosen, 1993). For example, vocational training institutions provide education that helps students acquire skills, pass tests, and graduate (all of which are outputs), which, in turn, helps their students get better jobs (an outcome). The distinction is relevant because organizations often have more control over outputs than outcomes.[1]

Efficiency is defined as the *ratio of outcomes (and outputs) to inputs.* It describes the cost per activity to achieve given outcomes, for example, the number of counseled clients per counselor who find employment or the number of graduating students per teacher. Efficiency is a ratio of the resources used (inputs) to accomplishments (outcomes or outputs), O/I. Efficiency is important for helping budgets stretch further and for choosing among competing service providers. It should be noted that the ratio "caseload per worker" is *not* an efficiency measure. Caseloads are not outputs or outcomes but are activities that are also called workloads. The measure "caseload per worker" is known as a *workload ratio.* The distinction between outcomes and workloads is important because, as many caseworkers know, high workload ratios are important only when outcomes or outputs are maintained.

The terms *productivity* and *productivity improvement* are not synonymous. The former is concerned with the level of productivity, whereas the latter is concerned with changing it. Productivity involves the level of present effectiveness and efficiency, and the processes to achieve it. Productivity *improvement* involves diagnosis of productivity problems, knowledge of alternative productivity improvement strategies, analysis of the receptivity of organizations to productivity efforts, implementation skills and strategies, and outcome assessment. This book deals with both productivity and productivity improvement.

The definition of *productivity* suggests that managers should be concerned with *both* goal attainment (i.e., effectiveness) and the efficiency of efforts (Morley, 1986; Rosen, 1993). However, public, nonprofit, and for-profit organizations vary in their relative emphasis on effectiveness and efficiency. (Although this book does not focus on for-profit organizations, they are discussed here for illustrative purposes.) Effectiveness is often of paramount importance in the public sector; for example, the public (and thus elected officials) expect 911 emergency services to respond promptly, teachers to teach well, traffic jams not to occur, museums to be open, space shuttles to fly, environmental toxins to be regulated, and defense systems to work. Although efficiency is important, it is often less important than effectiveness. Indeed, many citizens are more concerned with the effectiveness of 911 services (for example, that services arrive on time with appropriate personnel and equipment) than with efficiency of 911 services (e.g., the cost of timely response). The public nature of government organizations, their responsibility to a broad and diverse population, and the emphasis on effectiveness cause them to pursue productivity improvement efforts that are consistent with these conditions; strategies for deciding which goals to pursue, and evaluating how well they have been accomplished, are of great concern. Effectiveness is an important measure of public sector productivity, and agencies frequently seek ways to improve it.

Indeed, the lack of attention to effectiveness can bring severe repercussions to public organizations. Public organizations that are perceived to have low levels of effectiveness often encounter pressures to increase their workloads. In one such instance, a municipal unit of police detectives that had not communicated its effectiveness to the community faced significant pressures from elected officials to determine the "right" caseload for its detectives. Elected officials were also considering reallocating resources in favor of community-based policing efforts. The lack of sustained efforts to demonstrate and communicate its effectiveness—indeed, no such data had ever been gathered—contributed to the concern about caseloads, which, in this case, was also seen as a prelude to downsizing. In short, public organizations need to make the case that they are effective.

This does not mean that efficiency is unimportant in public organizations. For example, the cost of environmental regulation, and its impact on business, is clearly an important concern. Moreover, efficient organizations stretch their resources further and thus can be more effective. Efficient detectives solve more cases with the same resources. However, there is consensus that efficiency is typically a more important goal in the for-profit sector, where success tends to be more singularly defined as profit. Some business texts even define productivity *as* efficiency. Efficiency improvements are important because they result in cost savings that directly contribute to profitability, competitiveness, and corporate survival. Most productivity improvement efforts in for-profit organizations focus on applications that increase employee output, reduce inventories, speed up production, and reduce rework. Productivity efforts in public and nonprofit organizations emphasizing efficiency are frequently adapted from for-profit applications. In recent years, productivity definitions in the for-profit sector also emphasize "quality" in relation to customer responsiveness and error-free processes (specifically, as regarding performance, conformance, timeliness, accuracy, and reliability of services and products). These applications, too, are often used by public and nonprofit organizations. It should be noted that some situations cause efficiency to be an important concern in the public sector: when budget pressures are severe, such as in health care and prison organizations; when private sector providers compete for service delivery (for example, regarding office printing and park maintenance); when regulatory burdens are thought to be too high (such as in drug regulation); when public embarrassments occur (e.g., $800 toilet seats for the Navy); and when high-overhead agencies pursue efficiency gains through procurement and contracting processes.

Agreement exists that nonprofit organizations often seek effectiveness and efficiency in equal measure (Drucker, 1990; Kennedy, 1990). Donors, public agencies funding nonprofit organizations, and employees and managers who work for these organizations often have high expectations about their ability to make an impact on the areas that they are involved in. The extent to which they provide services and affect important community issues is an important measure of the effectiveness of nonprofit organizations. Tax laws require that nonprofit organizations reinvest excess revenues, which furthers their commitment to effectiveness. However, efficiency is equally important. Resources are frequently very scarce in nonprofit organizations, in part because their aims are huge (such as resolving homelessness) and in part because revenues streams are small (for example, based on membership fees). Resource scarcity causes nonprofit organizations to seek out "free" resources such as volunteers and community donations. This can turn nonprofit organizations into highly efficient providers. Productivity efforts aimed at better use of volunteers and greater success at fund-raising are especially important to these organizations.

Finally, organizations also differ with regard to the extent that they value *equity* as an important goal. For-profit organizations usually have very little commitment to equity, other than avoiding discrimination lawsuits from their employees or clients. By contrast, public organizations often have great commitment to equity; they must provide services to all citizens, regardless of their ability to pay for them. Public organizations must also ensure equal access to services, and they often help disadvantaged populations use services. Nonprofit organizations also often serve disadvantaged populations, but they are seldom obligated to provide services to the entire population. Of course, both public and nonprofit organizations must avoid discrimination as well.

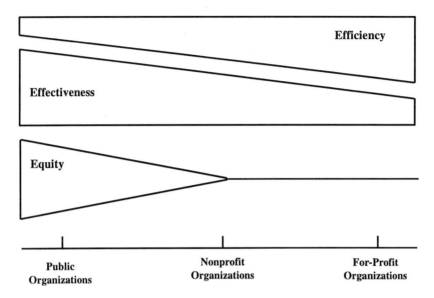

Figure 1.1. The Importance of Productivity Values

In sum, productivity is defined as the effective and efficient use of resources. Effectiveness is typically of great importance in the public sector, and nonprofit organizations often emphasize effectiveness and efficiency in equal measure. Public sector organizations also value providing services to all populations groups, that is, ensuring equity. The relative emphases of these values are shown in Figure 1.1.

An Example:
Orange County Corrections Department

There are many highly productive public and nonprofit organizations. A characteristic of such organizations is that they view their mission in a broad, societal context, and they use cost-effective methods for accomplishing goals. One such example is the Orange County Corrections Department in Orlando, Florida. This department transformed itself from a holding facility for inmates doing time to one that understands its mission in broader context: to transform individuals so that they can better perform in society and not return to prison.

To this end, the Orange County Corrections Department assesses each individual with regard to his or her abilities and barriers. Many inmates can't read, and so they are taught to read and write. Correction officials argue that without these basic skill, inmates will not be able to survive in society and will likely return to prison. Other inmates have alcohol and substance abuse problems; they are put through rehabilitation programs. Upon dealing with such problems, inmates are selected to participate in a variety of vocational training programs. For example, the prison's car repair program is a state-of-the-art facility, and many inmates readily find employment upon release. The prison also houses a state-of-the-art computer facility where inmates learn relevant job skills. Further, these training resources are obtained in part through donations from the community, thereby minimizing direct tax expenditures. The prison also uses advanced electronic surveillance techniques, thereby minimizing employee costs too.

The Orange County Corrections Department is not unique in its development of a broad mission and use of cost-effective approaches. In fact, many public and nonprofit organizations have transformed themselves in recent years. Nonetheless, many organizations have yet to improve themselves in this way. What is remarkable is that managers are finding the tools and resources to make a difference.

Is Productivity Improvement a Fad?

Productivity improvement sometimes receives a bad rap. Employees are often concerned that managers are managing by the "fad of the month," thereby introducing and abandoning different productivity efforts in rapid succession. Employees call such aborted efforts BOHICA–"bend over, here it comes again." Half-completed efforts often damage organizations by disrupting effective work activities and by reducing trust and confidence in management. The perception of productivity improvement as a fad is also reinforced by media reporting. Newspapers often report new tools that promise to solve important problems. Success stories and "how-to" articles soon appear in professional trade journals and, sometimes, in the popular press and even TV. Organizations hire managers who are competent in implementing the new strategies. However, success is often followed by the realization that challenges exist as well. Not all organizations and managers experience total success. Subsequent reports discuss negative impacts of efforts as well as instances of outright failure and rollback. Scholars contribute their views too. When such critical assessments occur, the judgment of the field changes from enthusiasm to caution about these strategies. However, the lack of articles about successful applications merely reflects that the applications are no longer *newsworthy*. Success is now routine. But eventually failure is also no longer newsworthy, and the media rush to report some new effort. The pattern repeats itself: The hot ticket of today is the dog of tomorrow. Does all of this mean that productivity improvement is a fad?

A reassessment is in order. We must better understand how organizations come to improve themselves through productivity. An article titled "Total Quality Management Is Dead" in *USA Today* (1995) notes that despite the alleged demise of Total Quality Management (TQM), "some tenets of quality management are so ingrained that they aren't even recognized as such anymore" (p. B1). Government organizations are increasingly customer oriented. Most organizations spend a considerable period planning and discussing, applying only parts of efforts, or applying the main idea of new strategies without much attention to specific techniques. In time, as more organizations acknowledge the importance of change objectives and the viability of response strategies, productivity strategies find wider use. Indeed, bookstores continue to sell many books on TQM nearly 15 years after its introduction. A 1992 study by the U.S. General Accounting Office (GAO) found that although 68% of federal units had some familiarity with TQM, only 13% of employees were actually involved in implementation (U.S. GAO, 1992). Likewise, a survey of local governments found that only 11% had a "substantial" commitment to TQM, although 79% undertook activities to identify customer needs, which is part of TQM (Berman & West, 1995). Organizations learn in small steps, from trial and error, and from the replication of successful efforts elsewhere. Many initial efforts are small-scale pilot efforts that are undertaken with greater success later. Widespread use often takes five to eight years from initial introduction and media hype. Thus, whereas the above strategies are only haltingly used, many older productivity improvement practices are now staples of management: Performance measurement is used by 67% of local governments, evaluation research by 80%; strategic planning by 64%; financial forecasting by 76%; employee involvement efforts by 74%; and management by objectives (MBO) by 47%. Some of these efforts are organizationwide, whereas others are used only in some departments (Poister & Streib, 1994). While 66% of state budget offices use effectiveness analysis, 94% use some form of productivity analysis (Lee, 1991).[2]

Such use over time suggests that productivity improvement is not a fad but a body of slowly diffusing knowledge and management practice. Poister and Streib note that in the last two decades, more and more techniques are being used. One reason that productivity improvement strategies are increasingly used is because they are *useful*. In a recent survey, 48.6% of city managers agreed or strongly agreed with the statement that productivity improvement strategies "are a useful vehicle of change" and an additional 41.7% "somewhat agreed" with this statement.[3] Likewise, 43.9% of directors of large social service organizations agreed or strongly agreed with this statement, and 37.98% "somewhat agreed" that productivity improvement is a useful vehicle for change. Half of the museum directors agree or strongly agree that productivity improvement is a useful vehicle for change, and more than a third somewhat agree with this statement.

Not surprising, many managers also regard productivity improvement as an opportunity for increased visibility and career advancement. Familiarity with productivity improvement strategies is also consistent with broader norms of both the American Society for Public Administration (ASPA) and the International City/County Managers Association (ICMA) that managers should strive for professional excellence. Table 1.2 reports the results of a 1995 survey among city managers and chief administrative officers in all 502 cities with populations of more than 50,000 (Berman, 1995). Respondents report widespread competence in a broad range of productivity improvement strategies. Given that these data are self-assessments, they might be interpreted to mean that, at the very least, managers believe that they ought to be competent in these areas. Of interest, those reporting higher levels of competence also report a stronger sense of job security—a critical concern in a profession that has a high turnover rate.

A Strategic Perspective

This book argues that a strategic perspective is needed. Managers must clearly identitfy which goals they are pursuing, the strategies for attaining these goals, and conditions that may affect the implementation of the strategies. This situation is somewhat analogous to medical diagnosis, which asks: What illnesses does the patient have? Which illness should be addressed, and how should the others be prioritized? What is the best strategy for dealing with this illness? How will the treatment be implemented, and how is progress to be measured? And, as in medicine, there is usually an abundance of problems or possible problems worthy of attention. Problems must be identified and decisions made about which productivity strategies should be implemented, taking into account conditions that will likely affect their success.

The strategic perspective is threefold. The first step is identification of productivity problems that are specific to the organization. There are numerous problems that may beset organizations. Some problems stem from inadequate

TABLE 1.2 Competencies of City Managers: Self Assessments

Productivity Strategies	Percentage of City Managers Competent in Strategy [a]
Management by objectives	73.4
Employee empowerment	71.4
Ethics training	68.6
Community-based strategic planning	65.5
Public image campaigns	59.5
Employee career development	59.1
Total Quality Management	57.8
Benchmarking	45.6

SOURCE: Berman (1995).
a. Indicates being competent or expert in area.

alignment of actual organizational processes with the needs of stakeholders. Organizations often state that they are customer or citizen oriented, but how well do they measure up? How do customers or citizens assess the organization's responsiveness? Other problems involve misalignments between goals and the organizational structures and resources to achieve these goals. An important source of problems also consists of politics and cynicism that cause departments to fight against each other at the expense of collaboration toward common purposes. Dysfunctional key actors are another source, such as those who ignore important problems and facts facing organizations.

Second, managers must choose from among different productivity improvement strategies to address the most important problems facing their organizations. This book discusses various strategies, such as quality management, strategic planning, partnering, organizational alignment, performance evaluation, use of information technology, and strategies for improving productivity through people. Each has its stated purposes. However, they can also be used to address a variety of concerns as well. For example, quality management is often implemented to redirect agency objectives as well as to increase communication among different units. However, other managers use TQM as a means to further delegation and empowerment practices or to increase performance measurement. Productivity improvement strategies often solve a variety of problems. Furthermore, productivity goals that are not fully reached through one strategy are often reinforced when using another strategy; for example, the need for measurement is furthered by strategic planning, continuous improvement, program evaluation, and benchmarking.

Third, managers must address the manner in which they implement targeted improvements. Organizational realities and external constraints cannot be ignored. Neither can the strengths and weaknesses of managers who assist in implementing improvements, or the efforts needed to obtain the commitment and motivation of employees. Cynicism must be overcome; old and new foes must be reckoned with. There now exists a wide range of top-down, bottom-up, mixed, and planned change models, each of which provides perspectives on implementing change. Choosing a good implementation strategy is essential to success, as important as the productivity improvement strategy.

Another way of understanding the implementation challenge is as follows: Many productivity improvement strategies affect existing *values* (e.g., increased customer orientation, openness in decision making), *systems* (rewards, information technology, etc.), *tools* (use of surveys, scheduling, efficiency analysis, and so on), and *behaviors* (courtesy to clients, etc.). In this regard, productivity improvement is viewed less as an external event that is done to an organization or individual and more as a nurturing and shaping of already existing values, infrastructure, tools, and behaviors. That is, *productivity improvement is an intervention in the existing state of the organization.* The magnitude of the required change effort not only depends on the nature of the productivity improvement effort but also on the current state of values, systems, tools, and behaviors. Organizations whose values are already consistent with various productivity improvement strategies probably experience less resistance to using, say, benchmarking than those that are committed to, for example, getting by with the least effort. Depending on the organization, some changes will take multiple efforts over time. Discontinued efforts are not necessarily evidence of fads or failures but, like all efforts, must be evaluated in terms of their impact on existing cultures, practices, behaviors, and skills.

In sum, the strategic perspective requires that managers (a) identify specific productivity problems, (b) identify a range of appropriate productivity improvement strategies, and (c) develop an implementation strategy for successfully effecting change.

The Evolution of Productivity

Productivity is a body of knowledge and management practice aimed at improving the effectiveness and efficiency of organizations. This section discusses the evolution of different productivity improvement strategies (Bouckaert, 1990). Productivity strategies are typically developed in response to specific challenges

TABLE 1.3 The Evolution of Productivity

Period	Problem	Selected Strategies
1900-1939 "Industrialization"	Growth of organizations	(a) Hierarchical designs, (b) Rationalizing work process, (c) Supervising and motivating workers, (d) Functions of executives: PODSCORB
1939-1945 "World War II"	Quality war products	Quality production and control
1945-1965 "Postwar growth"	Controlling growth Human motivation	Program and performance budgets Research: Theory X versus Theory Y
1965-1980 "Program analysis"	Increasing program efficiency and effectiveness Human motivation	Operations research, cost-benefit analysis, PPBS/ZBB, strategic planning Organizational development
1980 to present "Quality paradigm"	Increasing effectiveness and efficiency through organization Stakeholder trust	Outsourcing, partnering, flattening organizations, use of IT Broad-based strategic planning, Total Quality Management and related strategies

or conditions; therefore, to understand the evolution of productivity is in large measure to understand the challenges that organizations face, in appropriate historical context.[4] The development of productivity involves five periods.

Many productivity strategies date back to the first period between 1900 and 1939, which is called the "industrialization" period (see Table 1.3). During this period, the scale and scope of many organizations dramatically increased. In the for-profit sector, factories grew much larger, and companies became more complex as they added new divisions and departments (e.g., personnel). Increased size reflected both demand (many consumers wanted a Ford Model-T) as well as competitive advantages arising from economies of size and scope (e.g., integration with suppliers and distributors). The challenge of increased demand was revisited on federal agencies such as the departments of Army and Navy and the Internal Revenue Service. The for-profit experience created many new productivity strategies relating to the rationalization of work processes, supervisory management skills, the roles of executives, and principles of organization.

Productivity strategies associated with the rationalization of work processes are often discussed in connection with Frederick Taylor's scientific management. The purpose of this approach, described in 1912, is to increase the efficiency and effectiveness of operations by identifying the best work practices, selecting employees to perform these practices, and ensuring implementation. Taylor also discussed economies that resulted from working in teams. An important challenge was the impact of new work processes on supervisory management, which was required to deal with more employees in a more impersonal manner than under previous craftsman-apprentice systems. Mary Parker Follett described in 1926 how supervisors can best get employees to follow instructions without creating resistance: Requests should be depersonalized, and bad work habits such as slothfulness or not following procedures should be examined for their consequences (Shafritz & Hyde, 1992). This is congruent with Dale Carnegie's work on making friends and influencing people by creating areas of agreement, cooperation, and conformed desires. According to Follett, psychology is an important part of scientific management, and managers require training and testing in both.

Another problem of the time was defining the functions of executives and departments. For example, the role of personnel departments (now renamed human resources departments) was defined as managing the flow and effectiveness of employees through such as activities as designing job descriptions, recruitment, selection, hiring, training, appraisal, support, and exit. Effective and efficient strategies were developed in each of these areas. The job of the executive was described by Gullick and Urwick in 1937 (based on the work of Henry Fayol) as POSDCORB, or planning, organizing, staffing, directing, coordinating, reporting, and budgeting. Organization of the new bureaucracies was a critical concern. The "correct" design of organizations was advocated based on the need for specialization (hence different departments for personnel, marketing, etc.), the need for authority to coordinate different departments, and limits regarding the number of employees or departments that one person could effectively oversee. Although these principles help, they were later challenged as being somewhat vague and sometimes inconsistent. For example, the principle of clear and undistorted communication suggests that supervisors should deal directly with many subordinates, but the principle of a limited span of control suggests that managers must limit the number of subordinates that they directly oversee.

These principles of scientific management and organizational design were used in public agencies as well as nonprofit organizations. Hospital administrators used the new techniques to distinguish themselves from doctors, even though most hospitals continued to be run by doctors. Bouckaert (1990) and others describe these strategies as serving as the basis of the reform movement to create a government that was less influenced by politics and corruption and more by professional, efficient management.

During this period, schools of public administration were created to train public managers in these new techniques (e.g., the Maxwell School of Citizenship at Syracuse, New York), and various commissions were created to further the use of business techniques in governments at all levels. The principles of organization and scientific management were widely applied during World War II (1939-1945), especially by the federal government. This is the second period of productivity improvement. The war effort also created a need for increased performance and reliability in manufacturing. Consumer products sometimes malfunctioned, but higher standards were required on the battlefield for tanks, planes, and communications. Domestic manufacturers who converted to war-time production developed the new techniques of quality control in mass production. These approaches were discontinued in the United States after the war because they were considered too costly and unnecessary for consumer goods. However, these strategies were absorbed by Japanese companies, refined, and later reintroduced in the United States in the late 1970s as Total Quality Management. This is discussed later.

The third period is called "postwar growth" and occurred between 1945 and 1965. An important concern was the sharp rise in government spending, and new budget strategies were introduced to control costs. Specifically, traditional line item budgets (used primarily for accountability in spending) were complemented by functional and performance budgets. Functional (or activity) budgets link resources to activity levels (e.g., expenditures related to street maintenance). Performance budgets relate resources to outcomes (e.g., cost per street mile cleaned); they are efficiency budgets. Although these techniques had only limited impact at the time, the development of these budgets and measures has increased over time.

During this period, researchers undertook significant efforts to increase their understanding of human motivation as relating to productivity. Maslow (1954) discussed a hierarchy of needs, suggesting that whereas some people only work to satisfy their physiological and safety needs (e.g., for food and shelter), others require social acceptance, recognition, and even self-actualization. Workers could not be adequately motivated without their needs being met. They might comply with management but have little commitment. This causes productivity to slump. McGregor discussed Theory X versus Theory Y people, whereby the former are presumed lazy and the latter highly motivated. These theories would become the foundation for later experimentation during the 1970s.

The fourth period, between 1965 and 1980, focused on program improvement, with five major developments. The first one is the development of Operations Research. These analytical techniques, invented during World War II, were greatly advanced by progress in computers, mathematics, and statistics. They include simulation and queuing modeling, linear programming, and decision analysis, as well as advanced tools of project management. Operations Research techniques are often used for logistical problems, such as those found in defense and transportation. These techniques optimize resources and outcomes, such as by identifying the optimum number of buses serving multiple routes, which minimizes waiting and transfer periods and limits expenditures (Chapter 8). A second development was the use of economic techniques, specifically, cost-benefit/effectiveness analysis and risk assessment, which are often used in environmental management and infrastructure investment decisions. In addition, program evaluation was developed and refined to assess program outcomes, identify community needs, and evaluate service efficiency (Newland, 1972). These became relevant to nonprofit organizations in their work under federal grants. A third development was the introduction of elaborate budget processes to better control costs and "force" discussion about the effectiveness of programs, such as through Planning-Programming-Budgeting and Zero-Based Budgeting. These budgeting processes relate program expenditures to other broader goals, other programs, and alternative spending amounts. These budgeting approaches failed to take hold. They were too encompassing and cumbersome, and often failed to take into account the incremental and political nature of programs. With few exceptions, these budget approaches are not much used today, but vestiges still shape some decisions in agencies.

A fourth development concerned the link between organization and strategy. Many companies diversified and became multinational. The disparate mix of services and products created a need for the strategic management of highly diversified portfolios and decision-making processes for making strategic decisions. From this challenge developed strategic planning. This was later adapted by the public sector as a broad-based, consensus-building strategy among public and private organizations (Chapter 5). Finally, during this period research ideas about human motivation were put into practice through Organizational Development (OD). Early OD applications emphasized increased human expression, open communication, and team-building (e.g., T-groups). Because these practices were not perceived as directly contributing to productivity, many were discontinued in the mid-1970s. However, later applications pioneered concepts of Planned Organizational Change for diffusing new processes throughout entire organizations. These are currently central to productivity improvement strategies (Chapter 4).

The current period since 1980 is the called the "quality paradigm" and focuses on broader and decidedly strategic concerns. Concern with client relations and the quality of services causes many organizations to consider TQM. First adopted by large U.S. multinational firms largely in response to competition from Japan, this practice rapidly spread through other sectors of the U.S.

economy. As of the mid-1990s, many governments have had at least a first brush with TQM, and many nonprofit organizations are experimenting with it now. TQM is a comprehensive management paradigm that emphasizes a customer orientation, empowerment, objective data in decision making (including performance measurement), and a holistic view of delivery and production processes. Many organizations have found TQM to involve too much change initially. Instead, they embark on different aspects over time: Benchmarking, reengineering, timeliness, empowerment, customer orientation, and so on are all part of the TQM paradigm.[5] In this sense, TQM, or Reinventing Government (ReGo), is increasingly used in public and nonprofit organizations (Chapter 7).

The current period also involves rethinking organizational designs. Increased use of information technology eliminates the need for middle managers who deal primarily with data or information processing. This enables flatter organizations with lower overhead costs. Continued budget pressures also create increased use of partnering and networking strategies: Many organizations are "shedding" functions to other organizations with whom they contract or partner. This allows new organizations to specialize and develop economies of scale and hence superior and more cost-effective services.[6] Although partnering has long been used by nonprofit organizations, many of these organizations are finding new opportunities with government and business. As a result of budget pressures and information technologies, the closed model of organizations is being replaced with a fluid, flatter, and networked model of organizations. The history of productivity continues to evolve. By comparison with earlier approaches to productivity improvement, the current efforts are decidedly more strategic in nature.

Some Challenges to Productivity

Various authors describe barriers to improving public and nonprofit organizations that have persisted over time (e.g., Ammons, 1992). Such challenges often are political, bureaucratic, personal, or philosophical in nature. The importance of barriers and challenges to productivity should be neither exaggerated nor minimized but viewed in terms of the coping ability of managers and their organizations to deal with them or to get around them. Not all challenges are present in every case.

The wrong-headed problem. Frederickson (1994) challenges recent efforts to reinvent government through TQM, reengineering, and so on, as being misplaced. He believes that most problems are political rather than administrative or managerial. For example, improvements in education require tough political decisions about the length of school days, training of teachers, school discipline, and so on. These political decisions lie outside the scope of TQM and other productivity efforts. He also believes that what is most needed is an increased citizen orientation in government, and that current efforts inadequately address this. In addition, TQM is sometimes used to bash the effectiveness of public employees. Osborne (1995) further notes that emphases differ between business and government. In business, TQM may lead to greater cooperation with vendors, but government must also ensure adequate competition for services should be advocated.

Leadership. Almost all productivity improvement strategies require some level of management support, and many require top management support. When such support is not forthcoming, important decisions cannot be made and productivity efforts flounder. Authority, legitimacy, and resources matter. Short-term time horizons are also mentioned as a barrier to productivity. Officials who seek quick solutions may be impatient with TQM or program budgeting. Such productivity improvement strategies often are characterized as having a long-term focus, but most improvement efforts are structured to provide tangible benefits within 6 to 12 months. Yet even such periods are sometimes too long. Shifts toward greater customer service and employee empowerment also require ongoing leadership commitment. Turnover among senior managers, directors, and elected officials also hurts productivity improvement efforts: Momentum is lost when new managers fail to support new efforts. Leadership is also required for dealing with challenges from other units or stakeholders. For example, efforts by corrections departments to provide more training to inmates sometimes causes resistance among elected officials who prefer policies and programs that are tough on criminals. Leadership is also needed to overcome bureaucratic rigidities and resistance from lower managers who may fear losing control or power.

Another challenge is simply that leaders may not be interested in promoting productivity improvements. Nonprofit directors often find fund-raising and board relations to be more pressing problems. Public leaders are also often less concerned with productivity improvement. They may also have inadequate skills in implementing productivity or they may be ingrained in cultures that reject new ways of doing business. Leaders in cultures that stifle innovation and openness find it difficult to undertake productivity improvement efforts.

Human resource issues. Civil service regulations and other human resource practices, such as limitations on performance bonuses, are also frequently mentioned as barriers; it is said to be especially difficult to reward competence and to punish incompetence in the public sector. It is sometimes also difficult to adjust duties. In the past, when organizations had more resources, they sometimes created "turkey farms," that is, programs of low priority and visibility that were staffed by incompetent employees (Cohen & Eimicke, 1995). However, today most organizations lack such resources as they are "lean and mean" following years of downsizing and retrenchment. Other practices include giving undesirable assignments to such employees until they finally leave the organization, or providing negative feedback. However, productivity also provides employees the opportunity to distinguish themselves and to improve their competitiveness. Thus some employees and managers may welcome change. Nonprofit organizations face different personnel constraints, specifically, working with large numbers of volunteers. Volunteers have high turnover rates, may be ill-prepared for their jobs, and may require extensive supervision.

Resources. The lack of resources is also a frequently mentioned barrier. Many productivity improvement strategies require resources for training and other purposes. The lack of resources stymies implementation even though, paradoxically, the lack of resources also gives rise to the need for productivity. Resources are needed for training, creating new units, reorganization, computer purchases, pilot projects, hiring, and so forth. The lack of monetary rewards is also mentioned as a barrier. However, incentives may be offered in other forms, such as superior assignments and promotion.

Personal. Personal barriers to productivity are also mentioned. Some managers are cynical about new strategies or fearful of losing their job security. Other managers are set in their ways (i.e., they will resist any change), lack necessary skills, or have adopted unproductive personal habits (e.g., lack of time management, poor interpersonal skills, tunnel vision). These barriers are hard to overcome when individuals are unable or unwilling to make necessary changes. They may also be the hardest to identify, because individuals mask negative traits and behaviors in the workplace. Some managers lack passion, that is, zeal and commitment to public goals. Such managers may be more interested in maintaining the status quo than in seeking improvement. These barriers often become evident when new productivity efforts are attempted.

The enumeration of the above barriers has led some authors to suggest that public and nonprofit organizations enjoy lower productivity than for-profit, private organizations. In fact, the sectors are not strictly comparable: Public schools may be required to educate a broader population than private schools.

When engaged in similar efforts, public agencies are often able to compete with private sector organizations for service contracts (e.g., municipal garbage collection). This result should not be surprising, because many of the above problems are also present in private companies. Short-term time horizons can be severe in publicly traded companies, which face pressures from stock markets to produce high returns for their shareholders. Yet these companies find ways to improve their productivity. Private companies also have rules and regulations regarding employees; although dismissal is easier, it too must based be on a sustained record of negative performance evaluations. Neither sector has a monopoly on bad personal habits, either. Although the profit motive to seek cost savings is stronger in private companies, public and nonprofit organizations have motivation to pursue effectiveness. *The importance of barriers to productivity should be neither exaggerated nor minimized but viewed in terms of the coping ability of managers and their organizations.* Chapter 4 discusses implementation strategies that help deal with many of these barriers.

The Sectors

Finally, we turn to the characteristics of public and nonprofit organizations, which vary in size and purpose. Nonprofit organizations are private organizations dedicated to serving public or membership needs rather than obtaining profit for owners (Salamon, 1992). Membership-serving nonprofit organizations exist primarily to provide benefits to their members, whereas public-serving organizations serve the public at large. Examples of member-serving nonprofit organizations are social clubs and various professional and business associations, whereas public-serving nonprofit, nonprofit organizations include churches, social service providers, funding intermediaries, and political action committees. This book focuses on public-serving organizations. These organizations fulfill various roles: (a) They often fill a need that is left unfilled by public organizations. Governments often fail to reach a consensus about the need for services, and nonprofit organizations can fill this gap (e.g., providing special care for AIDS patients). Sometimes nonprofit organizations predate government commitment to services (e.g., volunteer fire services). (b) They provide a vehicle for groups to organize themselves, and allow for providing services to specific groups. By contrast, government often focuses on service delivery to a general population. (c) Finally, nonprofit organizations provide a flexible way of public service delivery, with a minimum of red tape and with

TABLE 1.4 Public and Nonprofit Organizations

Organizations	Approximate Number
Public Organizations	
U.S. government	1
state governments	50
counties	3,043
municipalities	19,292
townships	16,666
school districts	14,556
special districts	33,131
total	86,739
Nonprofit, Public-Serving Organizations	
arts	4,930
health	18,080
education	36,159
civic and social	41,090
social services	64,100
total	164,359

SOURCE: Data from Henry (1995), Salamon (1992), U.S. Bureau of the Census (1991).

considerable knowledge of local conditions, opportunities, and needs; many government services are contracted out to nonprofit organizations. However, the resources of many nonprofit service organizations are very limited.

There are an estimated 86,000 public organizations and 164,000 nonprofit public service organizations in the United States (Table 1.4). The latter figure is based on those organizations that are eligible for tax exemption based on their nonprofit missions, which are sometimes referred to as 501(c)(3) firms, and have at least one paid employee (Salamon, 1992). Both government and public-serving nonprofit organizations are characterized by a small number of large organizations and a large number of small organizations. The public sector consists of the federal government, 50 state governments, 3,000 counties, 36,000 municipalities and townships, 14,500 school districts, and 33,000 special districts. Historical data show that the number of school districts has decreased by 87% since 1945 as a result of consolidation. By contrast, the number of special districts has quadrupled. Unlike municipalities and townships (which have remained nearly constant in number), most special districts perform single functions. Typical functions are the protection or development of natural resources, fire protection, housing and community development, water management and supply, cemeteries, parks, airports, and expressways (Burns, 1994;

Henry, 1995). Employment growth appears to be strongest in local government and large special districts.

Of the 164,000 public-serving nonprofit organizations in the United States, about 39% provide social services, 25% are civic and social organizations (including many neighborhood associations), 22% are educational institutions (primary and secondary schools and universities), 11% are health care organizations (hospitals, nursing homes, etc.), and 3% provide arts and cultural services (museums, orchestras, etc.). By expenditures, health service organizations account for 56%, whereas educational institutions account for 26%, social services for 12%, and civic and arts associations for a combined 6%. In recent years, health care organizations have grown the most quickly, reflecting federal priorities and overall expenditure growth in this sector.

Although there are many differences among public and nonprofit organizations, the common thread is commitment to some public purpose. Whether large or small, governed by elected officials or a private board, the dedication to public issues means that they must work collaboratively with clients, constituents, citizens, and other stakeholders to ensure continued support for, and effectiveness of, their services. Such collaboration suggests that public and nonprofit organizations are involved in maintaining and building network communities. This theme of community is further explored in Chapter 5.

Summary

This chapter discusses the need for productivity improvement in both public and nonprofit organizations. It defines productivity as the efficient and effective use of resources. It argues that productivity is connected with the need for increased responsiveness as well as working with tight budgets in public and nonprofit organizations. Productivity is not a fad, and organizations use a wide range of productivity improvement strategies over time. A threefold strategic perspective is suggested for productivity improvement that addresses the importance of assessing goals, identifying productivity challenges and appropriate productivity improvement strategies, and designing efficacious implementation efforts. This chapter also addresses challenges of productivity improvement, and it concludes that the importance of barriers depends on the coping abilities of managers and their organizations. Finally, this chapter discusses similarities and differences between the public and nonprofit sectors.

Notes

1. Chapter 3 discusses the measurement of outcomes in further detail and distinguishes between short-term and long-term outcomes. In this book, the term *outcome* is used generically to include outputs unless otherwise noted.

2. Comparable data for nonprofit organizations are not available. Approaches that are widespread are often used by 45%-75% of surveyed agencies or jurisdictions. There are many reasons that not all productivity strategies are used by all organizations: Implementation challenges are one aspect. In addition, not all organizations experience the same problems; many approaches command considerable attention and cannot be used simultaneously; and some strategies are complementary with regard to aims.

Strategies also show declining use as other, complementary, or newer strategies find greater acceptance. For example, MBO was used by 41% of local jurisdictions in 1976, 62% in 1987, and 47% in 1993. In this case, modern forms of empowerment and Total Quality Management may be displacing MBO, which was first introduced in the early 1970s.

3. This information is from a survey of city managers and directors of museums and social service organizations conducted in 1997. See Chapter 11, Note 1, for a discussion of the methodology of these survey results.

4. Public and nonprofit organizations experience some similar as well as different conditions.

5. This connection with TQM is sometimes denied by consultants, who seek to proclaim their wares as completely new.

6. Privatization is sometimes used ideologically to reduce the size of government, without due concern for productivity and other consequences. This is discussed in Chapter 6.

References

Ammons, D. (1992). Productivity barriers in the public sector. In M. Holzer (Ed.), *Public productivity handbook* (pp. 117-138). New York: Marcel Dekker.

Berman, E. (1995). [National survey of city managers]. Unpublished data.

Berman, E., & West, J. (1995). Municipal commitment to Total Quality Management. *Public Administration Review, 55*(1), 57-66.

Bouckaert, G. (1990). The history of the productivity movement. *Public Productivity and Management Review, 14*(3), 53-89.

Burns, N. (1994). *The formation of American local governments.* New York: Oxford University Press.

Cohen, S., & Eimicke, W. (1995). *The new effective public manager.* San Francisco: Jossey-Bass.

Drucker, P. (1990). *Managing the non-profit organization.* New York: Harper Business.

Frederickson, G. (1994). Total quality politics: TQP. *Spectrum: The Journal of State Government, 67*(2), 13-15.

Gullick, F., & Urwick, L. (1937). *Papers on the science of administration.* New York: Institute of Public Administration.

Henry, N. (1995). *Public administration and public affairs* (6th ed.). Englewood Cliffs, NJ: Prentice Hall.

Herzlinger, R. (1996). Can public trust in nonprofits and government be restored? *Harvard Business Review, 74*(3), 97-107.

Holzer, M. & Callahan, K. (1998). *Government at work: Best practices and model programs,* Thousand Oaks, CA: Sage.

Kennedy, L. (1990). *Quality management in the nonprofit world.* San Francisco: Jossey-Bass.

Lee, R. (1991). Developments in state budgeting: Trends of two decades. *Public Administration Review, 51*(3), 257.

Maslow, A. (1954). *Motivation and personality.* New York: Harper & Row.

Morley, E. (1986). *A practitioner's guide to public sector productivity improvement.* New York: Van Nostrand Reinhold.

Newland, C. (1972). Symposium on productivity in government. *Public Administration Review, 32*(6), 739-850.

Osborne, D. (1995). Why TQM is only half a loaf. In J. P. West (Ed.), *Quality management today.* Washington, DC: International City/County Management Association.

Poister, H., & Streib, G. (1994). Municipal management tools from 1976 to 1993: An overview and update. *Public Productivity & Management Review, 17*(2), 115-125.

Rosen, E. (1993). *Improving public sector productivity.* Newbury Park, CA: Sage.

Salamon, L. (1992). *America's nonprofit sector: A primer.* Washington, DC: Independent Sector.

Shafritz, J., & Hyde, A. (1992). *Classics of public administration* (3rd ed.). Belmont, CA: Wadsworth.

Total Quality Management is dead. (1995, October 17). *USA Today,* pp. B1-B2.

U.S. Bureau of the Census. (1991). *Statistical abstract of the United States.* Washington, DC: Government Printing Office.

U.S. General Accounting Office. (1992). *Quality management: Survey of federal organizations.* Washington, DC: Government Printing Office.

Foundations

CHAPTER

2

Problem Diagnosis

▓▓▓ Productivity improvement begins with the diagnosis of organizational and individual problems. The purpose of diagnosis is to ensure effective intervention based on a thorough understanding of problems. This chapter examines productivity problems in four areas: (a) stakeholder responsiveness, (b) organization and the efficient use of resources, (c) working through people, and (d) project and program management. Problems in these areas are among the most important productivity issues today, and all impair the ability of organizations to reach high levels of effectiveness and efficiency (Ammons, 1995; Covey, 1994; Herman, 1994).

Diagnosis begins with taking inventory of symptoms and developing understanding of the processes that cause them (Harrison, 1994). Diagnosis is a creative process that requires broad knowledge of organizational problems. Although some productivity problems are easy to identify, other problems masquerade as symptoms and hide important challenges to productivity. For example, a unit experiences frequent client complaints. This might be caused by inadequate client orientation, a sudden increase in the demand for services that the unit is unable to meet, or the result of recent downsizing. Although complaints are problematic, they do not constitute a problem in any diagnostic sense. The challenge for managers is to identify the underlying processes that give rise to the symptoms that are observed. To this end, managers frequently gather information from different sources such as employees, other managers, and clients. Information from different sources often adds new understanding and appreciation of conditions, and some sources may suggest solutions as well.

Organizational information must be carefully appraised. To evaluate the reliability of information, managers frequently look for consistency: One client complaint does not prove much, but 20 might. Consistency across different sources, such as between individuals and administrative records, also strengthens the credibility of initial hunches. Managers often make diagnostic mistakes when they rely on single occurrences on which to base their decisions, or when they fail to deal with information that is contradictory. Managers also use knowledge of frequent productivity problems as a background for evaluating organizational information. Information is used as evidence that either substantiates or invalidates the likelihood of suspected problems. This strategy helps address the problem that diagnostic information is often incomplete, and is similar to medical diagnosis, discussed in Chapter 1, in which doctors obtain information that is interpreted through a knowledge base of medical problems. This chapter provides a knowledge base of productivity problems. It should be noted that even when the diagnosis is correct, productivity efforts must also be informed by knowledge of implementation and other factors that are discussed in Chapter 4.[1]

Assessing External Relations

In recent years, organizations have been increasingly viewed as "open systems" that survive through exchanges with their environments; organizations must satisfy the needs of their stakeholders: clients, citizens, elected officials, and community leaders. When the needs of these stakeholders are met, organizations benefit from increased support for their missions. However, when their needs are unmet, organizations suffer the consequences through democratic processes and the loss of clientele.

Different Strokes for Different Folks

A frequent productivity problem is that employees and managers do not have a clear view of who their clients are beyond "the general population" or "anyone who walks through the door." Different populations have different needs and a need for different services as well. Every customer, client, or citizen is not the same. Organizations that do not have good knowledge of (a) who their clients are and (b) what they need cannot hope to provide effective and efficient services. For example, although police departments cannot pick and choose their markets—as many public organizations, they are chartered to serve entire populations—clearly the problems of low-income minority populations are different than those of people in affluent neighborhoods. Police departments need to ensure that their efforts are appropriate to different areas. Likewise, parks departments must provide services to teenagers, single mothers, and retirees. These groups are all part of the general population, but they have very different needs. Tax collectors' offices must serve people who are blind or those who do not speak English (say, only Creole); resources must be made available to serve these different populations.

A problem that is sometimes mentioned involves the conflicting needs of stakeholders (Linden, 1992). For example, most citizens like zoning regulations that beautify their neighborhoods, but as clients of zoning departments, they generally prefer fewer regulations. AIDS efforts must balance the needs of parents and children to increase prevention with the needs of those who are HIV positive for developing a cure. In addition, productivity improvement focuses on intended outcomes, but managers must sometimes consider unintended outcomes too; for example, school closures during winter storms impair the ability of some parents to earn income while looking after their children. The conundrum of conflicting and interdependent interests requires careful management of external relations. When stakeholders do not understand the ways in which organizations meet their specific needs, as well as the broader interests of public organizations, the credibility of organizations suffers and conflicts may occur in democratic decision-making processes.

It is often said that nonprofit organizations overstretch their resources in an effort to serve broad populations (Drucker, 1990). In so doing, they may fail to develop ties with population groups that further understanding of population needs as well as build support for programs. Overreaching also dilutes grant-writing and fund-raising efforts. Nonprofit organizations need to decide which target populations they will serve, and how they plan to do so. They need to understand the needs of different populations, how these needs are prioritized, and which needs the organization is able to address.

Table 2.1 shows some measures for diagnosing the above problems. Persistent stakeholder complaints often indicate a lack of responsiveness to stakeholder needs, but this is a crude measure because it fails to locate the source of problems. A frequent cause is top management failure to segment the needs of different stakeholder groups, or its failure to make meeting different needs a priority

TABLE 2.1 Indicators of Productivity Problems: External Relations and Organization

---

Stakeholders:

1. Who are your stakeholders? Do you and your staff understand their needs?

    Indicators: stakeholder complaints, employees/managers not understanding stakeholder needs, narrow view of stakeholders, no efforts to measure and improve satisfaction (e.g., surveys)

2. How are you improving your services? Are you better than your competition or comparable organization?

    Indicators: lack of efforts to seek continuous improvement, inadequate rewards for improvement, no efforts to get feedback about improvements, no comparison with other organizations, no analysis of contracting out

3. Who supports your organization ? How effective are they?

    Indicators: lack of public and client support when needed, lack of a group of supporters, ineffective support, lack of efforts to build a network of supporters

Organization:

4. What are your priorities? Are they shared throughout the organization?

    Indicators: lack of priorities, lack of periodic strategic planning, priorities unknown or contested by employees/managers, possibly in conjunction with low staff morale, complaints by stakeholders, loss of market share

5. What are those units doing?

    Indicators: competition among units, hostile relations among units, objectives that are outdated, insufficient autonomy for units, too much/too little oversight, duplication of activities among units, inadequate use of partnering with other organizations

6. Are resources and technology used efficiently?

    Indicators: periodic budget shortfalls, priorities not matched by resource reallocation, lack of a plan to ensure staying up to date in technology and expertise, lack of recognition for efficiency gains

7. What does your staff care about?

    Indicators: lack of commitment to professional values, apathy, cynicism, or short-term orientations among staff; lack of efforts by managers to promote professional values

8. Do those in charge exhibit leadership?

    Indicators: lack of goal setting by units, personality conflicts in units, lack of professional values, lack of authority, unfamiliarity with leadership roles and values, lack of followership by employees

---

among managers and employees. Interviews with employees can help identify the lack of such priorities. The absence of "in-place" strategies to improve customer service (including, but not limited to, satisfaction surveys) is often a good indicator that the needs of external stakeholders are not taken seriously, because it is unlikely that high levels of satisfaction occur by chance. Organizations that claim to have such strategies should show that the strategies are being used and also how their efficacy is being monitored.

Measuring Up and Getting Support

Customers, citizens, community leaders, and elected officials have increasingly high expectations of organizations. They expect services to be relevant, timely, and without error (McClendon, 1992; Rosander, 1989). Stakeholders are quick to sour on organizations that do not meet their needs or that do not meet their needs as well as other organizations. The need for improvement is also an imperative of professional management, namely, to serve one's clients in the best possible manner and to improve organizations. But it is also based on the realities of competition among service providers and, for public organizations, an antigovernment environment that favors privatization and contracting out. Organizations must continuously update and improve their services or face the consequences.

Continuous improvement in meeting client needs is seldom, if ever, achieved by decree. Rules, regulations, and policies are necessary but insufficient to create adequate commitment to improvement. Continuous improvement requires an attitude among employees and managers in which opportunities for addressing stakeholder needs are sought out, implemented, and rewarded. As mentioned in Chapter 1, productivity improvement requires a change in values, systems, tools, and behaviors. The productivity challenge is that positive attitudes about improvement may be absent. Continuous improvement and stakeholder orientation must be part of the organizational culture. As a value system, it is fostered by ongoing dialogue about the need for improvement as well as by top management leadership and support for initiatives (Halachmi, 1996; Kennedy, 1991). Trust must exist that mistakes will be tolerated as employees search for improvement. Organizations with high levels of commitment to their stakeholders usually have policies, regulations, and strategies that promote improvement, but they do not rely solely on these rules to achieve their aims.

An area of special concern for nonprofit organizations is improvement in fund-raising. Fund-raising is a critical part of their activities, in part because proceeds are often used to help spawn new activities. Rising fund-raising costs imply that these efforts must be increasingly efficient and effective. Continuous improvement in this area involves not only better returns on mailings and fund-raising events but also the use of more sophisticated marketing techniques to reach potential contributors. An important aspect is also making better use of members of the board of directors. They should be engaged in fund-raising, and their terms of appointment should include expectations about fund-raising.

Diagnosis of stakeholder orientation and commitment to continuous improvement includes the use of tools for managing continuous improvement (e.g., benchmarking), efforts by staff to seek and implement continuous improvements, and the extent that soliciting feedback from clients and other stakeholders is solicited to improve current services. Other diagnostics involve efforts to generate information about the effectiveness and efficiency of services of competitors as well as studies about privatization, contracting, and partnering opportunities. Although such studies are sometimes politically charged (e.g., they may reflect infighting among rival units), they nevertheless suggest that effectiveness is taken seriously. The absence of such activities suggests, in varying degrees, a lack of commitment to continuous improvement.

However, running programs well does not automatically guarantee a cadre of committed supporters. Public organizations (and programs) require supporters to see them through inevitable moments of controversy that are part of democratic processes (McClendon & Catonese, 1996). Nonprofit organizations need supporters to assist in fund-raising and to increase awareness in the community and among funding agencies about the efficacy of their services. Stakeholders come to expect certain services; for example, roads without potholes seldom generate spontaneous support. Also, public attitudes are somewhat cynical about the ability of many organizations to perform, and a recent survey of city managers finds that community leaders have only modest levels of trust in local governments to understand and meet the needs of community organizations (Berman, 1996, 1997).[2] Support must often be generated through intentional processes in such settings as social events, advisory groups, and board meetings. Organizations need a broad range of strategies for getting the word out that they are responsive to the needs of their stakeholders and that they are efficacious actors. Managers must make these arguments and evaluate whether their message is being understood. They must also ask community leaders, clients, and citizens for their support. When organizations fail to develop an adequate support base, they often encounter challenges and barriers in their development.

Diagnosis of a lack of support usually requires interviews with program and senior managers. The following are typical questions: "Which *ten* strategies do you use to promote the accomplishments and role of your organization? Who would you call for support in the event that your program or organization needed it? How effective do you know these supporters to be in public forums?" An inadequate answer may suggest the lack of an adequate support base. The diagnosis of effort in cultivating support involves such questions as these: "How much of your time do you spend cultivating new allies for your program or organization? Whom do you place on advisory groups and how do you use them?" Such questions get at the essence of deliberate activities to build a support base.

Organizational Challenges

Other problems of productivity are sometimes caused by not adhering to basic principles of organizational design. A wide range of symptoms such as infighting, lack of direction, and the inefficient use of resources may disappear when managers refocus on principles of design and structure. It is important to periodically reaffirm key tenets of organizational design, which are sometimes overlooked in daily practice.[3]

Form Follows Function

A principal task of management is to determine the function of organizations and units. In the public and nonprofit sectors, this is tantamount to deciding which constituencies they seek to serve and which needs they will address, developing an organizational structure to fulfill these needs, and reckoning with the limitations of resource constraints. A problem is that many organizations tend to develop new functions over time that are only loosely connected to each other. This is the result of continuing pressures and opportunities to provide new services. For example, schools face great pressures to provide an ever-expanding range of nonacademic services to students. Such diversification of effort dilutes the main objective of learning. It also causes units to emphasize their own goals, thereby leading to excessive intraorganizational rivalry over resources and priorities. For example, within schools, administrators often clash with teachers about funding for nonacademic pursuits. Such infighting is exacerbated when managers fail to reaffirm the purpose of the organization and build support for a common understanding of how different units contribute. Indeed, a primary purpose of many processes of organizational alignment is the restructuring around (new) purposes.

After the purpose of organizations has been decided on, a second principle of organizational design is that to get things done, *responsibility must be assigned and accepted for goals and tasks.* Goals are seldom accomplished in the absence of responsibility for them. Problems occur when leaders fail to delegate responsibility to managers; the latter feel that they are given inadequate direction and resources to accomplish their jobs. Significant tasks remain undone because leaders do not have sufficient time to accomplish everything by themselves. An interesting pathology is the resulting inversion of decision making through which operational decisions drift upward to top managers and policy decisions drift downward to lower managers, in part because of abdication by top managers and because lower units are searching for a clarification of their roles. This causes great confusion. Other problems of responsibility are assigning too little responsibility and frequent changes in responsibility, both of which cause managers problems in fulfilling their jobs.

Leaders must assign responsibilities and resources, and identify those tasks or units that are central to moving the organization into the future. In this regard, organization charts typically identify responsibilities for (a) services or products, (b) supporting activities such as those relating to human resources, technology, and cleaning, and (c) top management functions for allocating responsibilities, ensuring that responsibilities are fulfilled in appropriate ways, and negotiating relations with other organizations that affect the long-term survival of organizations. However, organization charts do not show which activities of which units are deemed critical for moving the organization forward to meet its critical goals and objectives at any point in time. When organizations do not have a sense of their priorities and resulting responsibilities, they are at risk of drift and, eventually, may lose their stakeholder support.

Many indicators of inadequate direction and assigning of responsibilities exist. Detection of these often requires interviews with managers and staff. When purpose or priorities are unclear, people at all levels are unclear about where their unit or organization is heading. People articulate the objectives of their own unit but cannot relate them to the bigger picture. They may respond to such questions as "What is the purpose of the organization?" by discussing their unit's processes and procedures rather than the objectives and goals of larger units. The presence of planning documents does not imply direction, because many documents are manufactured solely for public relations and by managers so that they will "look good." Ineffective leaders are often uncertain in what way their actions are perceived as leadership by others, and they typically find little support from others that their actions are meaningful examples of leadership. When responsibilities are unclear or not assigned, people are confused about expectations. When the problem persists over time, it is likely that some stakeholders are underserved, which gives rise to complaints. Some employees will state that they believe they could be doing a better job, and that morale is therefore becoming a problem; some employees become upset about their unit's poor performance, whereas others become indifferent: "If management doesn't know or care where it is going, why should we?" However, staff morale may also indicate other problems, and the diagnosis of inadequate direction must include other indicators mentioned in Table 2.1.

Organization

Another task of organizational design is organizing people, resources, and technology for fulfilling responsibilities. This might be called the *organization of responsibility*. There are many different ways in which activities can be organized. In general, activities should be organized so as to take advantage of

economies of scale (such as increased efficiency through larger production as well as meeting minimum requirements of critical mass),

economies of scope (that is, increased efficiency through diversification, for example, by leveraging expertise),

cost-effective production methods (including decisions about the extent of specialization, uses of information technology, etc.),

state-of-the-art standards, and

responsiveness to changes in the environment and customer demands.

Additional criteria of adequate information and devolution of decision-making authority are also used, reflecting recent developments in quality management. The above criteria seldom suggest one best way of organizing; specific, situational factors must be taken into account. What works well for one organization may not work well in another. For example, new technology often has economies of scale: Magnetic resonance imaging (MRI) equipment requires minimum use rates. Hospitals can organize this technology by purchasing it as equipment for individual service departments, by establishing new MRI units that are viewed as cost or profit centers, by purchasing it from third party providers, and by forming partnerships with other hospitals (thereby minimizing use uncertainty and avoiding third party profits). What is best depends on specific factors. For example, a research hospital may wish to purchase the equipment so that it can be configured for its research scientists.

Organizations frequently change because conditions change. For example, multiple research hospitals may decide to form a regional partnership to suit their needs, thereby causing the previous "solution" of purchasing to be obsolete. In recent years, the need for increased responsiveness has caused many organizations to reconsider their use of departments as basic units of organization. Departments are justifiably used when there are well-defined areas of responsibility that have continuity of purpose, and there are minimum economies of scale, scope, or critical mass that must be met. Departments can also shield organizations from resource uncertainty, for example, by ensuring a pool of qualified personnel. But concerns about the rigidity of departments as well as sometimes high cost structures (especially in the era of budget constraints) cause top managers to consider partnerships, alliances, and outsourcing as alternative ways for obtaining capacity. Although not all activities can be contracted out (e.g., law enforcement), many services can be cheaply obtained through third party providers. It should be noted that many authors caution against contracting out core functions. For responsibilities that are unstable over time, organizations emphasize a looser structure that can be created and abandoned as needed: Project management, coalitions, and networks are some approaches that are used to ensure flexibility and innovation.[4]

Another reason that organizations must change is the use of new technology. Information technologies are increasingly essential to meeting the challenge of higher workloads. Electronic databases allow employees to access client records across units; this increases responsiveness to clients and reduces labor costs. Internet "home pages" help organizations deal efficiently with many routine client inquiries. Such pages often are interactive, which enables organizations to deal with a broader range of transactions. As these tools become more widely used, so too do client expectations that all organizations use them. The implementation of these technologies requires considerable organization itself. Technical staff must be hired to help employees install and maintain these new systems, and employees must be trained in their use. The cost of such equipment is often considerable, which means that its acquisition must be budgeted and planned for. Moreover, because the speed of technological innovation is high, the rate of obsolescence is high too. Thus renewal of information technology infrastructure requires ongoing planning.

The ability to use new forms of organization to increase responsiveness and lower costs is a hallmark of modern organizations. When organizations fail to take advantage of these new forms, they often experience increasing resource-task mismatches. One such indicator consists of employee complaints about inadequate resources to meet demand. That is, the old structure no longer supports the higher workload, and people are overworked. The inability to meet expectations erodes confidence. Comparisons with past efforts can be used to show increasing resource shortfalls, for example, on a staff-per-client basis, and client interviews may suggest that service priorities are inadequately met. Also, technology is not being effectively used, and managers seem unwilling or unable to deal with the new challenge. These are clear indicators of the need to rethink the way that people and resources are being organized to meet existing responsibilities.

Communication

Organizations bring together people with different areas of specialization as well as resources and technologies to produce services and products. Coordination of resources and activities is essential. To succeed, the following principles apply. First, units, and individuals within units, need to have a *clear understanding of responsibilities,* what is expected from them in terms of both results and communication, and how their authority relates to that of others. Problems arise when people are confused about their roles and how they relate to others. People make assumptions, and some of these assumptions lead to conflict. Second, these understandings, expectations, and relations should be kept *as simple as possible.* Complex rules breed uncertainty and confusion. People forget their rules or are confused about how they apply in a variety of different situations. Rules should also be relatively constant over time, because frequent changes create confusion and demoralization, which, in turn, leads to decreased productivity.

Third, every formal structure depends on informal relations and much goodwill to produce high-quality results. Individuals must be willing to go above and beyond that which is expected of them to deal with unforeseen situations. *No formal structure is sufficient: Rewards, incentives, and norms must encourage productive behavior.* Incentives are necessary to encourage productive behaviors and to reward accomplishment. People need to know through material and other forms of recognition that they are doing well. When rewards are perceived as small and insignificant, managers lose an important tool of motivation and morale, and productivity may suffer. Thus managers need a broad range of rewards, such as opportunities for promotion, training, conference travel, and temporary experiences working in other departments. However, managers must go beyond incentives, too. Managers demotivate employees when they fail to give praise. They must lead by example and set the tone and standard for communications and interpersonal relations. Managers must also smooth the wheels of communication within and across departments.

Policy and procedure manuals are helpful but are insufficient to deal with the communication problem. Indeed, large manuals often breed confusion and reflect the lack of adequate verbal communication that is necessary to help people do their jobs. By contrast, interviews help identify job aspects about which employees are unclear and confused. Frequent work-related complaints about individuals or units often indicate uncertainty about expectations and the rules for coordinating activities. Manager-diagnosticians should also examine whether responsibilities have been assigned to interface with other departments, and assess how well these liaisons are functioning in ensuring cooperation. Finally, the reward structures of units and departments must be evaluated to ensure that employees and managers receive appropriate feedback and incentives that promote productive behavior and accomplishment.

People Problems

Employee motivation and skills are critical problems in the productivity of organizations. When people lack motivation, productivity suffers. The key is to get employees and managers to adopt professional orientations: This involves acquiring and using appropriate technical skills, adopting social skills that promote teamwork and getting along, and promoting values that support professional cultures that are characterized by openness, integrity, and responsibility, which are necessary for productivity improvement (van Wart, 1998). Once a professional orientation is accepted by an individual, professional standards of conduct help guide behavior with minimal and less costly supervision.

3-D Professionalism

Professionalism involves technical skills, social skills, and professionalism; it is multidimensional. For example, productivity problems occur when people lack up-to-date technical skills for the work they are expected to do. This causes work to be performed at substandard levels or to be performed inefficiently. As examples, a land surveyor who does not use the latest methods will take longer and be less accurate; mental health workers who are unfamiliar with the latest therapies may be less effective. Productivity problems increase when people avoid doing certain tasks because they lack skills, such as the secretary who avoids budget activities because of a lack of spreadsheet or basic bookkeeping knowledge.

The problem of ensuring up-to-date skills varies somewhat according to one's stage of career and job situation. People who recently graduated tend to have up-to-date skills, but they may lack experience in applying them. Mentoring or in-house training is crucial to acquiring this knowledge quickly. People who have been on the job for a long time may lack the opportunity to learn the latest methods in their field. Attending professional conferences and continuing education courses is essential to staying up to date. People who are transferring between jobs may find that they need both to update their skills and to learn new applications for existing skills. It is relatively easy to detect skill deficits by asking people to perform tasks that require the skills. It is usually not very effective simply to ask about skills, because people who seek a job or those who put up facades inevitably say that they do possess skills that they do not possess adequately.

However, professional skills alone do not ensure productivity by people. Many activities require teamwork, and the ability to work in teams and to get along is vital to productivity. Indeed, those who rub people the wrong way not only produce conflict or tension in group efforts, they also cause others not to use them in future endeavors. Thus productivity suffers twice. In this regard, employees whose background emphasizes professional skill development at the expense of social skills are often surprised to find themselves both heavily recruited and subsequently cast out of work groups.

A variety of different perspectives exist regarding critically needed social skills. Covey (1994) discusses the importance of refraining from saying unkind or negative things; the importance of exercising patience with others, keeping promises made to others, exercising love and assuming the best in others, seeking to understand before reacting, giving an understanding (rather than evaluative) response, admitting mistakes, apologizing and asking for forgiveness, allowing oneself to be influenced, and distinguishing between the person and the problem. These rules help to "grease the wheels" of social interaction, but they do not deny self; for example, understanding others first does not imply that we agree with others. Differences are discussed by seeking out common ground and mutual interests without blame. Goleman (1995) argues that the "emotional intelligence" of people determines professional success more than their IQ. According to Goleman, the fundamentals of EQ are self-awareness (about one's own feelings), controlling one's impulses, optimism in the face of setbacks, identifying and responding to the unspoken feelings of others, and social skills (e.g., handling emotional reactions in others, interacting smoothly, managing relations effectively).

In recent years, the role of organizational culture has been increasingly acknowledged as an asset for productivity improvement (Harrison & Beyer, 1993; Kotter & Heskett, 1992; Schein, 1992). Professionalism is more than the acquisition of technical and social skills alone. It is also a set of values. The term *organizational culture* is loosely defined as the values and norms of organizations as embodied by the beliefs and practices of its members. Cultures vary.

Professional cultures emphasize accountability, responsiveness, openness, and integrity. Integrity implies that people fulfill their word. Such values are consistent with many productivity improvement. By contrast, the absence of professional values and norms is often a barrier. For example, cultures of apathy and depression are slow to adopt modern practices, or to do so with the zeal and commitment that make a difference. Cultures of confusion lack constancy of purpose and hence the possibility of seeing good strategies through to completion. Cultures of greed are short-term oriented and lack sufficient social cohesion. Top managers play important roles in defining such values and instilling such values in lower managers.

There are several reasons for the lack of open communication, integrity, and respect that characterizes cultures of fear, greed, and confusion. For example, the "game" of organizational politics causes concern about exposing a variety of falsehoods. Communication and openness threaten to reveal skills that people claim but do not have. Openness in decision making also exposes flawed judgments and bad intentions such as efforts to discredit colleagues without good cause. Ill intentions require the cloak of secrecy (DuBrin, 1990). Although many employees and new managers object to such power games, they nonetheless are realities in many organizations. In addition, managers sometimes bring personal problems and dysfunctional orientations to their jobs, which impairs a positive culture. For example, managers may suffer from personal insecurity that causes them to seek positions of power and to be heavy-handed in their decision making and implementation. These activities aim to compensate for insecurity but are seldom successful because they do not address underlying problems. Such managers frequently fail to seek adequate input from employees and, as a consequence, often base their decisions on limited information. The lack of input and autonomy also causes distrust between employees and managers. This lowers employee motivation, which causes micromanagement by managers, which further lowers employee motivation in a vicious cycle. Insecure, authoritarian managers may suffer additional symptoms of anorexia or obesity, excessive overwork, a need to make derogatory comments, anxiety, unbalanced personalities, and inflexibility.

Other problems include rigid adherence to personal values that become dysfunctional when they induce secrecy or prejudice, substitute for professional judgment, or otherwise reduce trust. Some examples of values that may become dysfunctional when they are indiscriminately applied are that people cannot be trusted, that good is never good enough, that it's OK to lie, that it's never OK to lie, that feelings should not be expressed in public, that life is to be endured but not enjoyed, and so forth. Such values, when rigidly applied, produce results that may be a barrier to open communication (McClure & Werther, 1995). Schaef and Fassel (1988) also note that addictions are widespread in American society and that behaviors of secrecy and confusion are sometimes associated with addictive personalities. In some instances, power is itself the source of addiction. Characteristics of addictive behavior are being self-centered, thriving on confusion and a lack of communication, and promulgating cover-ups and untruths. Such behavior decreases productivity and productivity improvement. Overcoming these problems of addiction, dysfunctional rules, poor values, and false professionalism is an enduring challenge to productivity improvement.

Diagnosis

Only in rare instances can the diagnosis of skill deficits be determined through tests. Skill deficits are usually observed over time through sustained lack of performance, task avoidance, or client complaints about services. For example, insurance companies may note that some service providers fail to resolve particular problems. Supervisors note that some employees avoid administrative responsibilities, only to find out that they lack budgeting skills. Eventually, incompetence shines through. People claim skills because it makes them appear professional, and few others are willing to challenge them lest they be held to similar scrutiny as well. This problem is exacerbated in professions in which standards are somewhat subjective.

Some professionals are extensively educated in the technical aspects of their careers but lack interpersonal or supervisory management skills. Productivity suffers when professionals with limited interpersonal skills become supervisors or managers without appropriate training in this area. The diagnosis of troubled social skills is usually based on a person's record of social interaction. Signs of social skill deficits are being disliked by others in the absence of other specific causes such as policy disagreements or political infighting. People are usually quite clear about those they socially dislike, although they may hesitate or find it difficult to give specific reasons. The hesitation is because the reasons are not professional in nature; they are social.

Diagnosing value shortfalls is often a difficult task. One approach is to observe behavior. Professional values are proactive with regard to competence and responsibility, and adamant about honesty. Managers who consistently seek out opportunities for improving organizations, who seek to address stakeholder needs, and who implement strategies in an open and impartial way are more likely to be acting in accordance with professional values than those who fail to proactively undertake strategies or who implement them in secretive ways that promote favoritism. In this regard, apathy may reflect inadequacy in the professional values of being proactive. Apathetic managers are, for example, identified by the absence of mentoring or training for new staff and the lack of plans for improvement. A drawback is that diagnosis through observation is difficult and time-consuming. For this reason, hiring should always involve a thorough assessment, background checks, and detailed interviews of references and past employees.

An alternative is to interview employees and managers. Employees who operate in cultures of professionalism, openness, and integrity almost invariably comment about the honesty of their supervisors, the openness of information in the organization, the commitment to professional standards, and opportunities to make a difference. Employees who operate in other cultures often focus on nonprofessional elements, such as having nice colleagues, "getting along," and long holidays. Conversation about accomplishment and professional ethics is absent. They may also complain about confusion and self-centered behavior by supervisors. People who are not committed to professionalism frequently avoid direct discussion of their plans and accomplishments. However, the presence of professional statements alone does not necessarily indicate professionalism; it may be a facade.[5] Table 2.2 provides some further diagnostic measures.

Projects and Programs

Projects and programs are the focus of older productivity improvement strategies yet continue to offer numerous opportunities for improvement. Programs are defined as a set of resources, directed toward one or more common goals, under the direction of a single program manager such as in the Head Start program. Programs encompass projects, which are smaller in scope and typically have beginning and ending dates. Three common problems in project management are cost overruns, time overruns, and poor performance or quality. Indicators of poor project management often focus on these aspects.

Planning for Accomplishment

Programs and projects often experience delays due to unforeseen events. Delays reduce efficiency and may result in a loss of effectiveness. Planning is important for anticipating such events. The hallmark of properly managed

TABLE 2.2 Indicators of Productivity Problems: People and Programs

---

People Problems:

1. Is your staff professional?

   Indicators: lack of skills for performing tasks; avoiding tasks; lack of efforts to upgrade skills; lack of commitment to professional norms of competence, honesty, and responsibility; presence of apathy or carelessness

2. Which employees have insufficient people skills?

   Indicators: not getting along with people, complaints about personal interactions, being shunned, impatience, not keeping promises and commitments, personalizing events, interactions that cause stress and illness

3. Are relations healthy?

   Indicators: unclear communication, avoiding discussion about problems, persistent confusion, ill-intended behaviors, lack of performance, ridicule of ethics, overdrawn stories of heroism

Projects and Programs:

4. What is your time schedule?

   Indicators: lack of deadlines and due dates, lack of contingency planning, missing deadlines, lack of accountability for meeting deadlines

5. Are resources and technology used efficiently? What techniques are used?

   Indicators: lack of work redesign efforts, lack of use of analytical techniques for project management, lack of ground rules for teams, lack of empowerment/too close supervision

6. How are short-, mid-, and long-term outcomes measured?

   Indicators: lack of program evaluation, lack of stakeholder surveys, lack of performance monitoring and measurement, not meeting performance standards

7. Who supports the program?

   Indicators: lack of support for projects/program, lack of efforts to cultivate support, lack of effective support, not using support effectively

---

programs is that they achieve their objectives (a) on time, (b) within budget, and (c) at or above quality and performance specifications. Common problems are delays caused by faulty equipment and tardy vendors, errors in service due to poorly prepared staff or poor communication with clients about their needs and expectations, illness or departure of key personnel, and changes in rules and regulations. A great number of these problems can be prevented or anticipated.

Because delays have myriad causes, planning must be inclusive in nature. Planning is needed with regard to personnel, resources, technology, and management. Projects and programs typically have different phases or periods of activity (e.g., start-up), and planning must take the requirements of different periods into account. Planning must also include target dates for different activities. In this regard, time management is not only a planning activity but also a mind-set: Productive managers worry about meeting deadlines, and they do whatever it takes to keep their projects and programs on track with regard to cost, time, and quality. Diagnostics for the lack of planning include repeated slippage, cost overruns, and poor quality. Although planning is often done informally, concerns about delays increasingly cause managers to adopt formal approaches to planning that allow more detail. Examples of such planning for very complex projects involve space shuttle launches and defense logistical operations.

In recent years, efficiency gains have frequently been made through redesigned of work processes and the use of new technologies. Work process redesign focuses on the elimination of steps that cause delays and add little value to the project as a whole. Delays associated with unnecessary approvals are eliminated and, where possible, activities are undertaken in parallel rather than sequential fashion. Because work process redesign is increasingly commonplace, the lack of "reengineering" may qualify as a productivity problem. New technologies are also used to improve project management: Computers now allow for networking in ways that reduce the need for frequent meetings. Traditional analytical techniques help in the efficient use of resources, for example, those related to scheduling and inventory control. The absence of such techniques, where they should appropriately be used, might be a diagnostic of problems.

Empowerment and teamwork are essential to productivity. A source of great inefficiency is the lack of adequate empowerment, and managers need skills to help employees work as teams. For example, ground rules need to be established and maintained for agreeing to finish work on time, respecting the ideas of others, and attending meetings. New managers often have problems exerting leadership. Thus diagnostics include the use of empowerment techniques as well. It should be noted, though, that a lack of use of modern methods may indicate other productivity problems. Often, higher level managers introduce techniques that are disseminated at lower levels. In some organizations, inadequate emphasis exists about such diffusion, reflecting the incorrect belief that managers will pick up such new techniques.

Stakeholder Satisfaction

Stakeholders are often surprised and disappointed about the level of information that is available about program outcomes. The effectiveness of programs or projects often is not known with any accuracy. The reason is that many administrative records focus on control and accountability rather than improvement and responsiveness. Admittedly, outcome measures are sometimes difficult to specify (see Chapter 3), yet it is important to generate such information because programs and projects are funded in the expectation that they are effective (and efficient) in responding to public needs. Often, managers in public and nonprofit organizations fail to undertake outcome assessments because long-term impacts cannot be accurately assessed. This is unfortunate because knowledge of short-term outcomes (i.e., outputs) is relevant and affects long-term outcomes. Short-term outcomes are measurable and can provide feedback that helps improve programs.

Diagnostics focus on the frequency, thoroughness, and use of outcome assessments by project and program managers. Typically, these assessments involve surveys of clients, which provide information about the effectiveness of program efforts. Some assessment methods use focus groups composed of program clients. The use of these assessments is essential, and thus diagnostics include this aspect too.

As mentioned earlier, the development of stakeholder support is an important part of public and nonprofit management. What is true for organizations is also valid at the lower levels of programs and projects. Accomplishing outcomes at these lower levels provides no protection against politically inspired attacks from external sources and other program managers. Thus an important challenge is to create allies who support projects and programs. Important allies are higher managers who can provide cover from attacks by other units. Managers need to be persuaded that the program or project contributes to their goals for the unit or organization. Managers should also cultivate a cadre of clients and citizens who are likely to speak up in favor of the program when needed; advisory groups are often used. Diagnoses focus on awareness so as to create a cadre of supporters and to proactively undertake efforts to build a group of program or project supporters.

From Diagnosis to Improvement

Many productivity strategies serve multiple goals. For example, process reengineering, discussed in Chapter 7, helps solve problems of organizational realignment as well as increasing the customer orientation and openness. Motivational strategies affect values as well as orientations toward skill upgrading (Chapter 10). The above productivity problems can be addressed through a variety of different strategies, and managers sometimes address persistent problems through a combination of strategies over time. For example, problems of morale and professionalism might be addressed by parallel strategies of motivation and strategic planning, followed by empowerment and a customer orientation. It follows that because productivity strategies serve a multitude of goals, focus is of crucial importance in ensuring that productivity improvement strategies address and resolve the problems that give rise to their application.

Nonetheless, some general guidance exists for applying the productivity improvement strategies of this book to the above problems. Problems of goal-setting and customer focus are often addressed by strategic planning (Chapter 5) and quality management (Chapter 7). Problems of stakeholder support are addressed through broad-based strategic planning (Chapter 5), effective partnering (Chapter 6), and effective communication (Chapter 11). Problems of organizational structure are addressed through reorganization and privatization (Chapter 6), reengineering (Chapter 7), and the use of information technology (Chapter 9). Problems of individual motivation and behavior, communication, and the productivity of teams are discussed in Chapter 10. Problems of program and project management are addressed through project tools (Chapter 9), quality management (Chapter 7), and efficiency enhancement (Chapter 8). Problems of raising revenues and decreasing costs are also discussed in Chapter 8. Managers who take up productivity improvement causes find opportunities to address them in much of what they do, but the above strategies are uniquely focused on the above objectives.

It bears repeating that implementation is a critical determinant of successful productivity improvement. The best-laid plans comes to naught in the face of poor planning and resistance. Implementation strategy is a cornerstone of productivity improvement and is discussed in Chapter 4. Measurement helps evaluate and justify the use of productivity strategies and is discussed in Chapter 3.

Summary

This chapter discusses frequent productivity problems in public and nonprofit organizations as well as strategies for diagnosis. It discusses problems dealing with clients and other external stakeholders, various problems associated with organization and relations among units, problems of dealing with people, and problems of program and project management. Within each area, specific productivity challenges are discussed. This chapter also provides strategies for diagnosing problems. It cautions managers and diagnosticians to use multiple measures and to look for consistency among these measures.

Notes

1. A caveat is that this chapter does not take a developmental perspective on organizations. Organizations go through different stages, which causes them to experience different problems. Another caveat is that this chapter does not aim to provide an exhaustive overview of productivity challenges, only those that are frequently mentioned. Technically, most of this chapter is based on an open systems model of organizations. It focus on goal attainment and processes that affect that. It focuses less on system fits and other aspects that are discussed in Chapter 3, which focuses on change management.

2. On a scale of 3 = strongly agree to –3 = strongly disagree, respondents indicated that community leaders have only modest agreement with the statements that government understands the needs of community organizations (1.2) and that government services meet the needs of community organizations (1.5).

3. As pointed out nearly 50 years ago by Herbert Simon, every principle has exceptions. Still, the following principles are generally useful.

4. Matrix organizations combine elements of functional and service organizations but are increasingly less common for reasons mentioned in the following section on communication. Also, functional organizations are increasingly less common because coordination across areas of expertise causes frequent delays (see Chapter 7).

5. This raises the question of why organizations keep apathetic managers. One reason is that apathetic managers are less of a competitive threat to other managers.

References

Ammons, D. (1995). *Accountability for performance.* Washington, DC: International City/County Managers Association (ICMA).

Berman, E. (1996). Restoring the bridges of trust: Attitudes of community leaders toward local government. *Public Integrity Annual, 1*(1), 31-39.

Berman, E. (1997). Dealing with cynical citizens. *Public Administration Review, 57*(2), 104-112.

Covey, S. (1994). *Principle-centered leadership.* New York: Simon & Schuster.

Drucker, P. (1990). *Managing the non-profit organization.* New York: Harper Business.

DuBrin, A. (1990). *Winning office politics.* Englewood Cliffs, NJ: Prentice Hall.

Goleman, D. (1995). *Emotional intelligence.* New York: Bantam.

Gore, A. (1995). *Common sense government.* New York: Random House.

Halachmi, A. (1996). Measure of excellence. In H. Hill (Ed.), *Quality, innovation and measurement in the public sector.* Frankfurt, Germany: Lang.

Harrison, M. (1994). *Diagnosing organizations.* Thousand Oaks, CA: Sage.

Harrison, M., & Beyer, J. (1993). *The cultures of work organizations.* Englewood Cliffs, NJ: Prentice Hall.

Herman, R. (1994). *Handbook of nonprofit leadership and management.* San Francisco: Jossey-Bass.

Kennedy, L. (1991). *Quality management in the nonprofit world.* San Francisco: Jossey-Bass.

Kotter, J., & Heskett, J. (1992). *Corporate culture and performance.* Toronto, Canada: Free Press.

Linden, R. (1992). Meeting which customers' needs? *Public Manager, 21*(4), 49-52.

McClendon, B. (1992). *Customer service in local government.* Washington, DC: American Planning Association.

McClendon, B., & Catonese, A. (1996). *Planners on planning.* San Francisco: Jossey-Bass.

McClure, L., & Werther, W. (1995). Leadership and developmental interventions for dysfunctional workers. *Leadership & Organization Development Journal, 16*(1), 17-22.

Rosander, A. (1989). *The quest for quality in services.* Milwaukee, WI: American Society for Quality Control.

Schaef, A., & Fassel, D. (1988). *The addictive organization.* San Francisco: Harper & Row.

Schein, E. (1992). *Organizational culture and leaders.* San Francisco: Jossey-Bass.

van Wart, M. (1998). *Changing public sector values.* New York: Garland Press.

3

Measuring Productivity

The Need for Measurement

Funding agencies, elected officials, and citizens want to know what public and nonprofit organizations are accomplishing. Through measurement, public and nonprofit organizations give accountability for their results, show responsiveness to clients and constituents, improve the planning and budgeting of programs by obtaining an objective assessment of what is working and what is needed, and determine the effectiveness of productivity improvement efforts. Measurement is also used to provide cost justification for investment decisions, and it helps with the oversight of contracts by keeping contractors accountable for their results. Measurement is a foundation of productivity improvement. It is consistent with professional norms of accountability, openness, and maintaining high standards, and many organizations need managers and employees with the ability to measure program outcomes (Ammons, 1995; Greiner, 1996; Hatry & Fisk, 1992; International City/County Managers Association [ICMA], 1995; Kanter & Summers, 1987).

Productivity measurement can be either a one-time event or an ongoing activity. As a one-time effort, it frequently uses program evaluation strategies that were developed in the 1960s and 1970s, which provide a detailed and comprehensive analysis of outcomes. These approaches also seek to determine the unique effect of program activities on program outcomes. Examples of program evaluation include many assessments of the Head Start program, crisis response programs, and technology development efforts. Although some evaluations are repeated over time, they are nonetheless understood as discrete studies (Rossi & Freeman, 1993). Since the early 1990s, however, productivity measurement is increasingly used as an ongoing activity, called *performance measurement,* and is increasingly demanded by the U.S. Congress, state legislatures, local bodies, and grant agencies. For example, the 1993 Government Performance and Results Act requires federal agencies to establish quantitative performance measures and targets. Agencies are required to submit annual reports that monitor their performance. Usually, performance measurement is not as comprehensive as program evaluations. Only a few key indicators are used. Some cities and organizations provide quarterly performance measurement reports and have developed a detailed infrastructure for generating and analyzing outcome-oriented performance data.[1]

As an ongoing activity, performance measurement is increasingly tied to budgeting and strategic planning in public and nonprofit organizations. Performance measurement allows units to show how they are making progress toward strategic objectives, and this information feeds into the funding decisions of the budget process. In a recent survey, 73% of cities more than 50,000 indicated the use of performance measurement, and 44% used it citywide in all departments (Berman & West, 1997). Likewise, 78% of large social service organizations report the use of performance measurement, and 43% use it in all departments. Of the large museums, 67% use performance measurement, and 36% do so organizationwide (Berman, 1997).[2] The growing use of performance measurement is furthered by the continuing importance of accountability, the diffusion of modern management information systems that reduce the cost of acquiring performance information, and the increased use of client surveys.

Regardless of whether productivity is measured once or as a monitoring system, the principles of scientific measurement remain much the same. The following section discusses methods and examples of measuring the productivity of public and nonprofit organizations. This chapter also discusses issues related to the quality of measurement, to data collection, and to the implementation of strategies for productivity measurement.

Measures of Productivity

Measuring Effectiveness

Effectiveness is vital for productivity in public and nonprofit organizations. Effectiveness is defined as the *level of outcomes* accomplished. For example, the number of clients that are successfully served, the level of satisfaction that clients or citizens experience with program services, or the number of visitors to museum exhibitions. Outcomes are accomplishments, not efforts. Long-term outcomes are distinguished from outputs, as discussed in Chapter 1. Long-term outcomes (or goals) measure the ultimate objectives of organizations and reflect basic rationales for programs and organizations. The time horizon of such goals is often three to five years and sometime even more. For example, some long-term outcomes of museums are to increase the quality of life in cities and increase support and appreciation for local artists. Goals of many teacher improvement programs (which help teachers teach better) are to increase the reputation of school districts and to help students learn more. A long-term outcome of teen courts (a pretrial diversion program for first-time juvenile offenders) is to produce responsible and productive citizens (Brinkerhoff & Dressler, 1990; Hakes, 1996).

Outputs are defined as outcomes that are the direct, immediate consequences of strategies. They are sometimes called short-term outcomes. It is a tenet of productivity measurement that all activities produce short-term outcomes. All activities have consequences. For example, teacher training programs often increase the skills of teachers to communicate difficult material, to conduct classes in an orderly manner, to better prepare lesson plans, and so on. AIDS awareness programs produce greater knowledge among target populations about how the virus is transmitted, how the possibility of infection is reduced, where to go for testing, and the availability of community resources in the (unfortunate) event of HIV infection. Outputs occur as a result of program activities and are subsequently linked to long-term outcomes. For example, greater awareness of how HIV is transmitted is intended to affect sexual behavior, which, in turn, is aimed to reduce the incidence of future HIV infections—a program goal.

Productivity measurement efforts begin by (a) specifying the activity that is being evaluated and (b) identifying outcomes and outputs that are to be assessed. An important distinction between ad hoc program evaluation and ongoing performance measurement is that program evaluation attempts to measure all outcomes and outputs, including those that occur but are not intended. Such elaboration is an extensive, but justified, process because program evaluation seeks a complete and comprehensive assessment of the program. By contrast, performance measurement focuses only on key outcomes. Only those outputs and outcomes are measured that are most important to the program and that can be measured within the context of current or slightly expanded management information systems. For example, some easily measured outputs of crime control are the clearance rate of burglary, murder, robbery, rape, and narcotics cases as well as the percentage of cases closed, the timeliness of responses to 911 calls, and the number of arrests. Some outcome measures are the actual burglary and other crime rates, citizen fear of crime, teen participation in gangs, the level of illegal drug use, and death and injury resulting from automobile accidents (Tigue & Strachota, 1994). These data are often available but some may require citizen surveys. Although many different measures exist, programs seldom use more than five to ten of such measures to gauge their performance.

A practical challenge is sometimes identifying key outcomes and outputs (Poister, 1992). Program outcomes are sometimes unclear, for example, when managers are placed in charge of already existing programs. Wholey, Hatry, and Newcomer (1994) suggest asking questions of employees and stakeholders to clarify outcomes. Discussing program effectiveness measures with key stakeholders is also instrumental in building a cadre of supporters. The purpose of questions is to clarify the importance of different outcomes and outputs according to client and citizen needs. The latter often have clear ideas about what programs should accomplish that are markedly different than notions held by managers and employees. This helps build a balanced perspective about which outcomes are essential. Employee input is also useful in suggesting outputs and ways in which they might be measured. Another challenge is that some outcomes are very difficult to measure, such as crimes that are prevented or improvements in mental health. The usual strategy in these instances is, first, to focus on those outcomes that can be measured and, second, to use subjective assessments of clients and citizens to collect data about these more difficult to measure outcomes.

The relationship between long-term outcomes and outputs is not always singular. For example, a reduction in AIDS cases (an outcome) may be caused by campaigns to increase awareness or the use of new drugs, or both. That is, outcomes are affected by program activities as well as other occurring events. Whereas program evaluation designs take great pains to isolate program effects from other effects (see below), performance measurement acknowledges these other effects but focuses on outputs. The reasons for emphasizing outputs over outcomes are (a) that managers have more control over outputs and (b) that program outcomes occur over time horizons that are very long from the vantage point of program development. Program outputs are more relevant for today's decisions. Current program outcomes are shaped by past program activities, not those of the present. However, program outcomes are useful to increase understanding of the salience of current program goals. Program outcomes help assess the relevance of proposed activities and output measures.

In some instances, it may be necessary to consider midterm outcomes too. These are defined as outcomes that link outputs and long-term outcomes. For example, it is plausible to hypothesize that improved teaching increases school reputations through improved test scores and student/parent satisfaction with classroom learning environments. The latter are midterm outcomes that are caused by increased teacher skills. In HIV/AIDS awareness programs, an important midterm outcome is change in sexual behavior. As previously mentioned, such change may be caused by increased information (i.e., short-term outcomes) and is intended to reduce the number of new AIDS cases—a program goal. The time length of short-, mid-, and long-term outcomes varies across programs. For example, teacher improvement programs may take six weeks and thus too have short-term outcomes. However, the impact of AIDS awareness campaigns takes much longer. Generally, short-term outputs occur within 3 to 18 months, midterm outcomes in one to three years, and long-term outcomes usually require at least three years.

A useful analytic technique in program evaluation is a program flowchart or model that provides a comprehensive view of resources, activities, outputs, and outcomes. Figure 3.1 shows an example of a program model, based on Wholey, Hatry, and Newcomer (1994), that identifies outcomes as well as strategies and resources associated with a local program that brings recreational opportunities to disadvantaged neighborhoods through mobile units (called Rec 'n' Roll). This program is operated by the Orange County Parks and Recreation Department, Florida. When used in performance measurement, program models help (a) to communicate in a visual way the nature and importance of the program and (b) to link key performance indicators to specific outcomes.[3] It is important to reiterate that performance measurement identifies only key outcomes and outputs for which data are readily available.

Measuring Efficiency

Efficiency is defined as the ratio of outcomes or outputs to inputs (O/I), for example, the number of client problems solved per counselor, the number of crimes solved per police officer, or the number of completed health inspections per health inspector (Halachmi, 1992; Rosen, 1993).[4] Efficiency calculations

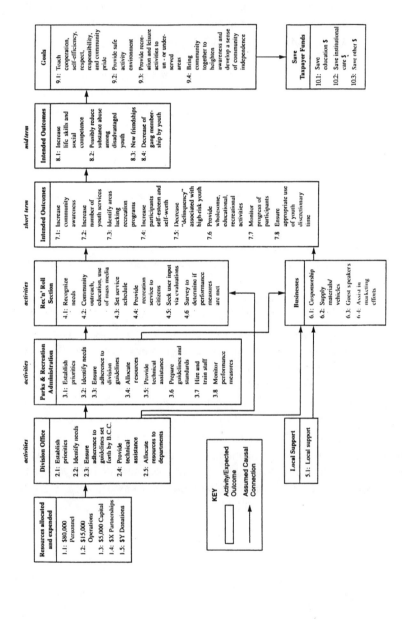

Figure 3.1. Orange County Parks and Recreation's Rec 'n' Roll Program: Resources, Outcomes, Goals

require that managers have data about outcomes and inputs. It bears repeating that efficiency measures focus on outcomes, not activities; caseloads or service calls per employee are not measures of efficiency. (They are discussed further.)

Efficiency can be measured in many different ways. It is seldom possible to measure the efficiency of an entire public or nonprofit organization. In its simplest approach, conceptually, efficiency is calculated by identifying all outcomes and dividing these by all inputs. This is called *total efficiency.* For example, a measure of total efficiency is the total cost per counselor of solving all client problems, or the total cost per completed health inspection. Total efficiency requires that all costs be taken into account, hence salaries, overhead, materials, and so forth. It also requires enumeration of all outcomes. When multiple outcomes are produced, then these too must be taken into account. For example, when a second outcome is the processing of insurance claims, total efficiency is the average cost for solving X problems and Y insurance claims per counselor. Total efficiency is a simple but impractical measure when multiple outcomes exist that are not readily aggregated in the same units. This is often the case in dealing with public and nonprofit outputs that are not readily expressed dollar or other common units.

For this reason, most efficiency measures focus on single outcomes. These are called *partial efficiency* measures. For example, teacher outputs include student test scores, graduation rates, as well as student counseling and advancing community interests through volunteer efforts. The number of students who pass standardized tests per teacher is a measure of partial efficiency. It does not assess other outcomes, such as counseling or volunteer services. Performance measures are often based on such practical considerations as the availability of data. For example, student test scores may be available but not other measures of student ability or attitude. Other examples, drawn from public safety, are the cost per cleared case, cost (or hours) per arrest, cost per emergency response call that is attended to, number of executed warrants per employee per day, cost per collected traffic citation, average time per completed assist to other agencies, and so on.

Managers must choose in what ways they will measure inputs. The basic efficiency formula assumes that all inputs are taken into consideration, that is, salaries, overhead, materials, and so forth. This approach is complicated by the fact that while such data are often available at the level of organizations, they are seldom readily available for subunits. Also, using such data for lower units requires that managers allocate fractions of overhead and capital expenditures to different units or even individual employees. Lower units of analysis frequently use salary cost or number of personnel as input measures. This is called *labor efficiency.* Such measures are justified because lower level managers often have little control over overhead. In the above examples, a measure of labor efficiency is the number of client problems solved per counselor or the fraction of students who pass tests per teacher. A common problem in calculating labor efficiency is dividing outcomes into labor totals without appropriately allocating the fraction of labor that is responsible for producing the output. This is justifiable only when units that are compared are assumed to have the same labor allocations. For this reason, efficiency measures are often controversial when used to make comparisons across organizations. For example, some schools have higher graduation rates per teacher but also make more use of teacher assistants and computer resources. Efficiency measures are usually used to compare the development of organizations over time.

Although measures of partial labor efficiency are widely used, some other measures bear mention as well. *Marginal efficiency* is the cost of producing an additional increment of output, for example, the cost of serving an additional client or servicing a larger student population. Marginal efficiency often ignores costs that are essentially fixed (e.g., costs of buildings or staff support) that do not change when increasing outputs incrementally. Another distinction related to the valuation of inputs is the concept of social versus private efficiency. Inputs can be calculated from the perspective of society or that of the organization. For example, from society's perspective, building and building maintenance costs should be included in efficiency measures, even when they are not paid for by an agency or program. Likewise, the use of volunteers might be regarded as a free resource for program officials, but from the perspective of society, the use of volunteers requires management and oversight time that should be valued, because this time cannot be used for other purposes. Most efficiency measures consider private costs, that is, costs that occur from the perspective of programs or organizations.

Efficiency measures also vary to the extent that they consider the quality of inputs and outputs. For example, teachers may have similar student graduation or pass efficiencies but may vary according to the quality of students that they start off with or with regard to their own skills. Experienced teachers may cost more but produce better results. Such differences should be taken into account. Quality should be specified to better compare among organizations or units. Finally, it is common to calculate efficiency indices that assess the development of productivity over time. For example, if in time period I, 50 units are produced by 60 employees, and in time period II, 60 units are produced by 55 employees, then the productivity measures for each period are, respectively, $(50/60 =)$ 0.83 and $(60/55 =)$ 1.09 units per employee. The productivity index in period II is $(1.09/0.83 =)$ 1.31, a significant gain in efficiency.

Clearly, efficiency can be measured in many different ways. In most areas of public and nonprofit activity, there are few standard, agreed-upon ways of measuring efficiency. Most professional organizations do not recommend or mandate the use of certain measures. Thus organizations must often design their own measures. However, in many instances, relevant measures often suggest themselves. For example, parks departments often measure the cost per acre of lawn care or mowing. Police departments often measure the cost per cleared case. Many productivity improvement efforts suggest additional efficiency measures. For example, the efficiency of a new social service partnership might be measured by its cost of treating patients. To assist in the development effort, this chapter discusses standards for measurement (see below). It is also a good practice to engage stakeholders and employees in a dialogue about the feasibility and relevance of different measures to ensure acceptance. Managers must decide which measures they will use, acknowledging the strengths and weaknesses of each.

It is important to note that many employees experience an excessive emphasis on efficiency as demeaning and demotivating. Employees often measure their job satisfaction by standards of effectiveness (i.e., solving an important problem) rather than by how fast they did it or how many client problems per hour they solved (that is, efficiency). Efficiency measures are therefore seldom used in isolation from other performance measures and are never used in lieu of comprehensive performance appraisals. Nevertheless, measures of efficiency are increasingly important in justifying program costs as well as productivity improvement efforts that require investment: In the world of competing top management priorities, proposals that promise efficiency as well as effectiveness gains are likely to be more favorably viewed than those that only yield effectiveness gains. Hence proposals for productivity improvement frequently provide balanced objectives of both effectiveness and efficiency gains, and productivity improvement efforts are frequently designed to produce both. (See the section "Analytical Techniques for Continuous Improvement" in Chapter 7 for sources of efficiency gains.) However, undue emphasis on efficiency may generate perverse behavior that should be avoided. For example, teacher efficiency measures should not draw teachers away from devoting time to students with special needs.

Other Measures

Workloads are defined as the activity levels of departments and organizations, and workload measures assess activities or strategies, such as the number of classes taught, the number of parks maintained, the number of patrols conducted, the number of fire inspections, and so on. Workloads are often related to inputs, for example, the number of classes taught per teacher, the number of full-time equivalent ground maintenance personnel used per acre of park, the number of patrols per police officer or the number of officers per patrol. These are workload ratios, although some authors refer to these measures as efficiency or productivity measures, even though they do not measure outcomes (e.g., Ammons, 1996). A useful feature of workload measures and workload ratios is that often they are readily available from administrative records. Some examples of workload ratio measures in public safety are the average number of bookings per day, the number of emergency calls received per day, the number of hours spent in court per case, the number of citizen volunteer hours used per police unit, the number of minutes per inspection, and the time spent per suspect sketch. Note that none of these concerns outputs or outcomes.

Equity measures are important. Workloads and outcomes are sometimes compared across different target groups, and these measures often have political ramifications. For example, police departments often must show that they serve different neighborhoods in an equal manner. Different arrest rates in black versus other locations must be explained, for example, on the basis of emergency calls, robberies, or substance use rates. Although it is not always possible to explain equity differences, they should be noted. For example, differentials in student test scores must be explained across gender and race divisions, even though it is not always possible to explain why these differences occur.

Benchmarking has also increased in recent years. Benchmarks are standards rather than measures of actual performance. Benchmarks exist for outcomes as well as for workload ratios. For example, a benchmark for fire serve response time is usually 3.5 minutes, and the minimum staffing for trucks and engines is about three firefighters. Standards for parks maintenance are 2.0 to 2.8 hours mowing per acre, and there are many detailed standards for tree, lawn, and weed control. Published standards must be adapted to specific local conditions. However, for many services, no benchmarks are available or published. In these instances, the term *benchmark* usually refers to an organization's own best practice or that of a comparable organization. Although almost anything can be measured, many authors recommend adopting about 20 measures that encompass important strategic and operational objectives; employees and managers find it hard to focus on more than 20 measures, and adopting fewer may cause efforts to be channeled in the wrong ways (Ammons, 1996; Epstein, 1984; Hatry, 1977; Keehley, Medlin, MacBride, & Longmore, 1997).

TABLE 3.1 Productivity Measures

Name	Type	Example*
Effectiveness	Short-term outcomes	Increased teaching skills
	Midterm outcomes	Student test scores
	Long-term outcomes	School reputation
Efficiency	Total efficiency	All improvements/total program cost
	Partial efficiency	Specific improvements/prorated cost
	Labor efficiency	Improvements/teacher
	Marginal efficiency	Incremental improvement/incremental cost
	Social efficiency	Improvements to society/total cost to society
Equity	Race equity	Student performance by race
	Geographic equity	Student performance by district
	Sex equity	Student performance by sex
	Income equity	Student performance by family income
Workload	Activities	Number of students taught
	Activities/input	Students per teacher
Cost-benefit	Benefits/costs	Student performance/total cost per teacher
Benchmarks	Workload standards	For example, 30 students per teacher
	Effectiveness standards	For example, 96% graduation rate

NOTE: *Teacher improvement program.

Finally, the above efficiency measures are readily transformed into cost-benefit or cost-effectiveness estimates. Cost-benefit measures require that benefits are expressed in monetary values: Because this is often extremely difficult with public and nonprofit services (What is the dollar value of improved school ratings?), measures often involve cost-effectiveness in which outcomes are not expressed in their own units (e.g., as ratings). Cost-benefit/effectiveness analysis requires that all costs and outcomes are identified. These are usually valued from the perspective of society rather than the organizations or programs, as is the case with many efficiency measures. Program opponents frequently call for cost-effectiveness analysis, but receiving such analysis seldom allays their concerns. This is because many concerns focus on effectiveness rather than efficiency. For example, concerns about inmate vocational training often deal with recidivism (i.e., effectiveness), even though opponents express a "need" for cost-benefit analysis of inmate training programs. Thus managers do well to critically analyze calls for cost-benefit analysis.

Table 3.1 provides a comparison of various kind of measures. In conclusion, (a) most efficiency measures are determined by the availability of data; (b) measures of partial labor efficiency (units per employee) are widely used; and (c) measures of efficiency are seldom used in isolation from other performance measures.

Further Issues in Measurement

Guidelines for Measurement

Scientific criteria exist that assist in the development and evaulation of measures. First, measures should be valid, that is, they should measure what they are supposed to measure. A measure of the efficiency of policy response teams should take into account a broad range of their activities, not just one activity. Valid measures are sufficiently specific. They should have a meaningful range of response categories, for example, a valid measure of response time should include different degrees of being on time. Second, measurement should be reliable. Reliability means that, on repeated measurement, measurements should show little variation. Reliability is an issue when using observers to rate the cleanliness of streets or parks. To overcome this problem, raters must be trained and have accuracy of their rating verified. Reliability in surveys means that different samples of the same population should yield similar results. This is ensured by using random sampling, discussed below.

Third, measures should also be simple and easy to understand. Complex measures are often confusing to those who use them such as senior managers, elected officials, and board members. When stakeholders do not understand measures, organizations fail to increase their accountability and demonstrate their responsiveness. Measures should also be relevant to those who will use them. To deal with this problem, some managers pilot-test proposed measures among citizen groups and other potential users. Fourth, measures should reflect program activities that managers can affect. It is senseless and anxiety-inducing to hold managers accountable for things they cannot change. Fifth, measures should be practical. Data should be relatively easy to collect, and such data should conform to the above standards. The way in which measures are collected should also be foolproof. To increase the credibility of data, program evaluation frequently uses external consultants, and performance measurements are often audited by budget departments that, in some instances, are also responsible for gathering data from administrative records.

Multifaceted Indicators

Whereas some measures are highly specific (e.g., number of students taught), other measures are abstract. For example, two short-term outcomes in Figure 3.1 are to increase community awareness and to provide wholesome educational activities. What exactly does "community awareness" mean? What are "wholesome" activities? They are appropriate outcomes, but they also require further specificity before they can be measured. When managers are able to influence the design of their measurements, the first step is to identify different dimensions of such concepts. There is seldom one best way to measure such concepts. For example, "awareness" may mean that parents are aware of the existence of the Rec 'n' Roll program, but it may also mean that they are aware of the need for recreation. Another dimension is that schools and community organizations are aware of the program. Likewise, what are the different dimensions of "wholesome" activities? Are wholesome activities those that develop self-esteem? Do they include sports, with the possibility of injury? The first step in constructing measures is to be clear and specific about the different aspects that are being measured. Of course, not all outcomes are abstract in nature, but those that are need to be further specified. Managers need to think about the way in which different concepts are measured.

The second step is to identify how different, specific outcomes will be measured. By what means will data be collected? Typical data collection strategies are surveys of clients, staff interviews, and the use of data from administrative records. For example, awareness might be assessed through a survey of parents, whereas measurement of safety might be assessed by using data from administrative records. These different measurement approaches are discussed later in this chapter. Table 3.2 shows an example of the operationalization of measurement constructs.

Using Comparison Groups

The measurement of outcomes alone does not necessarily prove that program strategies cause outcomes. Such proof is sometimes sought, especially in the context of program evaluation. For example, in programs for the homeless, the aim is often to reduce the number of homeless persons, but does a reduction in homeless persons "prove" that the reduction occurred because of assistance efforts to the homeless? Perhaps the reduction occurred because the economy improved. At stake is the need to deal with a variety of "rival" explanations about

TABLE 3.2 Sample Operationalization of Measurements

Outcomes* →	Dimensions →	Measurement
7.1 Increase community awareness	Parent, school, and community leaders' knowledge of Rec 'n' Roll programs	Annual survey, number of program inquiries
7.2 Increase number of services	Number of game activities offered, types of game activities offered, sports and social interaction activities offered, locations served	List of activities
7.4 Increase participants' self-esteem and self-worth	Participants make positive statements about self, participants recognize positive/negative comments	Observation, survey of parents
7.6 Provide wholesome activities	Activities that increase self-esteem, activities that minimize injury	List of activities, survey of parents regarding activities
8.1 Increase life skills and social competence	Knowledge of rules of social interaction, conflict management skills, knowledge of ways to search for information, recognition of value differences	Survey of attitudes, observation of behaviors
8.4 Decrease gang membership	Attitudes about gangs, participation in gangs	Survey youth about gang preferences, statistics on gang membership

NOTE: *Numbers refer to items in Figure 3.1.

the impact or lack of impact of strategies or interventions. For reasons explained earlier, the problem of causality increases as the time frame of outcomes increases as well. Program skeptics are apt to raise questions about the efficacy of efforts, especially concerning mid- and long-term outcomes.

One approach is to identify all such rival hypotheses and to deal with them one at a time. For example, the impact of economic growth on homelessness might be estimated by comparing homeless populations in similar cities that experience different levels of economic growth, or by comparing homelessness in cities that have experienced changes in economic growth over time. The impact of efforts to mitigate homelessness needs to be assessed as well. For example, an estimate might be made based on program files of the number of homeless persons who are helped off the street and the number of those who are not recidivists after, say, 6 or 12 months. An obvious challenge is to identify all relevant rival hypotheses, and to respond to them effectively.

An alternative strategy is to conduct an experiment in which subjects are randomly assigned to either a control or an experimental group. Random assignment eliminates the possibility of systematic differences between the groups; chance differences are very small in large samples. However, experiments are seldom applicable to public or nonprofit organizations: For example, cities cannot be randomly denied programs for the homeless, nor can students be made to "suffer" from teachers who have been denied training (e.g., Campbell & Stanley, 1963; Sylvia, Meier, & Gunn, 1985). At best, test scores of different schools can be compared that vary according to the use of teacher education programs. Likewise, homelessness rates can be compared for cities that are broadly similar, except for the use of programs for the homeless. The key is to locate similar control groups, called comparison groups. However, when using comparison groups, managers must ensure that they are able to gather data about these other organizations. They also need to anticipate that the results of nonrandom comparisons will be contested on the basis that groups are different. They will need to show in what ways such groups are sufficiently similar to allow meaningful comparison.

Implementing Performance Measurement Systems

The implementation of performance measurement is usually a gradually unfolding process in organizations. Organizations must often build the capacity for gathering and analyzing data, and they must allow for changing initial performance measures as new measures are proposed and improvements are made in existing ones. Initial efforts frequently use only one or two measures as managers increase the capacity for performance measurement. Initial efforts often are limited in scope and subject to data gathering glitches; they are experimental in nature (Schwabe, 1996; Tracy, 1996).

The implementation of performance measurement often raises fears and concerns that managers must address. Performance measurement is often positioned by managers as an effort to increase accountability, to support ongoing program development, and to inform budgeting and other decision-making processes. Performance measurement is but one of several tools for this purpose. Managers find it necessary assure employees and lower managers that decisions will not be made in isolation from other measures, and that initial efforts are understood to be experimental and not written in stone. Units should have considerable input in deciding how their performance will be measured. Managers will also need to assure employees that the performance measurement effort will not impose undue burdens.

Top leaders also need to show that they are serious about performance measurement. To this end, they often assign responsibilities to different units for developing necessary expertise. Budget offices are often used for this purpose in public organizations because they have expertise in measurement and data analysis. They also have the capacity to audit performance measures submitted by other departments, and they can coordinate the need for surveys among different units. The use of surveys often involves outside experts to ensure objectivity and provide guidance regarding appropriate procedures. Technical consultants are also used to provide the "legwork," that is, the actual data collection.

The development of performance measurement can also tie into other efforts to increase stakeholder support. Key decision makers who affect the future of programs can be involved in measurement through ad hoc working groups that guide measurement and planning efforts. Key decision makers seldom object to efforts to assess and improve programs, and are apt to give their opinions about needed changes. In addition, measurement efforts can use an ad hoc "external advisory" group of program clients and community groups. This external advisory group provides feedback and a testing ground for measurement items (survey questions, etc.).

Data Collection

Productivity measurement requires the collection of data. Some principal data sources are agency records, surveys, focus groups, and the use of experts, actors, and observers. Each is discussed below.

Administrative Records

Organizations frequently produce a plethora of information in the process of managing programs. Administrative data include information on (a) staffing levels and qualifications, (b) budgets (program, indirect costs, etc.), (c) level of service provided, and (d) complaints, requests, and compliments. In addition, data from client files provide information on (e) progress, backgrounds, needs, use of services. Data from event files (e.g., repair logs) provide further information on activities. For example, to know what the most common problem is in parks, managers can examine supervisory and inspection reports about park maintenance. In these reports, managers can examine events (e.g., broken benches) as well words and phrases (e.g., things vandalized). Such events can also be examined through time or across different neighborhoods.

Administrative data are most frequently used for workload measures and workload ratios. For example, caseload data are frequently available from work logs and other administrative records (e.g., billing). These data are also readily transformed into workload ratios, such as caseloads per worker. The widespread availability of such data makes them ideal for benchmarking, and many benchmarks (or performance standards) are indeed based on workload rather than outcome data. For example, benchmarks exist for the number of calls that receptionists can handle, the number of hours needed to cut grass in public parks, and the number of swimmers that lifeguards can effectively oversee in swimming pools. However, administrative data are usually designed for the control and accountability of resources and activities, not for measuring outcomes. Outcome data are seldom collected except when the program practices Total Quality Management or benchmarking. Thus additional data collection efforts are usually needed.

Working with administrative data often involves the following challenges: (a) missing or incomplete data, (b) data that are available only in highly aggregated form, (c) data definitions that have changed over time and cannot be compared, (d) data that cannot be linked to particular events or clients, (e) data that are confidential, and (f) data that are inaccurate. These problems can be overcome to varying degrees; for example, records with missing data can be eliminated from analysis; raw data can be used to disaggregate reported data; reasonable adjustments are made to link data across time or cases; permission can be obtained to access confidential data. Overcoming these problems usually requires close relations with agency staff, in particular, record keeping staff.

Information technology systems provide important advantages in measuring productivity. They reduce the need for analyzing data from separate case files and other paper records, and they ensure that data are captured at the point of contact. These systems also facilitate data analysis and can be programmed to produce monthly or even weekly reports of key output measures. Organizations that lack adequate information technology systems greatly increase the amount of effort involved in data collection and analysis, which may be an insurmountable obstacle. In one such instance, a social work director in a hospital instituted a productivity measurement system to better measure and communicate to hospital administrators the contribution of her department. However, social workers did not use computers in documenting their cases and additional staff efforts were needed to gather and input such information from case records. Employees were required to provide this information daily to an administrative assistant, who spent 20 hours a week to input these data into a computer. The amount of additional effort quickly generated staff resistance and the productivity effort was aborted. Without information technology systems, only incidental studies are possible, such as through analyzing a sample of cases to determine organizational productivity each quarter. By contrast, information technology allows for monitoring of productivity in a routine manner with a minimum of additional staff effort.[5]

Surveys

Surveys are increasingly used to obtain information about citizen needs and client satisfaction. Such information is often central to outcome assessment and is seldom provided through administrative records. Most surveys should be conducted on an annual basis, and some even quarterly. The following issues are involved in conducting surveys.

Sampling. Most surveys are sample surveys. This involves drawing representative samples to make generalizable statements about populations of citizens, clients, or employees. The best way to obtain a representative sample is to give each member of the population an equal chance of being selected for the sample, so that the sample is not biased toward including any specific individuals or groups. This is achieved through random sampling. A key issue is determining the appropriate sample size. Samples usually range between 200 and 800 completed responses. Sampling size is determined by sampling error, which indicates the magnitude by which survey findings will vary in 95 out of 100 samples. Large samples better mirror the population from which they are drawn and thus have smaller sampling errors. The sampling errors of samples of 200 and 800 responses are, respectively, 7.1% and 3.5%.[6] That is, results vary for a survey of 800 completed responses by plus or minus 3.5%. Sample sizes of fewer than 200 have large sampling errors (e.g., the sampling error of 100 respondents is 10%), and sample sizes above 800 show relatively small declines in sampling error (e.g., the sampling error for a sample of 1,500 respondents is 2%). For most purposes, samples of 400 suffice; they have a sampling error of about 5%. However, when subpopulations are sampled, then each subpopulation should have an appropriate sample size, hence the total sample may be larger. Finally, sampling errors are almost independent of the population size. The above sampling errors refer to large populations (more than 20,000), and managers err on the side of caution by relying on these numbers. Small populations require somewhat smaller samples: Populations of 5,000 have sampling errors of 5% for samples of only 357, and populations of 1,000 have sampling errors of 5% for samples of 278.

In practice, four complications may occur in sampling. First, managers may not have a list of program clients. This is frequently the case in walk-in clinics or park services. In this instance, various days and times should be randomly selected throughout the year, and a random sample of (or possibly all) users should be surveyed during these periods. The second problem is that the list that exists does not exactly match the population. This too is often the case. For example, local governments frequently use tax rolls as the basis for selecting citizens. However, tax rolls are biased against renters. Such defects cannot be overcome but must be acknowledged. Managers must also explain their approach for randomly selecting persons within households: One approach is to interview those who most recently had a birthday (and are 18 years or older). This is tantamount to a random selection. The third problem occurs when the program has a very small number of clients (e.g., fewer than 400). In this case, no sample is necessary. Rather, a census of all clients is undertaken.

Fourth, the above discussion of sampling error assumes completed responses. A larger initial sample is selected to account for nonresponses. For example, if a final sample of 400 is desired, and the expected response rate is 55%, then the initial sample should be (400/0.55 =) 727. Nonresponses are an important issue in surveys because the respondent group must be representative of the sample that was drawn. Response rates below 60% merit concern about possible response bias, that is, differences between respondents and nonrespondents that could greatly affect findings. Two approaches for examining nonresponse bias are (a) comparing demographic characteristics of respondents with those of the population (e.g., using census data to compare sex, gender, and age distribution) and (b) comparing responses between respondents and nonrespondents. This requires a subsequent survey among initial nonrespondents, for example, a short telephone survey on selected items. Such "nonrespondent surveys" are increasingly used when response rates are low (Berman & West, 1995; Miller & Miller, 1991).

Types of surveys. There are three types of surveys: mail, phone, and in-person surveys. Each has somewhat different features, which are shown in Table 3.3 (based on Miller, 1994; modified). When many data (i.e., survey questions) are required, either in-person or mail surveys should be used. The length of most phone calls prohibits long interviews. In-person surveys are more expensive.

TABLE 3.2 Types of Surveys and Their Characteristics

	Mail	*Phone*	*In Person*
a. Response rate	30%-70%*	65%-80%	70%-95%
b. Amount of data	highest	low	low or high
c. Data collection	6-8 weeks	2-3 weeks	4-6 weeks
d. Cost**	$7-$10	$4-$7	$15-$25
e. Interviewer bias	lowest	medium	medium

NOTES: *General citizen surveys have response rates of 25%-40%, whereas surveys of program users and experts have response rates of 40%-70%.
**Per completed interview, includes management, training, printing costs; excludes phone toll charges, survey design, data analysis, and report writing.

Mail surveys almost always raise issues about response rates, and many cities are now using phone surveys, which are faster and usually have adequate response rates. Dillman (1978) suggests increasing the response rates of mail surveys by making them short and attractive, providing return envelopes, conducting follow-up telephone calls, and including a cover letter from senior officials (e.g., the mayor, school principal, and so on). When a quick response is needed, mail surveys should not be used because mail surveys usually require multiple mailings to ensure an adequate response rate. However, in person and phone surveys raise concerns about interviewer bias. Interviewers must be neutral and consistent in their questions. This requires training and supervision. The above concerns about response rates have caused an increasing use of telephone surveys.

Unbiased questions. Surveys often raise concerns about biased questioning. To avoid bias, questions should (a) be clear (i.e., unambiguous, specific), (b) avoid double-barreled phrasing, (c) be relevant and answerable by respondents, (d) be without inherent bias, and (e) avoid negative statements (Welch & Comer, 1988). Examples of these problems are shown in Table 3.4. Of equal importance is the selection of response scales. Closed-ended scales are preferred, because the analysis of many open-ended responses is cumbersome and prone to error. Response scales should be unbiased and complete. That is, they should include all relevant categories and have as many positive as negative response categories. A popular scale is the so-called Likert scale. For example, the question, "How satisfied are you with the services that your received?" would use the following response scale: Very Satisfied-Satisfied-Somewhat Satisfied-Don't

TABLE 3.4 Problems in Sample Survey Questions

Questions should be clear.

   *Question: "What do you think of recycling?"

   *Problem: The verb *think* is unclear.

   *Better: "Do you believe that your community should increase or decrease its household recycling efforts, or that its current level of recycling efforts should stay the same?"

Questions should avoid double-barreled responses.

   *Question: "Please state your level of agreement with the following statement: The city should contract with the private sector for wastewater treatment and spend the savings from that on improved household recycling efforts."

   *Problem: These are two separate issues, namely, about privatization and spending priorities.

   *Better: Ask questions separately.

Questions should be relevant.

   *Question: "Should the city increase funding for the midnight basketball program?"

   *Problem: Most respondents are unlikely to possess requisite information to respond.

   *Better: Ask respondents whether gang activities are a problem.

Questions should avoid biasing words.

   *Question: "To what extent do you approve of welfare programs?"

   *Problem: The word *welfare* has negative connotations

   *Better: "To what extent do you approve of providing assistance to the poor?"

Questions should avoid negatives.

   *Question: "Please state your level of agreement with the following statement: The U.S. should not recognize Cuba."

   *Problem: Some respondents will read over *not.* This will cause confusion.

   *Better: "Please state your level of agreement with the following statement: The U.S. should recognize Cuba."

Know-Somewhat Dissatisfied-Dissatisfied-Very Dissatisfied. Other Likert scales use Important/Unimportant; Good-Poor/Bad, Agree/Disagree; Adequate/Inadequate. Likert scales are also used that omit the "somewhat" categories (these are called five-point scales). A strategy for formulating questions is to (a) decide what information is needed, (b) decide what information target respondents can provide, (c) write preliminary survey questions, and (d) improve questions according to the above guidelines. Although existing surveys are helpful, each survey effort requires a survey that fits the unique situation.

The most common problems in doing surveys are (a) underestimating the time and resource requirements for successfully completing survey efforts and

(b) failing to address significant concerns of bias, response rates and sampling, and reliability. For this reason, survey efforts frequently include outside experts hired to guide the effort (see above, "Implementing Performance Measurement Systems").

Focus Groups

The purpose of focus groups is to generate understanding of program or client needs. They do not provide information that is representative, but focus groups do provide information about the range of concerns on which information should be collected. Thus they are usually done prior to conducting surveys. Focus groups involve semistructured, in-depth, group discussions. This technique was pioneered by companies in their marketing efforts. It is generally recommended that focus groups are homogenous, that is, that group members are selected from the same target group. This is because different target groups are likely to have different experiences, needs, and views. Different populations may also inhibit and drown each other out.

A typical use of focus groups is the following. A parks program operates and maintains park grounds and provides a full range of services and programs for park users. Services and programs include various sporting events, educational programs, and collaboration with the local department of health and human services, which sponsors self-help and social services on the park grounds. The parks program seeks to better understand how the neighborhood community uses its activities as well as which activities should be discontinued and which should be increased. Because this is an exploratory question, the parks program decided to use focus groups. A generalizable neighborhood survey or needs assessment might be used later. Some typical questions that might be asked of focus group members are as follows:

Which services did you use? Why?

How satisfied are you with these services? Specifically, how do these services help to meet your needs?

Do you have any suggestions for further improvement?

Which services would you like to see added? Here are some new activities that have been recently suggested: Are there any that you would use? Why or why not?

The park has certain regulations. We would like know which of them you are familiar with.

Did you have any contact with park officials while visiting the park? If so, which ones? What happened when you approached them? Did you get the information or service you requested? Were officials friendly?

Moderators should be impartial and assist focus group members to fully explore all matters that they have agreed to discuss. Thus moderators often steer discussions back to original agendas; focus groups are not meandering conversations. Moderators are usually assisted by a note-taker who records the comments of participants.

Other Approaches

Experts are used when objective, factual data are insufficient to make judgments about program outcomes and activities, or when the assessment of such data requires the judgment of experts. Some examples in which expert judgment might be used are the maintenance of landfills, the analysis of medical records (e.g., treatment of patients), the quality of a higher education program, or the use of management techniques. Experts should only be used when it is likely that their recommendations will be acted on. A criterion for accepting expert judgment is that it is shared by other experts; hence program evaluation always uses a range (or panel) of experts. Typically, no fewer than three experts are consulted.

Trained observers are used to evaluate the condition of facilities (e.g., parks, public rest rooms, public housing, nursing homes, beach maintenance, street cleanliness) as well as events (pickpockets, unauthorized ticket sales, etc.). Trained observers provide unobtrusive observation. The steps in undertaking trained observations are (a) deciding what is to be observed (e.g., street cleanliness); (b) deciding the dimensions of what is to be observed (working order, paint, weeds, repair, etc.); (c) developing a standardized rating scale (usually only three or four levels such as No Problem, Limited Problem, or Widespread Problem, in which terms are carefully defined—i.e., *widespread* indicates more than two thirds of an area outside a sandbox that is covered with sand); (d) training and supervising raters (trainee and trainers should agree 90% of the time); (e) carrying out the ratings; and (f) using random resampling to determine the accuracy of ratings.

Role-playing is a form of observer-based rating whereby observers pose as clients. Such observers are usually unknown to employees, although many do identify such "ghost" clients. The use of observers allows for spot-checks of service quality. Sometimes actors are matched with regard to race, gender, or age to observe patterns of differential treatment. An example of matched role-playing is the use of minority actors who pose as home buyers to detect discrimination in home buying or real estate services by comparing services provided to majority and minority clients. Matched role-playing is also used to detect bias in job hiring.

Role-playing involves several considerations. First, the transactions that are to be sampled must be clearly determined. Second, the number of cases must be decided on; 15 is usually sufficient to bring about legal action but larger samples are needed to substantiate the incidence of discrimination. Third, the training and practice of observers must be carefully monitored: All actors must act consistently.

Summary

This chapter examines the measurement of productivity. Measurement is needed to determine the level of productivity and the efficacy of productivity improvement efforts. It also provides accountability and helps show responsiveness to clients and citizens. The chapter discusses the need for considering short-term as well as long-term outcomes, and it discusses effectiveness, efficiency, equity, and workload measures. It examines such issues as the quality of measures and the implementation of performance measurement systems. This chapter also discusses a variety of data collection approaches for productivity measurement, including administrative records, surveys, focus groups, and the use of experts and raters.

Notes

1. Historically, program evaluation preceded performance evaluation. Program evaluation was developed in the 1960s in response to increasing accountability for large federal programs. It was criticized in the late 1970s for being expensive, untimely, and divorced from decision making. During the 1980s, new approaches focused on intermediate outcomes rather than long-term goals—to increase timeliness—and involved key stakeholders in the design and use of evaluation. Performance measurement developed from these efforts.

2. See Chapter 11, note 1, for a discussion of the methodology of these surveys.

3. Organization-level figures, which encompass multiple programs, can be created too. Then, activities are replaced by different programs, and outcomes are associated with different programs. In program evaluation, some models also identify "external" influences on outcomes as well as unintended outcomes.

4. Efficiency measures are sometimes called productivity measures, following the emphasis on efficiency in for-profit productivity measurement. This book takes a broader perspective on productivity, as discussed in Chapter 1.

5. This excludes efforts and costs that are involved in maintaining such information technology systems.

6. These are maximum estimates, assuming a 95% confidence interval. See Babbie (1995) for a more detailed discussion. Actual sample errors are sometimes 20%-30% smaller than those shown in the text. However, it is common to use the larger measures shown in the text.

References

Ammons, D. (1995). *Accountability for performance: Measuring and monitoring in local government.* Washington, DC: International City/County Management Association (ICMA).

Ammons, D. (1996). *Benchmarking for local government.* Thousand Oaks, CA: Sage.

Babbie. E. (1995). *The practice of social research.* Belmont, CA: Wadsworth.

Berman, E. (1997). [Survey of museums and social service organizations]. Unpublished raw data.

Berman, E., & West, J. (1995). Municipal commitment to Total Quality Management. *Public Administration Review,* 55(1), 57-66.

Berman, E., & West, J. (1997). [Survey of cities]. Unpublished raw data.

Brinkerhoff, R., & Dressler, D. (1990). *Productivity measurement.* Newbury Park, CA: Sage.

Campbell, D., & Stanley, J. (1963). *Experimental and quasi-experimental designs for research.* Chicago: Rand McNally.

Dillman, D. (1978). *Mail and telephone surveys: The total design method.* New York: John Wiley.

Epstein, P. (1984). *Using performance measurement in local government.* New York: Van Nostrand Reinhold.

Greiner, J. (1996). Positioning performance measurement for the twenty-first century. In A. Halchmi & G. Bouckaert (Eds.), *Organizational performance and measurement in the public sector* (pp. 11-50). Westport, CT: Quorum.

Hakes, J. (1996). Comparing outputs to outcomes. *PA Times, 19*(10), 1-2.

Halachmi, A. (1992). Evaluation research: Purpose and perspective. In M. Holzer (Ed.), *Public productivity handbook* (pp. 213-226). New York: Marcel Dekker.

Hatry, H. (1977). *How effective are your community services?* Washington, DC: Urban Institute.

Hatry, H., & Fisk, D. (1992). Measuring productivity in the public sector. In M. Holzer (Ed.), *Public productivity handbook* (pp. 139-160). New York: Marcel Dekker.

International City/County Managers Association (ICMA). (1995). *Applying performance measurement* [CD-ROM]. Washington, DC: Author.

Kanter, R., & Summers, D. (1987). Doing well by doing good: Dilemmas of performance measurement in non-profit organizations. In W. Powell (Ed.), *The nonprofit sector handbook* (pp. 154-166). New Haven, CT: Yale University Press.

Keehley, P., Medlin, S., MacBride, S., & Longmore, L. (1997). *Benchmarking for best practices in the public sector.* San Francisco: Jossey-Bass.

Miller, T., & Miller, M. (1991). *Citizen surveys: How to do them, how to use them, what they mean* (Special report). Washington, DC: International City/County Management Association (ICMA).

Miller, T. (1994). Designing and Conducting Surveys. In J. Wholey, H. Matry & K. Newcomer (Eds.), *Handbook of practical program evaluation* (pp. 271-292). San Francisco, CA: Jossey-Bass.

Poister, T. (1992). Productivity monitoring: Systems, indicators and analysis. In M. Holzer (Ed.), *Public productivity handbook* (chap. 10). New York: Marcel Dekker.

Rosen, E. (1993). *Improving public sector productivity.* Newbury Park, CA: Sage.

Rossi, P., & Freeman, H. (1993). *Evaluation: A systematic approach* (5th ed.). Newbury Park, CA: Sage.

Schwabe, C. (1996). *Development of use of performance indicators in the city of Coral Springs, Florida* (Unpublished case study). Washington, DC: ASPA Task Force on Governmental Accomplishment & Accountability.

Sylvia, R., Meier, K., & Gunn, E. (1985). *Program planning and evaluation for the public manager.* Prospect Heights, IL: Waveland.

Tigue, P., & Strachota, D. (1994). *The use of performance measures in city and county budgets.* Chicago: Government Finance Officers Association.

Tracy, R. (1996). *Development and use of outcome information in Portland, OR* (Unpublished case study). Washington, DC: ASPA Task Force on Governmental Accomplishment & Accountability.

Welch, S. & Comer, J. (1998). *Qualitative methods for public administration.* Chicago, IL: The Dorsey Press.

Wholey, J., Hatry, H., & Newcomer, K. (Eds.). (1994). *Handbook of practical program evaluation.* San Francisco: Jossey-Bass.

4

Achieving Success

The previous chapters discussed strategies for identifying productivity problems and for measuring productivity. This chapter examines strategies for implementing productivity improvement efforts. Specifically, it focuses on the need to gain commitment and overcome resistance among employees and managers for productivity improvements. Achieving their support is essential to success in productivity improvement. For example, although executives can require or mandate an increased customer orientation, they often have very little power to achieve it in the absence of employee and staff cooperation and commitment. Grand schemes come to naught in the face of opposition or indifference. As an old Russian saying goes, "The Czar is powerful, but far away in Moscow." Employees and managers have many different ways and reasons to resist productivity efforts (Rosenberg, 1992).

Fundamentally, productivity improvement is an *intervention* in existing roles, relationships, or expectations. For example, some productivity efforts require that managers and employees work with the community to define program goals, develop new standards for services, and implement new uses of information technology. As discussed in Chapter 1, this requires changes in values (e.g., accepting increased citizen input), systems (such as processes for seeking such input and rewards that reflect using citizen-based decision making), tools such as citizen surveys (discussed in the previous chapter), and behaviors. Old practices and habits must be abandoned in favor of new ones. In many instances, productivity requires increased openness in communication, as well as empowerment and responsibility, so that employees and managers own up to problems and collectively work toward solutions. Futures are emphasized that differ in fundamental ways from those of today. To the extent that employees and managers are still deeply rooted in cultures of low communication and autonomy, fear, and futures that reflect incremental change, they are likely to experience considerable stress as they respond to new expectations, behaviors, and roles that are appropriate to changing values and increased productivity.

Productivity interventions usually cause reactions that vary among employees and other managers. Managers need to be familiar with different ways in which support and opposition are expressed. Overcoming resistance and gaining support requires a *strategy* for ensuring success and dealing with issues that surface. For example, managers need to identify problems of resistance and develop plans for overcoming them. They must also develop strategies for support by identifying applications, units, and individuals that are likely to respond well to new productivity improvement initiatives. In so doing, they must support managers and employees in applying new approaches and provide consistent rewards and acknowledgment for efforts and outcomes. Managerial implementation strategies must also be applicable in a wide variety of contexts, for example, in dealing with employees who like challenges as well as those who prefer daily routines. Effective implementation must also deal with the realities of constrained resources and incentives.

Basic Causes of Resistance

The issue of support raises a fundamental question: If productivity improvement is such a good thing, why is it being resisted? Organizations have many counterproductive processes that give rise to resistance or minimal compliance rather than commitment. First, undiscussibility is a feature of most organizations. Many issues are undiscussable; managers agree that they are undiscussable; and it is undiscussable that what is undiscussable is undiscussable. An example of something that is often undiscussable is the competence of one's boss. Undiscussibility helps to maintain civil, peaceful relations (or bottled-up aggression), and it enables managers to concentrate on their objectives and exercise control over employees. However, in the context of implementing productivity, undiscussibility generates resistance because it denies employees the means to resolve the contradictions or uncertainties that they experience (Argyris, 1990; Argyris & Schön, 1996).

In this regard, a second basic cause of resistance is asking people to do things that they do not fully understand. Productivity requires new behaviors and roles, and these must be carefully explained. A need exists for concrete examples. Encouragement is necessary, and tolerance for mistakes must exist. Feedback must be constructive, not punitive. When managers ignore processes of adult learning and the need for positive encouragement and reenforcement, productivity improvement is seldom possible and employees will resist change. This problem is exacerbated in cultures that emphasize undiscussibility, but it occurs in other situations as well.

Third, productivity improvement feeds already existing employee cynicism, thereby furthering resistance. Some employees see productivity improvement as a means of exploitation—of organizations gaining something for nothing. Many factors cause employee cynicism, including widespread beliefs that they are undervalued and not listened to by managers. This also causes a cycle of cynicism in which employees reduce their motivation and effort because they feel underappreciated by managers, who then underappreciate employees more and thus listen to them less and micromanage them more, and so on. Past failures to improve organizations also make employees skeptical and cause resistance to change, and some employees view change from an "us versus them" perspective. Cynicism generates resistance or, at a minimum, passive compliance (or apathy) that is insufficient to achieve high levels of accomplishment. A national survey of city managers finds that 45% of respondents believe that employees feel their managers are dishonest or only "somewhat" honest; 41% believe that employees perceive managers to be *un*helpful in assisting them to be successful (Berman, 1995). Such negative attitudes clearly are a barrier to productivity improvement.

Fourth, managers may resist productivity improvement because they fear that it will diminish their power. Many managers persist in behaviors that aim for control, that aim to win, to dominate others, and to avoid upsetting people (Argyris, 1990). By contrast, the new productivity strategies go against these norms; they require that managers loosen control over employees (holding them accountable only for outcomes), that they support rather than dominate employee efforts, and that they proactively provide feedback, which may upset people. Productivity improvement also requires increased measurement and communication of results. Managers may be skeptical that productivity improvement will help them rather than hurt them. To the extent that managers use control-dominate-conflict avoidance to promote their careers, it is unreasonable to expect them to readily abandon these norms and related behaviors.

Finally, mindlessness is a basic and frequent cause of resistance to productivity improvement. When managers and employees are not fully aware of the conditions that are necessary for success, productivity improvement often flounders. For example, managers ask their employees to conduct a survey of program clients but fail to provide adequate time, resources, and training for the survey to be conducted properly. The lack of appropriate conditions gives rise to dissatisfaction and resistance. Obstacles occur that are not overcome. Mindlessness also causes complaints about insensitivity and authoritarian conduct. For example, managers often profess commitment to participatory decision-making processes, but they are mindless when they fail to consider that subsequent autocratic decision making will generate resistance.

Mindlessness is often caused by competing priorities, inexperience, and laziness. For example, competing priorities cause managers not to engage fully in what they are doing, and inexperience causes managers to underestimate the challenges that exist. Laziness causes managers to fail to think: Many people simply copy statements and conclusions made by others but fail to reflect on their applicability and implications for the situation at hand.[1] For example, the mindless adoption of recommended software programs causes resistance when implementation issues are inadequately addressed. Laziness also causes people to think in undisciplined ways, hence leading to conclusions that are not fully examined and warranted (i.e., jumping to conclusions). These conditions give rise to the mindlessness that generates resistance to productivity improvement.

Tactics of Resistance

Resistance is expressed in many different ways, and managers need to be astute in observing the signs of resistance.

Verbal Resistance

Employees use many ways to express their uncertainty, fear, disinterest, or resistance to productivity improvement efforts. Verbal expressions usually provide the public reasons that employees give others for not doing what managers would like them to do. According to Fournies (1988) and others, some expressions of resistance are as follows:

- We don't need this.
- We didn't do this before.
- What's in it for us?
- You don't understand the process.
- We are understaffed.
- There is not enough time or money.
- It has been tried elsewhere and it didn't work.
- It's too complicated.
- Other things are more important.
- We don't have the skills.
- It will never work.
- It's an effort to control us.

Expressions of doubt and resistance are not always made directly to managers and sometimes must be teased out from oblique comments or body language. Verbal resistance should be taken as a cue that managers need to proactively explore the possibility of unclear goals, strategies, reasons, and obstacles among employees. Usually, verbal comments hide underlying concerns and issues. For example, employees may not know why they are being asked to adopt new productivity improvement strategies: Lacking knowledge of the necessity of specific benefits or outcomes, they may feel that existing approaches are adequate or that other objectives are more important. Employees may also be uncertain how to proceed or, when told how, feel that they have a better way. They may also be upset about feeling inadequately consulted about the new proposed changes or may harbor past resentments against the managers who are leading the change efforts.

Other underlying concerns may reflect concerns about consequences. The above questions may be an indirect way of getting information from management about rewards. Other comments may be driven by concerns about punishments for trying, not trying, or trying and failing. Some questions may concern obstacles and beliefs about the difficulty of dealing with them. In this regard, other concerns are that employees may lack essential abilities to perform well in the new tasks. For example, performance budgeting usually requires the use of surveys to identify client satisfaction, yet employees (and managers) may have little knowledge of survey techniques and even less familiarity with data analysis. Some employees respond by seeking out new skills, but others will deal with the issue through resistance.

The above comments suggest a need to distinguish between the symptoms of resistance and their causes. Verbal resistance should be taken as a cue that managers need to proactively explore the possibility of unclear goals, strategies, reasons, and obstacles among employees. Employees may voice only a few concerns, perhaps because they feel uneasy or unable to express their concerns. The issue is more than sensitivity and hand-holding: Many of these concerns reflect legitimate issues that, when addressed, improve the success of productivity improvement efforts. Managers do well to search for other concerns as well: Responses that take the above concerns and questions at face value may not only be unwise (they may be pouring fuel on the fire), they may sorely miss underlying concerns.

Nonverbal Resistance

Nonverbal resistance is harder, and often takes longer, to detect. It can also do greater damage to productivity efforts. The problem of detecting nonverbal resistance is exacerbated because it is often cloaked in apparent commitment to productivity improvement. Resisters do not want to be discovered and they are skillful in avoiding detection. They smile and give the appearance of going along but may sabotage efforts when given the opportunity.[2]

A form of nonverbal resistance is foot-dragging. Employees and managers usually generate good excuses for not producing, and some staff spend considerable energy creating the conditions that cause delays and nonperformance. The implementation of productivity improvement falls behind schedule and, characteristically, there is little that the manager can do to speed matters up. For example, the installation of software is delayed because the vendor is asked to examine alternative packages, and doing so requires a new contract, which necessitates further delays, and so forth. When confronted with delays and nonperformance, savvy employees feign their own disappointment. They promise to do better next time. Everything is said to be under control—except that, the next time, some other excuse is given. The character and actions of employees who engage in foot-dragging often are above reproach.

A second form of nonverbal resistance is agreeing to do something, but instead doing what is actually believed to be important. Smart employees may even comply with requests to avoid blame, get praise, and pursue other efforts. They may also provide the manager with irrelevant or false information, complicating efforts to assess what is actually going on. To complicate matters, employees may even seek support from other managers, thus playing managers off against one another. Absenteeism is a third form of resistance. Faced by requests they do not want to respond to and commitments they do not want to make, some employees become ill; this avoids both the task and possible blame for nonperformance. By informing managers of their absence in a timely way, they may even convince the manager to give the task to someone else.

A more aggressive form of resistance is organized group resistance. Typically, employees come together and brainstorm about possible forms of resistance. One outcome of group resistance is that employees back each other up regarding the "impossibility" of getting the job done. Such consensus is often reiterated in group meetings. Employees spread false rumors to other managers and departments about the incompetence of their managers; such rumors eventually reach their own managers. Even more aggressive are acts of filing complaints and grievances. The quid pro quo sometimes is that such actions will be dropped when the manager concedes not to implement the proposed productivity improvement strategies.

Managers-as-resisters have additional tools for dealing with their superiors. For example, managers may decrease budgets for productivity activities, thus attaining only limited progress. Such underspending is easily justified in times of budget scarcity. Although higher spending levels might be demanded in future years, resulting delays from underspending can be sufficient to derail efforts. Another strategy is assigning staff to implementation tasks at hand. For example, if the first step is to develop guidelines for empowerment, staff might delay and prepare a draft that is unrealistic. The manager then intervenes as a "knight in shining armor" and rescues the productivity improvement effort. By then the project is three to four months behind schedule.

Obviously, such efforts do little to promote productivity improvement. Managers do well to diagnose resistance, even when the evidence is uncertain or just based on a hunch. For example, managers may be alert to tasks that fall behind schedule or are performed sloppily. Some tasks are complex, and not discussing progress and challenges may be a sign that efforts are not being implemented as they ought to be. Hearing rumors about problems is also a sign of resistance. The following sections discuss strategies for overcoming resistance and increasing commitment.

Intervention Strategies

Productivity improvement is an intervention in existing organizational processes and individual roles, expectations, norms, behaviors, and habits. As previously discussed, the purpose is to change existing processes, roles, behaviors, and values in favor of new ones. This section discusses principles of intervention as well as strategies for implementing such interventions.

Principles of Intervention

Principles are vital to successful implementation. Principles provide general direction and guidance and are designed to deal with the myriad situations that managers may experience as they implement productivity improvement efforts. Application of principles complements change strategies, discussed below.

Facilitate learning. Changes in behaviors, norms, and expectations require learning. Managers must teach others to see things in new ways and attain a committed following for the proposed changes. Great educators do a number of consistent things. Many great leaders were great educators, such as Gandhi, Churchill, Kennedy, Roosevelt, Buddha, Christ, Moses, and Mohammed. If managers can learn something from these leaders, they will make dramatic headway in implementing productivity, which is surely less encompassing and challenging than the political and religious objectives of these leaders.

It is useful to recall personal experiences with a teacher who *really* impressed you. Here are some of things that probably occurred: (a) Students were told why the subject matter was important. (b) Students were told how the learning would benefit them (e.g., by acquiring new skills, solving key problems, or receiving high grades). (c) The teacher didn't build any hills that students couldn't climb. (d) The teacher had an endless range of examples to prove his or her point. (e) The teacher involved students in the learning, through exercises, sharing of contributions, or critical self-reflection. The teacher also stimulated student curiosity through involvement. (f) The teacher welcomed contributions from all students, *regardless of their motives* for doing so. (g) The teacher knew when there was enough support from the classroom to continue the lesson. (h) The teacher was enthusiastic and stubbornly persistent about the lesson (also, the teacher didn't expect everyone to be as enthusiastic as he or she, but clearly appreciated those who were). (i) The teacher treated everyone with human dignity, even though he or she was superior in terms of the subject matter (you were *never* put down when you asked a dumb question). (j) The teacher was always in control of the classroom and knew how to draw the line with resisters.

There are many parallels with managerial efforts to ensure commitment. Managers must be patient, knowledgeable, prepared, persistent, kind, and in control (Lynch, 1992). The reason that these skills and attributes are required is that in their absence, resistance occurs: People do not like being treated as inferiors, and they disrespect those who lack knowledge. Managers, like teachers, also need to get a critical mass of support. Patience is a key virtue of all great educators and is also required of managers. The *rule of seven* is that people become masters of new skills only after they have tried applying them seven times. The *rule of three* is that people only hear things that have been said three times. Thus managers must be consistent in their message and always present to help employees to apply new skills. However, a problem is that managers are required to be impatient in many other ways; many things need be done *now.* But when it comes gaining support and commitment, managers must gain control over their impatience. This takes discipline.[3]

Obtain commitment from top managers. The reality of hierarchical power requires that managers get support from top managers. This is necessary because productivity improvement frequently requires resources and, most important, requires changes that some employees are apt to resist. Top management support legitimates changes at lower levels and eliminates end runs by disgruntled employees. Top management support empowers lower managers to act. Top managers who implement productivity improvement strategies frequently seek support from elected bodies or their board of directors for the same reasons.

The need to obtain top managers' support implies that lower managers must sell their idea for productivity improvement to top managers. In this, lower managers often find themselves competing against other proposals for funding. Although productivity improvement proposals that emphasize effectiveness gains are important, those that also provide efficiency gains and have a low chance of failure are even better (see Chapter 3). Thus managers need to identify efficiency savings, which often causes them to rethink or retarget initial productivity improvement efforts to highlight these gains. Some sources of efficiency improvement are current errors and delays that cause rework and a loss of employee time. Table 4.1 shows an outline for a Productivity Improvement Proposal that addresses these issues, although proposals are not always this thorough.

When managers fail to obtain support, they diminish their ability to make necessary changes. Rather than being able to follow a planned, proactive course of action, managers must then react to events and situations and make improvements whenever possible, for example, using employee turnover or new workload demands as opportunities to make improvements. This passive approach lengthens the time that is required for improvements and may cause some improvements never to occur.

Top management support is often a necessary condition for productivity improvement. Table 4.1 also distinguishes between conditions or obstacles that

TABLE 4.1 Productivity Improvement Proposal (Outline)

1. Background: Current Activities
Discuss key activities or work processes.
Add any diagram or flowchart that clarifies current activities.
Identify improvement needs or opportunities.

2. Productivity Improvement Effort
Define the productivity improvement effort and relationship to improvement opportunities or needs
mentioned under Step 1.
Discuss how the productivity improvement effort (a) increases effectiveness, (b) increases efficiency,
and (c) pays for itself (or is otherwise imperative to undertake).
Discuss any standards that the improvement effort seeks to attain and compare with existing
performance.

3. Measurement Matrix
Identify key performance measures (including quality) of program outcomes, productivity improvement
objectives, and efficiency savings.
Use examples of measures (with past trend data, to the extent available).
Discuss data collection strategies.

4. Implementation Strategy
Summarize the purpose of the implementation effort and discuss the steps of the overall implementation
strategy.
Discuss the feasibility of Implementation Plan I: Manager identifies obstacles that can be overcome and
discusses how this is accomplished.
Discuss the feasibility of Implementation Plan II: Manager identifies constraints that are fixed and cannot
be overcome, and shows that the plan stays within these constraints.
Approximate milestones and time frames for implementation.

5. Summary
Recap the purpose of the intervention, the need for the intervention, and the expected outcomes and
benefits of this effort for the organization.

can be overcome and those that are constraints that cannot be overcome. Managers must find opportunities within constraints that they cannot change. For example, many states have recently overhauled their welfare regulations. Managers who seek improvement of these new programs must work within the constraints of existing laws because they are seldom empowered to change them. Existing laws, however imperfect, should not be used as excuses for not seeking improvement, and identifying opportunities for improvement often requires knowledge of current work processes and their shortcomings. Managers increase their case for productivity improvement when they show an understanding of fixed constraints, when they show that suggested productivity improvements do not require changes of such constraints, and when they have plans for overcoming challenges that they can change.

Establish trust through action. Managers need to make a few friends. Productivity requires a degree of trust, that is, the expectation that managers and coworkers will not take advantage of employees (Barber, 1983; Carnevale, 1995). Some managers believe that trust is caused by innate character and values. However, good people have been known to behave in ways that produced distrust. Rather, trust and friendship are increased by *actions:* (a) showing employees that managers are using their powers to further their interests, rather than being indifferent or harmful; (b) including employees in decision making about aspects that affect them, and delegating; and (c) demonstrating to employees that managers are efficacious in their actions and that they produce at high levels of accomplishment (McClelland, 1985). When these actions are consistently undertaken, trust increases. Comparison with Argyris's "normal" management values of control-dominate-avoid explains why many workers report low levels of trust in the workplace: It is uncommon to experience feelings of trust and friendship for people who use their power to control and dominate.

Building trust also requires that managers get tough on cynics and persistent resisters. Trust and commitment are a two-way street. Allowing dissenters to engage in negative tactics decreases the atmosphere of trust and hence productivity. Actions may be necessary to physically or otherwise separate such individuals from the rest of the group. Such employees cannot be allowed to spoil the atmosphere of trust and friendship (Ehrenhalt, 1996)

Selective use of rewards. Economic theory greatly emphasizes the importance of incentives such as rewards for increasing motivation; people do alter their behavior and goals in the face of incentives. But it is important to understand why incentives motivate: They (a) signal commitment by the organization to efforts to change and (b) help employees meet their needs in other areas. For example, increased salaries allow employees to better meet their needs for leisure and to support their families such as by providing better education or clothing, and can also bolster the ego by allowing employees to afford luxury items.

Financial rewards are often limited in public and nonprofit organizations. Managers must therefore often rely on nonsalary incentives and persuade employees that these are worthwhile. Even in for-profit organizations, financial rewards are balanced with other rewards because employees get used to salary raises and bonuses and then want more; the ability of any company to afford such rising costs is limited. Managers must look for alternative ways of meeting employees' needs. For example, when money is unavailable, managers may be able to restructure employees' schedule to give them more time off. This helps employees who have a need for leisure as well as those who are looking for an opportunity to work a second job (Chapter 10). By better understanding employee needs, creative managers find alternative ways of matching limited financial and other rewards to employees' needs. Senior managers need to be certain that lower managers are using a broad range of motivational strategies (Champagne & McAfee, 1989).

Although rewards are necessary, they are seldom sufficient. Rewards do not deal with the need for trial and error and support. In addition, overreliance on rewards may be counterproductive. First, the ability to reward implies the ability to punish. Overemphasis on rewards seldom increases the climate of trust because withheld rewards are perceived as punishment and reduce employee-manager cooperation, and employees may be fearful of losing future rewards. Second, employees have a need to be respected for their ability and individuality. An employee is more than "economic man." Overemphasis on money as a means of effecting change is a not-so-subtle way of denying the importance of people as individuals. Material rewards without employee participation and understanding often buy little commitment. As one review of studies of incentives plans concludes: "Changing the way that workers are *treated* may boost productivity more than changing the way they are *paid,* although (combining both) may be the best system of all" (Binder, 1990, p. 13).

Commitment to accomplishment. Many tactics of resistance aim to reduce attainment of the goals of productivity improvement—whatever they may be. A foundation of implementing productivity improvement is commitment to results. Managers must be like sports *coaches* who consistently and persistently focuses their players on the importance of goals and goal attainment. Such accountability requires *specific* outcomes to be accomplished at *specific* target dates that are viewed as deadlines.

Two problems of accountability are under- and overperformance. Employees often avoid overaccomplishment because they do not wish to be branded "rate busters" or "overachievers." Underperformance occurs when employees lack integrity and agreement with the goals and objectives that are set. Lack of integrity means that employees do not have a commitment to fulfilling their promises, and that they will have many excuses for why they fail to perform. Lack of agreement means that they do not make commitments: Astute managers are aware that employees try to get managers to buy into outcomes or target dates that are ill-specified, thus allowing for a variety of excuses ("I tried my best, but . . . "). When agreement exists, the door is closed on many excuses for failure.[4] It should be noted that new entrants into the workforce are often very surprised about these "games" between employees and managers, and that accomplishment is *not* always the norm in organizations.

However, overzealous commitment to accomplishment may cause managers to become impatient with the rights and needs of others. Such impatience detracts from necessary learning experiences, discussed earlier. Impatience may also lead to callous disregard for the rights and ethical treatment of others. Managers may fail to consult with employees and clients about their needs and expectations. They may unknowingly trample on laws whose existence they failed to discern or respect because of their impatience. To avoid this problem, managers need to combine their commitment to outcomes with intermittent consultation of stakeholders and analysis of laws, rules, and ethical principles. Failure to do so can cause resistance and even legal entanglements that are a source of great embarrassment to both managers and their organizations.

Strategy for Broad-Scale Intervention

During the last 20 years, new strategies for implementing change have been devised. Although managers are often encouraged to make changes swiftly and decisively, they must also lay a foundation of acceptance and commitment. Intervention strategies are increasingly based on a multistage process known as Planned Organizational Change. This process incorporates the above principles and has been used to implement productivity in small settings (20 people) as well as very large organizations (20,000). Although different authors use some-what different steps, the following steps typically are present (Kolb, 1995; Powell & Friedkin, 1987).

It cannot be said too often that single tactics often fail to generate success. Managers sometimes rely on simple adages such as treating others like you want them to treat you. Such axioms are relevant but usually provide inadequate guidance in the face of specific situations and the need for exceptions (indeed, another principle is that every rule has exceptions). Platitudes and praise are also sometimes used to motivate employees, but they are seldom sufficient. More-over, false praise poisons the climate for subsequent efforts. As previously mentioned, pay and rewards are important, but alone they seldom generate sustainable enthusiasm for productivity. People also get used to pay and rewards, and then want more. Managers need an arsenal of different approaches that are seamlessly applied in a variety of contexts. The following strategy incorporates a wide range of different tactics.

Some managers avoid planning because they do not believe that future events can be foreseen. They prefer to react to events as they occur and rely on their abilities in the process. Implementation strategy helps managers to succeed by anticipating likely problems and proceeding in a logical way. It is somewhat akin to the planning that generals undertake to succeed in war. Such plans cannot anticipate all unexpected maneuvers and events, and often must be revised. However, these plans do prevent many problems, such as engaging the enemy with inadequate supplies. Likewise, planned change provides a structure for achieving success.

1. Feasibility and impact assessment. Managers identify productivity challenges by developing initial "hunches" and checking these against different indicators and multiple sources (Chapter 2). After an initial productivity diagnosis has been made, managers must develop a clear perspective about the consequences of proposed change with regard to existing *systems* (including rewards, information technology, customer processing procedures, billing, etc.), *values* (core beliefs, priorities, and practices associated with organizational culture), *behaviors* (such as being courteous, doing things that help others, and being on time), and *tools* (including surveys, productivity measurement, and various computer applications). Kolb (1995) suggests that managers should also be alert to changes in existing power structures (such as the chain of command) and any physical changes that may be needed (e.g., improved office layout). Such challenges often affect the success of proposed productivity improvement efforts. As a result of this assessment, managers may conclude that underlying problems must be addressed first. For example, managers may conclude that initial efforts are required to improve technology before instituting improved billing processes. When managers have inadequate skills in implementing change, or cultures exist that lack openness, trust, cooperation, and integrity, these deficiencies must be resolved first, before productivity improvement is undertaken.

Some authors also believe that managers need to assess forces that impede and promote the implementation of new productivity strategies (Armenakis, Harris, & Mossholder, 1993; Harrison, 1994). Negative forces include threats to employee job security or prestige, opposition from external stakeholders such as councilpersons and board members, conflicts with existing values or traditions, relatively high start-up costs (e.g., need for training or a new building), the "cost" of dealing with opposition, and the availability of opportunities for removing managers. Identification of obstacles may cause managers to conclude that key forces cannot be altered and that they are better off pursuing some other productivity problem. It should be noted that not all forces that give rise to current problems are necessarily obstacles to change; some forces disappear

TABLE 4.2 Feasibility Assessment

People:

Are the people who will implement the change effective change agents?

Do employees have adequate skills for the intervention? If not, how will required skills be obtained? Is training required? When will staff get it? How successful is training likely to be?

Which incentives and rewards are required? Are they adequate? Are there promotion and compensation opportunities?

Who will likely resist, and how will resisters be dealt with?

Can proponents be shielded from possible retaliation?

Who will monitor the change effort? Do change agents know what is expected from them? Who will evaluate the change agents?

How will staff be evaluated?

How will the change be explained to others in the organization? About how many interactions will this take? Over what period? What arguments explain the reason for change? What counterarguments might be raised? How will these be dealt with?

Is there sufficient support outside the organization for the proposed change?

How does the change affect current expectations, roles, and responsibilities? Are there role models within the organization that can be assigned leadership responsibilities for implementing change?

Other:

What changes of policy does the intervention require, if any?

Are the resources sufficient for the intervention (staff, technology, etc.)?

Are adequate resources available to sustain the intervention?

Are existing information, delivery, feedback, and other systems adequate to support the intervention? If not, what changes are needed?

Are any physical plant changes needed that prevent the intervention?

How will change affect decision-making structures within the organization? Can change be used to improve decision making?

How does the intervention affect relations among units? Are new liaison functions needed?

How does the intervention affect basic missions, goals, and objectives of units?

How and when will we measure the success of the intervention?

Is there a plan for the intervention? A time line for accomplishment?

---

upon implementation of new efforts, for example, unproductive behaviors or attitudes that are replaced by productive ones.

Table 4.2 shows a feasibility assessment instrument that addresses the above concerns.

2. Increasing acceptance for change. A key to building commitment for productivity is acceptance of (a) the need for and (b) the feasibility of change. Creating acceptance requires interaction and dialogue with others. Employees must come to see change as inevitable and accept the undesirability of maintaining the status quo (Stanislao & Stanislao, 1983). Managers must try to "unfreeze" currently held views about the current status quo (Lewin, 1951). By presenting evidence about the need for change and challenging assumptions and beliefs ("your clients tell me that our service is no longer meeting their needs . . ."), managers create openings for the possibility of change. In so doing, managers do well to focus on the interests of the organization ("I want our organization to serve the community as well as it can . . .") and to maintain trust by showing commitment to employees' and managers' broader interests.

Managers have different ways to present their case for moving beyond the status quo. For example, they can discuss client complaints, downward trends in workload or efficiency (see Chapter 3), persistent sloppiness, high levels of absenteeism, decreasing resources, outdated technology, low commitment from the community for efforts, litigation, and so on. Managers communicate this information through articles, reports, and meetings. Managers should also communicate the desirability of positive outcomes and their commitment to achieving them through persistent and consistent messages. To further commitment and improve decision making, input should also be sought from employees and managers about their assessment of current situations (Beer, Eisenstat, & Spector, 1990; Werther, 1989). The purpose of such involvement is to get employees and managers to accept the need for moving beyond the status quo: Managers should refrain from suggesting specific strategies, which is discussed in the following step.

3. The initial project. There are dangers in trying to implement change throughout an organization at once. Across-the-board change precludes the possibility of learning by trial and error. It also increases the likelihood of introducing errors that are magnified by the scale of application as well as those that affect the efficacy of subsystems of people or tasks. For these reasons, most authors recommend going slowly and using pilot projects whenever practicable. The purpose of an initial project is (a) to identify and weed out unforeseen bugs in the productivity improvement effort, (b) to create a model of successful application, and (c) to generate a cadre of supporters who are instrumental in diffusing further applications throughout the organization (Kanter, Stein, & Jick, 1992; Quinn, 1980).

Managers should choose initial projects that are likely to produce positive outcomes and can serve as a model for efforts elsewhere in the organization. This is sometimes referred to as the "ripe apple" theory of initial deployment. Thus atypical applications should be avoided, as well as those that have a high chance of failure. Test sites should be avoided that are confounded with other challenges, for example, other productivity improvement strategies. It is important that managers identify a suitable project champion and enthusiastic employees. They must be willing and able to produce positive outcomes. The project champion is usually someone who is respected throughout the unit. Managers must be certain to provide this individual with adequate authority and resources to complete the pilot project.

Initial projects should result in replicable experiences and a cadre of individuals to lead in such efforts. For this reason, upper managers frequently assign an advisory group of senior managers to pilot project efforts. The purpose of the advisory group (or learning team) is to increase the involvement of senior managers who may be asked to lead in deploying subsequent applications. The advisory group also assists the actual project team in developing applications of the intended productivity improvement strategies. It is a sounding board for possible solutions, including those that deal with overcoming resistance. Advisory team members also share their observations of the pilot team with members of their own unit, thereby increasing dialogue about productivity improvement within the organization and increasing awareness. The pilot project is usually concluded with presentations about outcomes and strategies that were used.

In some cases, pilot projects are not feasible. For example, reorganizations, by their nature, must often be performed throughout an entire unit or organization. Managers are often encouraged to make such changes swiftly and thoroughly. However, even in these instances, managers do well to acknowledge that they may not be able to foresee all of the consequences of change. Adjustments and incremental learning will be necessary. For example, a police detective unit reorganized itself from individual responsibility for a wide range of crimes within specific districts to responsibility for specific crimes within the entire city. This resulted not only in a need for cross-training in the event that individual detectives were unable to meet their responsibilities (e.g., due to vacation or sick leave), but an unforeseen problem arose in dealing with detectives whose performance was unsatisfactory and who had been given sole responsibility for certain crimes. In this case, further adjustments were needed to deal with this situation. The need for learning causes organizations to implement even small changes in a few units before implementing them throughout other units.

4. Diffusion. Upon completion of the initial project, managers and employees who participate in the pilot project identify and head up subsequent applications. Diffusion is often a cascading process in which one completed pilot project can lead to as many as 10 new projects. Of particular concern is the selection of managers and employees for such subsequent efforts. The 25-50-25 rule is that in most organizations, about 25% of employees will enthusiastically embrace change, 50% will sit on the fence and participate only when, in due time, the benefits of doing so are clear to them, and 25% of employees are cynical, withdrawn, and likely to resist any change. Managers should choose the road of least resistance; they should start the diffusion effort with those employees who are enthusiastic. In due time, the fence-sitters will follow. Indeed, a critical difference with the initial project is that whereas the former is characterized by learning the ropes, diffusion is characterized by the challenge of getting the support of managers and employees who thus far have stood on the sidelines.

Some managers prefer to diffuse new approaches by swiftly abandoning old approaches, whereas others prefer a "phase-in" period where both old and new processes coexist for a limited period. The choice ultimately depends on unique conditions. Regardless of whatever approach is selected, successful diffusion depends on top management commitment and adequate resources: Top managers must visit different units to show their support. Lower managers must be given adequate resources to reward employees for their commitment and accomplishments as well as means to deal with persistent resisters; they must have support from top managers to prevent end runs by such employees. Strategies for dealing with resisters are discussed further. Top management must also critically evaluate the willingness and ability of managers to implement productivity. A principal barrier to diffusion is a lack of follow-through by top managers, which is sometimes caused by frequent turnover among top managers and officials.[5]

5. Institutionalization. There is agreement that the gains of productivity improvement should be canonized into written policy and procedures. This provides for continuity in the face of turnover and the development of new priorities. For example, performance appraisal criteria affect performance expectations, and changes in these criteria are often enduring. Institutionalization acknowledges what many people are already doing. Institutionalizing rules and policies helps new managers and employees to become clear about the expectations and procedures of their organizations. Although policy and regulations are sometimes used to drive and encourage change, people and units tend to ignore, resist, or pervert rules and regulations to which they have little commitment.

The duration of planned change strategies varies according to the size of the organization and the need for overcoming any prior shortfalls. Feasibility assessments often last from two weeks to three months, depending on the magnitude of change, the extent to which others are consulted, and the development of empirical evidence about the need for change. Efforts to increase awareness often begin in a small leadership group and are extended to those who are likely to be involved in pilot projects. These efforts often last three months, during which managers refine their strategies and objectives and identify a cadre of committed managers. Pilot projects often require three to six months, depending on the nature of change. Diffusion processes last six months to three years, depending on the size of the organization and the number of times that efforts are replicated elsewhere. Institutionalization processes are usually brief but sometimes require organizationwide training.

Thus organizationwide change processes often take three to five years. However, it is important to note that benefits from productivity improvement occur immediately during pilot projects and thereafter as diffusion occurs through further application. Results do not require three to five years, only the diffusion of strategies does. Managers must show results following each productivity improvement effort. It should also be noted that many managers do not participate in the entire process. They may be transferred to different units or even leave the organization during the productivity improvement process. Others may join the organization and be asked to take responsibility in the middle of the change process. Some processes are aborted when leadership changes or after disappointing results from pilot projects. Such aborted efforts are often retried later. Thus the actual process is often chaotic from the perspective of individual managers and employees, and those who join such efforts need to be briefed about the prior process.

Although planned change is often discussed in the context of organization-wide change, it is applicable to small group settings as well. Supervisors of work teams practice the same steps but they are undertaken at a faster pace. According to the above model of change, managers of small work teams need to assess the consequences of proposed changes before they are undertaken. They must then get a group of employees to agree that change is desirable, or at least inevitable. They should then undertake initial efforts as a pilot project so that employees and managers can learn from early efforts. Only after the initial problems have been overcome are subsequent efforts attempted. Finally, the new approaches become an expectation that is reflected in reward and other decisions.

Dealing With Resisters

Managers must also plan for dealing with employees who resist change. This includes employees who do not wish to adopt modern values but instead use tactics of self-aggrandizement, intimidation, backstabbing, and other means to reach their goals. The first response to such "resisters" consists of a rational process of identifying and addressing underlying reasons for resistance. The goal is to reach an accommodation with the employee about these concerns. For example, an employee might resist change because it would require him or her periodically to work during weekends. An arrangement is made whereby the employee is promised that he or she will not be required to work weekends more than once every other month. However, what can managers do when employees make unreasonable demands or resist for the sake of resisting, to settle old scores, or because of a need to act out their malice and need for domination?

The second response is (a) to separate the individual from the change process and (b) to deal with the individual separately. Resisters and others who are obstacles to change should be identified early in the change effort. As noted above, change processes begin by identifying those who are enthusiastic about change, not those who resist. Change is created by involving more and more employees in changes over time. Resisters are usually not involved until the very last. By then, a majority of employees should be supporting the change effort and, ideally, many resisters will now have become isolated. Resisters may yet fall into place when they lose their audience. However, when this does not occur, managers must consider other alternatives.

One alternative is doing nothing. Managers might ask whether they actually need to have all employees on board for productivity improvement. Do these employees actually do more harm than good? The first priority of productivity improvement is to isolate such employees from influencing the success of efforts. If this can be accomplished, then it may be worthwhile to tolerate the imperfection of some persistent nay-sayers. Doing nothing is often attractive in view of other alternatives that involve personnel action. A second alternative is trying to transfer resisters whose services are no longer needed. Employees who resist are often poor performers and they may welcome a change of unit or supervisor. Their talents might be better suited to another position. Personnel managers often assist in finding alternative positions for such employees. But what is the manager to do when employees resist being transferred and no other manager wants them?

A third alternative is to seek dismissal of resisters. However, the complications of firing are well documented in the public sector, and firing is no panacea in the private sector either, because of the prospect of expensive lawsuits later. The road to dismissal typically begins with progressive discipline and the documentation of poor performance. Legally, managers must create a paper trail documenting unacceptable behavior or performance. Employees must be given an opportunity to improve and be provided with feedback about these efforts. However, management signals must be consistent; for example, dismissals are easily challenged when employees are also given satisfactory performance evaluations or when managers fail to inform employees of poor behavior as soon as it occurs. When repeated written notices fail to produce desired results, managers must provide notice of discipline. Most public agencies have arbitration processes, but a common complaint is that these processes include numerous appeals that are very time-consuming. However, some organizations such as New York State now have expedited processes that provide a final ruling in about two months. In some cases, downsizing is used as an alternative to dismissal by eliminating employees with poor performance records.

Managers need to focus on their objective of improving productivity. From this perspective, the best strategy often is initially to ignore resisters and isolate them over time. Strategies of transferring and dismissing resisters usually come into play at the end of implementation efforts *after* significant gains have already been achieved through employees who are committed to change. Although this implies that some productivity is lost due to the presence of resisters, in this imperfect world, the incremental cost of dealing with resisters is frequently not worth the incremental gain in productivity improvement.

A Note on Consultants

Productivity improvement efforts frequently involve consultants. Although most experts come from outside the organization, internal consultants are sometimes used too. Consultants fulfill different roles in implementing productivity: (a) technical expert, (b) organizational expert, (c) training and development specialist, and (d) change agent. Technical experts share knowledge such as developing a plan for implementing productivity, surveys of client satisfaction, interviews of employees to determine readiness for change, and so on. Regardless of whether they gather data or present existing data, the goal is to increase knowledge. Organizational consultants do much the same, except that they provide insight into human nature; they are a sounding board for testing new arguments and intervention strategies. Other consultants provide training and development that ranges from short awareness seminars to multiday workshops. The latter help "coach" managers and employees in new skills that are required. Finally, change agents work with managers to implement productivity improvement. They keep processes on track and usually fulfill various expert and training roles, too. They are also instigators of change ("Let's see what happens if . . .").

Managers should carefully choose consultants who are consistent with their needs. Consultants should be credible and respected in their field, and managers should feel comfortable working with them. Consultants should complement managerial strengths and weaknesses with regard to both technical skills such as statistical analysis and performance measurement as well as human and strategic skills.

Toward Self-Learning Organizations

This chapter argues that successful change involves identifying and overcoming resistance as well as implementing productivity improvement according to a plan. It also argues that resistance occurs in part because of traditional managerial values of seeking control and dominance and avoiding upsets. Resistance also occurs because some employees have their own agendas or prefer continuity over change. This raises a fundamental question: What would an organization look like in which resistance did not occur and in which managers and employees were naturally motivated to improve their outcomes?

Senge (1990) describes such organizations as "self-learning." These organizations are naturally predisposed to innovate. Self-learning organizations seek out interactions with their environments (e.g., with clients) through which they hope to learn how they can do better (Kettl, 1994). They reward employees who find things that are wrong, and managers empower employees to carry out new ideas. Self-learning organizations are network organizations; they aim to create new capabilities and to connect existing capabilities toward common goals (Benveniste, 1994). They work through teams of internal and external employees (that is, employees of other organizations). Communication is frequent, plenty, and purposefully aimed at producing better outcomes. To produce open communication, a climate of trust and mutual support is maintained. Loyalty is demonstrated and rewarded by achieving results, not by writing endless memos and attending meetings. Both employees and managers seek continuous self-improvement; incompetence is not tolerated. Careers are advanced when people are asked to serve on teams with successively greater levels of responsibility. Teams are rewarded according to what they achieve; hence a strong incentive is given to ensure positive, open, and productive work environments and to use productive employees (Van Wart & Weschler, 1996).

Self-learning organizations thrive on ethics. Honesty and integrity are the characteristics that are most often mentioned as desirable in surveys of employees and managers (Burke & Black, 1990; Kouzes & Posner, 1993). Integrity means commitment to the task and responsibilities at hand, and thus increases productivity. Commitment ensures that tasks get done, and commitment to excellence means tasks get done at the highest possible level. Rewards reinforce commitment to performance. Honesty implies acknowledging shortcomings and playing it straight, and is thus a sound basis from which to seek improvement. It also allows for trusting relations with others and hence mutual support and improved communication. Self-learning organizations are committed to high standards of performance and hence to ethics (Odom, Boxx, & Dunn, 1990).

The concept of a self-learning organization is an ideal, a standard. Most organizations share elements of both traditional and self-learning organizations. For example, some hospitals routinely perform world-class surgery but repeatedly fail in their billing practices. Most organizations do some things right, some things wrong, and many things in mediocre ways. The challenge is to raise the standard. Managers must deal with the existing realities of resistance and control-oriented management styles, and lay the groundwork for moving organizations toward becoming self-learning organizations. Top management must identify and support managers and employees who personify and implement the new values of self-learning organizations. Reward structures and other policies should be brought in line with the requirements of new forms of organization. Units should be required to show evidence of change and improvement while adopting processes that emphasize openness and high performance.

Summary

This chapter examines the challenge of implementing productivity and overcoming employee and managerial resistance. It identifies specific verbal and nonverbal forms of resistance. It discusses that productivity improvement generates resistance in the face of managerial value systems and employee attitudes and beliefs. Effective implementation rests on mastery of both principles and strategy. The principles are to educate effectively, emphasize accomplishment, undertake strategies that build trust, and understand the role of rewards. Implementation strategy requires completion of the following successive steps: feasibility assessment, building awareness, a pilot project, diffusion, and institutionalization. This chapter also discusses tactics for dealing with difficult people and strategies that managers should undertake as well as steps that help foster "self-learning" organizations.

Notes

1. One reason they may fail to reflect is that they are afraid of the consequences of reaching conclusions that are contrary to common wisdom or widely accepted beliefs. Following orders and repressing one's own creativity (and hence thinking) is the price that is often paid for acceptance by others.

2. The expression "The wolf is dressed in sheep's clothing" is appropriate here.

3. It is useful to practice imitating and perfecting the skills of great teachers. The rule of seven suggests that managers might need some coaching to become better teachers themselves.

4. To obtain agreement, managers end their requests by asking employees whether they are OK with the task and its deadline. When this is so, then agreement for accomplishment exists. Agreement should also be reached regarding ways in which unexpected problems will be dealt with.

5. New managers sometimes worry excessively about how they will deal with resistance. Enthusiastic employees and "fence-sitters" constitute about 75% of employees. By focusing on these employees first, managers create a situation in which the cadre of persistent resisters eventually becomes small. They are then often isolated by other employees through such comments as the following: "Oh, here come the nay-sayers and doomsday critics again . . ." Arguably, the power of cynics is greatest at the early implementation stages when even enthusiastic employees may have second thoughts. Therefore, at early stages, managers must repeatedly explain the reason for change, and demonstrate both their and top management's support for change.

References

Argyris, C. (1990). *Organizational defenses.* New York: Allyn & Bacon.

Argyris, C., & Schön, D. (1996). *Organizational learning II: Theory, method, practice.* Reading, MA: Addison-Wesley.

Armenakis, A., Harris, S., & Mossholder, K. (1993). Creating readiness for organizational change. *Human Relations, 46*(6), 681-703.

Barber, B. (1983). *The logic and limits of trust.* New Brunswick, NJ: Rutgers University Press.

Beer, M., Eisenstat, R., & Spector, B. (1990). Why change programs don't produce change. *Harvard Business Review, 68*(6), 158-166.

Benveniste, G. (1994). *The twenty-first century organization: Analyzing current trends—imagining the future.* San Francisco: Jossey-Bass.

Berman, E. (1995). [National survey of city managers]. Unpublished raw data.

Binder, A. (Ed.). (1990). *Paying for productivity: A look at the evidence.* Washington, DC: Brookings Institution.

Burke, F., & Black, A. (1990). Improving organizational productivity: Add ethics. *Public Productivity and Management Review, 14*(2), 121-133.

Carnevale, D. (1995). *Trustworthy government.* San Francisco: Jossey-Bass.

Champagne, P., & McAfee, R. (1989). *Motivating strategies for performance and productivity.* New York: Quorum.

Ehrenhalt, A. (1996). The debilitating search for a flabby consensus. *Governing, 9*(10), 7-8.

Fournies, F. (1988). *Why employees don't do what they are supposed to do.* New York: McGraw-Hill.

Harrison, M. (1994). *Diagnosing organizations: Methods, models and processes.* Thousand Oaks, CA: Sage.

Kanter, R., Stein, B., & Jick, T. (1992). *The challenge of organizational change.* New York: Free Press.

Kettl, D. (1994). Managing at the frontiers of knowledge. In P. Ingraham & B. Romzek (Eds.), *New paradigms for government* (pp. 19-40). San Francisco: Jossey-Bass.

Kolb, D. (1995). *Organizational behavior: An experiential approach.* Englewood Cliffs, NJ: Prentice Hall.

Kouzes, J., & Posner, Z. (1993). *Credibility: How leaders gain and lose it, why people demand it.* San Francisco: Jossey-Bass.

Lynch, R. (1992). *LEAD! How public and nonprofit managers can bring out the best in themselves and their organizations.* San Francisco: Jossey-Bass

Lewin, K. (1951). *Field theory in social science.* New York: Harper & Row.

McClelland, D. (1985). *Human motivation.* Glenview, IL: Scott Foresman.

Odom, R., Boxx, W., & Dunn, M. (1990). Organizational cultures, commitment, satisfaction and cohesion. *Public Productivity and Management Review, 14*(2), 157-169.

Powell, W., & Friedkin, R. (1987). Organizational change in nonprofit organizations. In W. Powell (Ed.), *The nonprofit sector handbook* (pp. 180-194). New Haven, CT: Yale University Press.

Quinn, J. (1980). Managing strategic change. *Sloan Management Review, 21*(3), 3-20.

Rosenberg, D. (1992). Eliminating resistance to change. *Nonprofit World, 10*(5), 33-36.

Senge, P. (1990). *The fifth discipline: The art and practice of the learning organization.* Gardem City, NY: Doubleday.

Stanislao, J., & Stanislao, B. S. (1983). Dealing with resistance to change. *Business Horizons, 26*(4), 74-78.

Van Wart, M., & Weschler, L. (1996). *Being smarter under crises: Advanced learning as innovation in organizations.* Paper presented at the 57th National Conference of the American Society for Public Administration, San Francisco.

Werther, B. (1989). *Dear boss.* Deephaven, MN: Meadowbrook.

PART

III

Strategies

Broad-Based
Strategic Planning

If you don't know where you are going,
any road will take you there.

Chinese proverb

New developments and changing environments often prompt organizations and communities to assess their priorities and efforts. They need to make adjustments to better serve clients, citizens, and other stakeholders and to better position themselves for the future. Strategic planning is a set of procedures that help organizations and communities to align their priorities with changing conditions and new opportunities. Through strategic planning, organizations develop new goals and strategies, update their missions, and create shared commitment among leaders, employees, and others regarding present and future endeavors. Strategic planning is often used in organizations that find themselves in fast and ever-changing environments, and those that use it do so frequently (Bryson, 1995; Bryson & Crosby, 1992; Giles, 1993; Kemp, 1992; Ostrom, 1993; Wheeland, 1993).

Strategic planning does *not* assume that future events can be perfectly predicted. Rather, organizations and communities use strategic planning to design a future that better meets their needs and to develop paths and guideposts that help them in their quests. To this end, strategic planning asks such questions as the following: Which roles and missions should organizations seek to fulfill? Is the mission, and its rationale, widely shared by client groups and others inside and outside the organization? What are the unique competencies of the organization that make it qualified to fulfill this role? How do these competencies compare with the expertise and capacity of other organizations? How much external and internal commitment exists for goals that are pursued? How might future challenges affect the ability of the organization to fulfill its goals? Is collaboration with other organizations possible and desirable? Which objectives and strategies are being pursued to realize this vision? Are these objectives specific, feasible, and credible? What resources are available to assist organizations in their efforts, and are these resources adequate? By which target date will strategies be implemented and completed? How will success be measured?

This chapter examines strategic planning in two contexts: in dealing with community-wide issues that involve cooperation among multiple organizations and in dealing with the strategic adjustments of individual organizations. It also discusses analytic techniques that are used in strategic planning.

Community-Based Strategic Planning

In recent years, community-based strategic planning has become a well-defined approach that helps communities forge collective responses for dealing with communitywide problems. As one community activist observed: "No one person can solve our problems. . . . Traditionally, we looked for someone to be our answer. We are realizing that *we* are the answer" (Oliver, 1995, p. G1). Community-based strategic planning is an act of consensus-building among often disparate individuals and organizations (Etzioni, 1993; Fowler, 1991; Wood & Gray, 1991). For example, strategies to improve local economic development require coordinated efforts by businesses, government agencies, community colleges, and other organizations. Businesses and community colleges normally do not interact much with each other to address mutual, communitywide issues. Likewise, many public safety issues involve local police, schools, neighborhood associations, churches, and parent associations. Community-based planning is also used in other countries. For example, formerly centrally planned economies use it to improve their capacity for dealing with local issues (Berman, 1996a; Berman & Stephenson, 1996; Michigan Department of Commerce, 1990).[1]

Other examples of collaborative leadership are shown in Table 5.1. Community-based responses are increasingly used to address the growing complexity of many problems as well as to better use the capabilities of local organizations. A recent, 1997, survey finds that 52% of cities of more than 50,000 had used community-based strategic planning during the past 12 months. About 38% of large social service organizations and 30% of museums had engaged in such planning as well (Berman, 1997).

Community-based strategic planning involves distinctive steps and phases. The overall process is designed to build agreement and commitment to common goals. Strategic planning is based on the logic that leaders must (a) build trust and commitment among participants, (b) reach agreement about the nature of the problem or challenge, as well as the various solutions that can be used, and (c) show commitment through the implementation of proposed solutions. This usually results in four distinctive phases of community-based strategic planning:

- The decision to initiate a community-based strategic planning process and the selection of a strategic team of leaders
- A period of data collection and consensus-building among community leaders
- The formulation of missions, visions, priorities, goals, objectives, strategies, performance measures, and target dates of community-based responses
- Implementation of recommendations

Some authors divide these steps into smaller steps in the following manner:

1. Initiating strategic planning process
2. Identifying key community leaders for participation in the strategic planning process and providing this group with a mandate
3. Researching the environment for opportunities and threats and analyzing internal strengths and weaknesses
4. Identifying critical issues
5. Drafting mission and/or vision statements
6. Prioritizing alternative goals and developing an action plan of objectives, strategies (including resources), and target dates
7. Gaining acceptance of the plan from other actors
8. Implementing the plan
9. Reviewing and updating the plan

Strategic planning involves some unique vocabulary that distinguishes among *missions, visions, critical issues, goals,* and *strategies. Missions* are defined as the purposes of collective efforts that are expressed through mission statements.

TABLE 5.1 Examples of Collaborative Leadership

Economic Development:

- Local government develops comprehensive economic development strategies together with leaders of area businesses, schools, universities, neighborhood associations, county governments, banks, and community organizations (e.g., Futures Forum, Phoenix, Arizona; Hollywood, Florida).

- Local government works with area hospitals to create a regional center for biomedical instrument research and manufacturing (e.g., New Orleans, Louisiana).

- Banks work with neighborhood associations and governments to provide home improvement loans and to build homes for low-income families (e.g., Baltimore, Maryland).

- City works with insurance companies to ensure coverage for nonprofit vendors (e.g., New York City).

Human Services:

- County welfare agencies work with courts to provide integrated services for child care payments, noncustodial parent involvement in child care, and job skills training for custodial parent (e.g., Anoka County, Minnesota).

- Preventive services for poor women (e.g., breast cancer screening, prenatal care) (Urban-Care Partnership, South Bend, Indiana).

- Local government works with nonprofit organizations to provide comprehensive care for homeless families and adolescents (e.g., housing assistance to prevent eviction) (Portland, Oregon).

Education:

- Schools, parents, teachers, and employers collectively identify the educational needs of children (e.g., Boulder, Colorado).

- National Network of Educational Renewal brings universities and school districts together to renew the education of educators (Seattle, Washington).

- School boards work with local governments and planning commissions to reduce overcrowding by requiring growth management impact fees and building lead time (e.g., Dade County, Florida).

- Schools work with police and nonprofit organizations to provide early warning of domestic violence affecting their students.

Public Safety:

- Police works with middle schools to teach students to avoid becoming victims.

- Police works with neighborhood associations to provide community-based policing.

- Police works with manufacturers, insurance companies, and shipping companies to reduce auto theft.

For example, a mission in economic development is to increase economic growth, employment, and the attractiveness of a community as a place to live, work, and visit. Mission statements sometimes include a brief history or statement of guiding values or principles. Vision statements identify a future state that is desirable. For example, a community-based strategic planning effort for economic development may include in its vision increased tourism and attracting environmentally safe industries. Mission and vision statements are usually briefly stated, seldom exceeding one or two paragraphs each.

Critical issues identify specific results or problems that strategic plans must address and are often used by others as benchmarks to evaluating success. For example, local economic development planning often involves such critical issues as increasing downtown development, increasing the supply of workers with adequate skills, and creating new jobs. Goals are general ends that advance the vision in these specific issue areas. For example, some goals of downtown development planning are to improve its appearance and attractiveness to tourists and to make the downtown area attractive for new business development. Goals should be significant and meaningful yet broad.

Objectives are specific, measurable outcomes that advance goals. In the above example of improving downtown appearance, an objective might be to ensure adequate signage. A second objective might be to increase the number of trees, bushes, and flowers. A third objective is to reduce the amount of litter and graffiti. Objectives are limited in scope but, collectively, they effect progress toward goals. (In this regard, the relationship between objectives and goals is similar to that of the multifaceted indicators and measures discussed in Chapter 3.) Objectives usually have target dates as well as performance standards. Each objective usually has multiple strategies. Strategies are the actual efforts through which objectives are accomplished, for example, choosing among alternative signs and ensuring that signs are in place before a specific date.

Leadership is the operative word in forging a communitywide strategy. Leadership is required to get organizations to participate in planning efforts, to articulate common visions and develop consensus regarding strategies, to ensure that plans are implemented, to go first in announcing personal commitment, and to commit one's own organization to the outcomes of collective efforts. Local government leaders often play a key leadership role in starting community-based strategic planning processes because they are responsible for broad areas such as economic development, race relations, and social services. They must forge consensus among other community leaders unknown to each other (Berman, 1996b). The role of leadership as a condition for success is widely recognized in the literature (for example, Bryson, 1995; Chrislip & Larson, 1994; Gardner, 1991; Gates, 1991; Hay, 1990). It follows that communities that lack elective leadership or otherwise inhibit it also lose opportunities to address their myriad complex, interdependent problems through collective action.

Table 5.2 compares community-based strategic planning with "traditional" strategic planning efforts. A key differences between traditional, for-profit strategic planning and community-based strategic planning is that the latter involves facilitated (rather than directed) processes of planning and information gathering as well as consensual decision making and implementation (rather

TABLE 5.2   A Comparison of Traditional and Community-Based Strategic
            Planning

Traditional Strategic Planning	*Community-Based Strategic Planning*
Single organizations	Multiple, "networked" organizations
Involves a few decision makers (typically 1-7)	Involves many stakeholders (10-1200), who are often the leaders of their organizations
Assumes that goals, objectives, and strategies will be accepted by affected parties	Assumes that stakeholder participation is essential to acceptance and hence implementation
Assumes adequate information of threats, opportunities, strengths, and weaknesses by a few participants	Uses many stakeholders to provide needed information about participating organizations and their environments
Can be conducted in 2 hours to 2 days, although usually between 2 days and 3 months	Requires 3-6 months for ensuring awareness and consensus on problems, goals, objectives, strategies, and priorities
Requires commitment from the top leader	Requires commitment from the key public and private stakeholders
Planning leader leads the planning process and develops and decides on new strategic options	Planning leader is facilitative and relies on stakeholders to suggest and accept new options
Implementation is often top-down and ensured by hierarchical authority	Implementation is consensual and ensured by peer pressure
Outcomes occur during 6-month to 5-year period	Outcomes occur over 2- to 5-year period

than top-down management). Community-based strategic planning also has more decision makers (10 to 1,200 rather than a few executives). Historically, strategic planning was developed by for-profit companies to help them plan their production, marketing, and business development: In the 1960s and 1970s, strategic planning focused on helping large multinational firms better manage their diversified business portfolios, but in the 1980s, emphasis shifted to the management of strategic issues.

The Practice of Community-Based Strategic Planning

Getting Started

Public officials play a leading role in launching community-based strategic planning. Such officials include mayors and governors as well as chief appointed officials such as state and federal agency directors. Ranking elected officials are prominent in this process because they readily command legitimacy for dealing with public issues. They also hold forth a credible promise of public support through new policies, programs, or funding in the event that subsequent decision-making efforts lead to action. Sometimes chief executive officers of prominent nonprofit organizations also lead in initiating community-based activities (Berman & Werther, 1997).

As a practical matter, leaders must decide which problems or issues they will address through community-based strategic planning. These decisions often reflect three key considerations. First, issues are more likely to be addressed when they are seen as salient concerns by other citizen groups and organizations. Public support furthers the commitment of leaders. Elected leaders must also feel confident that leaders of other organizations are likely to follow their initiative and that they have support from their organizations too. A second condition is that issue areas and potential strategies must be consistent with the priorities and ideologies of elected and/or self-appointed leaders. Many elected officials enter office with a vision of future accomplishments, and issues that are consistent with these visions are more likely to be acted on. Third, elected officials must believe that community-based action is effective. They must feel comfortable with existing models for achieving community-based commitment and decision making. Managers of public and nonprofit organizations can play important roles by bringing to the attention of elected officials these successful practices of community-based planning.

After the decision has been made by a leader to "go forward" with an issue and deal with it through community-based strategic planning, a team of community leaders is created, called a strategic planning committee (SPC). This is usually done with the assistance of a process facilitator who guides the strategic planning effort. An example of a community-based strategic planning effort involved economic development in the City of Hollywood, Florida, population 135,000, in which the author was involved. The driving reason for the strategic planning effort was that the city had failed to capture its share of economic growth occurring in South Florida. The strategic planning process brought together 34 community leaders in an SPC: the mayor and four council persons, the city manager and one agency head, four leaders of neighborhood and housing associations, a prominent local lawyer, five leaders of educational and vocational institutions, the administrator of the largest hospital, seven CEOs of prominent businesses and banks, three leaders of business associations, four senior managers or editors of area newspapers, and two clergymen. These individuals represented organizations that have shown a commitment to Hollywood. The group size represented a balance between inclusiveness and manage-ability, and other community members who wished to participate served on various subcommittees discussed below (City of Hollywood, 1994).

Inclusiveness broadens support, but it also implies that officials must fre-quently interact with individuals or organizations toward whom some animus exists. Leaders sometimes have concerns about how they will deal with such persons and organizations. In this regard, the constitution of a new group of stakeholders for strategic planning allows for "fresh starts." To ensure broad participation, ground rules for decision making usually include that adversaries will have the opportunity to contribute their views. However, decisions are made by the majority, not with unanimity. Of concern also is having to deal with elected officials. Their participation greatly increases the likelihood that recom-mendations will be adopted in later public policy settings. Political opponents are usually invited, too. Political opponents often participate so as to be part of the process, to keep tabs on what is happening, and to share in the credit for results. In turn, they may be co-opted.

One of the very first issues facing SPCs is clarification of the group mandate: On whose authority is the group proceeding? Although public officials often play a leadership role in convening the group, the group is an informal network that generally does not fall under any public jurisdiction. The group must create its own mandate. This informal act is furthered when leaders state their organi-zation's commitment to the process. They must indicate their organization is willing to participate and that it will devote resources to the effort. Ground rules are clarified. A frequent concern is that mandates do not bind organizations to participate in recommendations or even to complete the process; such a require-ment would scare most organizations away from the table.[2] Group mandates are often very brief in lieu of further work on mission or vision statements. Mandates often identify the willingness of organizations to cooperate in studying the issue or problem and to work toward identifying strategies that address the problem.

Consensus-building is furthered by designing the strategic planning process to create a shared commitment to processes and outcomes. Initial meetings are designed for key leaders to show their commitment in word and deed, and to allow other leaders to easily agree with the process, rules, and agenda items. The process sometimes includes small assignments through which leaders signal their commitment and can be acknowledged by others. Consensus-building is an important part of community-based planning, and the above preparatory efforts may last several weeks. Table 5.3 indicates that the actual process may take six to seven months. Of course, these are but rough estimates; when fewer organizations are involved, the time is usually shortened.

TABLE 5.3 Time Line for Community-Based Strategic Planning

Preparatory Activities (about 4 months):

Week 1:	Elected leader identifies an issue or problem in need of communitywide support and participation (e.g., economic development or teenage drug use).
Weeks 2-5:	Elected leader explores alternative approaches for dealing with the problem with leaders of other organizations and internal managers. Discussions suggest that a community-based strategic planning (CBSP) approach is desirable.
Weeks 6-10:	Leader contacts experts about doing CBSP in his or her community.
Weeks 11-16:	A competitive bidding process is undertaken and a process facilitator is selected.

Strategic Planning Process (about 6-7 months):

Weeks 1-4:	Community leaders are identified and contacted to participate on the Strategic Planning Committee (SPC). Their agreement to participate is obtained.
Week 5:	First meeting of the SPC. The mandate is clarified. Concerns and observations about the problem are made. Issue areas are identified for further study. Media representative writes an article for the newspaper.
Week 6:	Facilitator discusses with SPC members subcommittee assignments, expertise, and staff participation. Community resources for data are identified.
Week 7:	Second meeting of the SPC. Subcommittee assignments are made, additional community leaders and staff are identified and invited to participate on data gathering subcommittees. Leaders discuss and coordinate their availability.
Weeks 8-16:	Subcommittees collect data. Surveys are undertaken, a community profile is completed. The SPC meets in week 10 to review ongoing activities.
Weeks 17-18:	The SPC meets to discuss and accept the analysis of the problem. "Critical issues" are identified. A Mission or Vision Statement is formulated. Media representative writes a second article about the CBSP project.
Week 19:	The SPC meets to identify different issue areas for developing goals, objectives, strategies, target dates, and performance measures. Strategic Planning Task Forces (SPTFs) are constituted for each area and assignments are made.
Weeks 20-26:	SPTFs meet three to four times to identify goals, objectives, strategies, target dates, and performance measures.
Week 27:	The results of the SPTFs are combined into a proposed Strategic Plan. The SPC discusses the proposed plan. Modifications, concerns, and so on are discussed and a vote is taken to adopt the proposed Strategic Plan. The SPC members are thanked for their service and the SPC disbanded. Media representative writes a third article.
Week 28:	The recommended Strategic Plan is formally adopted by participating jurisdictions. Implementation begins. Monthly or bimonthly review of progress. Leaders assess the need for a new CBSP effort after 2 or 3 years.

Data Collection

Strategy development requires the best possible understanding of the problem, its context, and causes. Three types of data are often collected for this purpose. The first type of data is past, present, or future critical events. For example, changes in federal laws, plant closings, and environmental catastrophes often are critical events in communities. The second type of data is trend analyses. Changes in population demographic characteristics and income levels often affect local economic development. A community profile is often prepared. A third set involves analyses of internal strengths and weaknesses as well as external opportunities and threats that affect the community (SWOT analysis). SWOT analysis is more encompassing than event and trend analysis: It focuses on community capacities in dealing with issues (for example, leadership, resources, organization, and coordination) as well as external factors that are political, economic, social, or technological in nature (that is, PEST). Although perfect information is seldom available, what exists should be gathered and brought to the attention of leaders.

Because the planning scope of SPCs is usually large, subcommittees are used to generate understanding for different issues. This also enables other community leaders and interested citizens to participate. Sources of data include public agencies (including higher level governments), staff reports and memos, studies by private organizations, and market research (see the section "Analytic Techniques," below). When few data are available, "hard" data are combined with "soft" interpretations and common knowledge to create an understanding of the problem and its context. Group participation furthers consensus-building about the significance of events and trends. The generation of shared knowledge typically requires several meetings during a two- or three-month period. These activities help forge community among otherwise disparate leaders. In the case of Hollywood, Florida, five SWOT analyses were conducted concerning tourism, neighborhood rehabilitation, commercial revitalization, training and employment, and municipal services. Each of these issue areas affects economic development. The number of committees formed reflected the number of additional participants that needed to be accommodated in the strategic planning process. About 150 persons participated, including the 34 original members. The data collection and analysis phase of strategic planning lasted about 10 weeks and group members met three to four times.

During the data collection phase, citizen and business surveys are often used to gather further information as well. These efforts serve a dual purpose, namely, to collect data and to inform citizens about the activities of the group. Managers contribute by ensuring that surveys are conducted in a timely and credible manner. Public support increases the legitimacy of such efforts, whereas the lack of such support sometimes creates obstacles to implementation. To ensure public participation, media representatives are also often invited to keep citizens informed about these activities. These journalists ensure that articles appear about the strategic planning effort. In some cases, public meetings are also used, although these are typically used later in the context of policy adoption by public bodies (Thomas, 1995).

The data collection and consensus building stage ends with the development of a shared understanding about the problem and its context. This is a creative process that involves techniques of brainstorming and reality-testing. Brainstorming ensures that problems and issues are fully explored. Relevant details are identified, and the knowledge of individual group members is brought to bear. After the subcommittees have completed their work, various reports are shared among members of the strategic planning committee. Although they have followed the data gathering efforts of the subcommittees, and most have participated in one such committee, the data are new for many leaders. The sharing and discussion of the data allow for the development of new perspectives. Typically, a process facilitator assists the consensus forming effort by providing summaries and suggesting "critical issues" for further development. Addressing these critical issues is central in further community-based strategic planning efforts.

Identifying Critical Issues, Developing Plans

Upon acceptance of the SWOT findings and critical issues, the strategic planning committee must identify the critical issues. This is necessary because more often priorities are identified than can be pursued and also because some critical issues exceed the mandate of the strategic planning committee: For example, neighborhood safety is an appropriate concern of neighborhood development, but public safety issues are neither the focus nor the mandate of most local economic development efforts. Identifying these issues is also a first step toward developing a mission statement because it causes the committee to focus the efforts of the group. For example, the Hollywood Mission Statement states (in abbreviated form),

> The mission of the City of Hollywood Strategic Planning Committee is to empower our citizens to adjust to economic change. . . . To accomplish our mission, we will establish new directions which will . . . retain jobs, create an environment that stimulates economic growth, maintain Hollywood's existing tourism industry, rehabilitate neighborhoods and provide effective municipal services.

After formulating the mission statement, new subcommittees or task forces are formed to develop goals, objectives, and strategies that address each critical issue (see definitions, above). This allows previous research subcommittees to be reconstituted to accommodate new participants and gain fresh perspectives. The activity of developing goals, objectives, and strategies is creative and usually occurs over three or four meetings. During this process, facilitators help participants to focus on goals, objectives, and strategies that are both feasible and within the mandate and mission of the group. Representatives from organizations that are involved in subsequent implementation participate, too. Their perspectives ensure that proposed strategies are "reality based." Likewise, experts are sometimes brought into decision-making processes, for example, to inform of experiences in other communities.

A concern of most planning processes is that plans do not "gather dust." Several strategies are commonly used to avoid this problem. First, facilitators often seek commitment for implementation from elected officials, agency heads, and the directors of organizations. This furthers legitimacy and the marshaling of resources. Second, where practicable, some organizations begin implementation prior to formal adoption. This creates some early successes and a positive climate of change. In other cases, the proposed strategies may be realized quickly because they already have the support of organizations, regardless of subsequent adoption by the strategic planning committee. Third, to ensure adoption by elected bodies, elected officials are involved in the planning process. This allows proposals to reflect their views and hence increases the likelihood of acceptance. Fourth, facilitators discuss barriers to implementation and assess ways in which these barriers can be overcome.

The final product of the task forces is a compendium of proposed goals, objectives, strategies, and target dates. The compendium is ultimately adopted by vote of the strategic planning committee. Because of the number of objectives, many strategic planning committees rank these in terms of priority. Table 5.4 shows some goals and strategies from the above Hollywood community-based strategic planning effort. The entire document contains over 125 strategies, each of which is linked to specific goals and objectives.

Implementation

The most important part of strategic planning is the implementation of proposed strategies by the implementing organizations. As discussed above, the implementation process often begins prior to the formal adoption of proposals. This is possible because many proposed actions fall within the existing purview of organizations or managers. There is no need to provide public organizations or managers with new mandates. The implementation process is also furthered

TABLE 5.4 Statements From a Community-Based Strategic Planning Action Plan

---

TASK FORCE: JOBS AND ECONOMIC DEVELOPMENT

Selected Goals:

■ Strengthen and broaden Hollywood's economy by supporting and encouraging the growth of existing businesses and encouraging new job creating investment

■ Create a pro-business environment within city government that distinguishes Hollywood from the cities with which it competes

■ Create an integrated economic development delivery system that reflects a partnership between the city, business community, and the Broward County Economic Development Council

Selected Objectives:

■ Increase the availability of funding for new and expanding businesses by creating new sources of debt financing

■ Implement a targeted marketing program directed at attracting companies in the health care industry, aircraft industry, and marine-related industries

■ Implement a business calling and retention program

■ Establish a City Business Center within City Hall

■ Assess the employment skills needed in Hollywood and develop a mechanism to coordinate economic development-related job training resources and activities

■ Develop a nonprofit public-private partnership for economic development, whose governance and financing will be shared between city government and Hollywood's business community

Selected Strategies:

■ Community Redevelopment Agency to issue bonds, setting aside 10% of the proceeds dedicated to funding a Revolving Loan Fund for businesses locating in the CRA area by September 1994

■ Economic Development Director and the Chamber of Commerce to design an ongoing retention/calling program, which will be coordinated with Broward Economic Development Council, by December 1994 to be implemented by March 1995

■ City Manager to initiate a Total Quality Management program beginning May 1994

■ Broward Employment and Training Administration (BETA) to identify job training partnerships and educational programs by August 1994

■ Strategic Planning Committee to appoint a committee to draft a business plan for the PPP by May 1994

SOURCE: City of Hollywood, Florida, Strategic Planning Task Force (1994).

by adopting specific start and completion dates for activities. Sometimes the services of the process facilitator are extended to help agencies organize and implement efforts.

In other instances, strategic management approaches are used. Strategic management involves identifying a few important, strategic issues that often cut across departments, and convening a high-level committee to ensure that the issues are dealt with (Hay, 1990). The previously formed *strategic planning committee* may become the *strategic management committee,* overseeing plan implementation. However, in most instances, community leaders wish to get on with other activities and leave implementation to the separate organizations. In this case, leading public officials must take responsibility for ensuring follow-through by different organizations. Within local government, strategic management teams are used to ensure implementation. Such teams consist of the mayor, city manager, department heads, and staff as required. It may also include the "held-over" process facilitator.

What outcomes does community-based strategic planning produce? The outcomes that result from these efforts are new commitments from a multitude of actors to work on community problems. Such coordinated efforts greatly advance communities into the future, and leaders gain recognition for assisting communities in setting new courses. First-year results usually include stream-lining of procedures and piloting of new services. For example, community colleges improve their planning outcomes through increased interaction with the business community. As is frequently the case in complex problems, final outcomes may require two or more years of implementation, such as with increasing neighborhood rehabilitation or improving skills of graduates. Thus the results of community-based strategic planning become evident over several years. It can be noted that turnover of community leaders, changing conditions, and progress toward goals implies that community-based strategic planning should be conducted on a recurring basis, for example, once every five years.

Strategic Planning Within Public and Nonprofit Organizations

Strategic planning is not only used for building communitywide consensus, it is also used in helping organizations to identify new goals, develop strategies, and move into the future. Strategic planning improves the alignment between stakeholder needs and organizational missions and between department objectives and broader, organizational thrusts. It is also used to align the role of the board with the needs of nonprofit organizations. Although the process of strategic planning within public and nonprofit organizations is roughly similar to that described above, the context of organizations is very different than that of loosely connected actors. This causes much more concern with such issues as the capacity of departments to fulfill their missions, rivalry among departments and managers over turf, the role of directors and boards in facilitating change, and so on. In other words, getting organizations to change is the preeminent challenge and objective of strategic planning. Another difference is that the time frame is much shorter. Because fewer actors and organizations are involved, strategic planning processes often last from two days to two months.

As noted in Chapter 1, strategic planning is widely used. A recent survey finds that 74% of cities of more than 50,000 had used strategic planning in one or more departments during the past 12 months (Berman, 1997). Strategic planning is also widely used by large social service organizations and museums; respectively, 81% and 76% reported such use. A variety of factors cause public and nonprofit organizations to undertake strategic planning. A frequent motivation is the need for increased responsiveness in the face of a changing environment. A typical example of this need was experienced by a county parks and recreation department that had been providing essentially the same services for about 20 years. Changing demographic characteristics and community conditions created a need for different services, including after-school programs for teenage youths, a program for single mothers, and community events that responded to the needs of a rapidly developing Hispanic population. At different times in the past, these needs had been expressed through disparate community leaders, including an occasional inquiry by an elected official, but these encounters were few and did not effect much change. Now, teenage violence and drug use are major issues, more Hispanics serve on the county board, and schools and community organizations have increased their leadership in dealing with community issues. Also, organizations sponsor leisure activities that duplicate those of the parks department. These changing conditions require that the parks department increase its responsiveness to community needs and that it reassess its priorities for programs and services.

Growth is another frequent reason for strategic planning. This was encountered by a local chapter of a large social service organization. Consistent with the vision of its director, this local organization had become very successful at obtaining grants and contracts to provide a multitude of services to different client groups. These services included running peer counseling programs in a high school, a suicide prevention hot line, family counseling services, and services to the elderly. The expansion effort was in part based on a policy that encouraged service providers to acquire grants and contracts in their areas of expertise. Staff then became divided among those who wished to emphasize adult services versus those who preferred adolescence programs. The difference has implications for priorities, such as decisions regarding marketing strategies, grant-writing activities, the selection of board members, and so on. It is clear that the organization must choose an area to focus on if it is to be successful in fulfilling its role. Strategic planning helps shape different viewpoints. Board members contribute to the process by sharing their expertise and commitment to the organization. Strategic planning rarely generates unanimity, but it does create an orderly process for generating understanding and consensus.

External change and internal growth are frequent reasons for doing strategic planning. Some other reasons are to take advantage of new opportunities; leadership changes, building enthusiasm (or at least support) for new initiatives; creating a political base (strategic planning frequently includes external, advisory groups whose members may become champions in time); and the need for consolidation, reorganization, or restoring balance among different services. These and other reasons are discussed below.

Laying the Foundation

A critical problem for strategic planning in many organizations is getting organizations to adopt and implement new goals. Mission (or vision) statements that emerge from strategic planning retreats frequently engender little support and enthusiasm outside the managerial ranks of those who participated in the vision/mission creation process. Strategic planning is sometimes DOA (dead on arrival) at lower levels of the organization.

Part of the problem is that many employees and managers have vested interests in the status quo. They feel comfortable in their knowledge of how things work and have acquired sufficient resources and skills to do their jobs well. They have friends and allies who share commitments to existing goals. Thus asking employees and managers to give up existing security for unknown futures draws resistance and opposition. Only those who are greatly disaffected will embrace change.[3]

As discussed in Chapter 4, employees and managers must understand the reasons for change (Vroom & Jago, 1988). Answers to the question "Why is change necessary?" must (a) increase the desirability or inevitability of future changes and (b) decrease the possibility or desirability of continuing the status quo. These reasons must change the cost-benefit equation of the status quo: Benefits of change must be enumerated as well as the costs of the status quo. Providing employees and managers with tangible support from clients in favor of change, or tangible evidence of stakeholder dissatisfaction and complaints, contributes to the mind-shift. By circulating such information at various levels of the organization over several months, and forcing informal discussion, managers and employees often become more receptive to the inevitability of change.

Leaders must also ensure employees and managers that their needs are being listened to and taken into account. The ultimate commodity is trust and commitment. Leaders must earn this trust by showing how they will deal with the negative consequences of change: eliminated positions and adaptation. Often leaders commit to new positions or attractive exit packages for those who lose their jobs. They must also ensure adequate rewards for those who commit to change. Such actions are necessary to gain trust and demonstrate commitment. Effective managers balance their commitment to change and organizational objectives with the needs and constraints of their staff; commitment to organizational goals alone does not necessarily ensure much cooperation from managers and employees.

Creating a Strategic Plan

Given that any significant amount of organizational change usually requires top leadership commitment, strategic planning almost always involves top leaders of organizations. It may also include representatives of stakeholder groups, for example, clients. Strategic planning in organizations follows the same steps as described earlier. The strategic planning team (SPT) usually consists of the director or chief executive officer and division heads. This is a much smaller number of participants than in community-based strategic planning; participation by five to ten managers is common. This leadership group is supported by staff who provide data about the organization and its environment to the SPT for SWOT, trend, and critical events analysis. A critique of some corporate planning practices is that they have become dominated by staff input and direction. Leadership by top managers is necessary to help direct discussion toward critical needs of the organization (Mintzberg, 1994).

Subcommittees are formed that bring lower managers into the decision-making process. Bringing other managers into processes of decision making not only improves the quality of information (Roberts & Bradley, 1991), it also arrests managerial in-fighting and faction forming. These outcomes are mentioned in the goals of a recent effort to restructure emergency medical services: to identify permanent, long-range solutions to issues that currently are not being effectively addressed, to assure support by all internal constituencies, to eliminate divisiveness and political manipulation, and to better meet changing service demands (Snead & Porter, 1996). The process of data collection and analysis takes three hours to three months, depending on the size of the organizations and the number of managers and departments that are involved in the process; the greater the participation and consensus, the greater the likelihood that subsequent plans and priorities will be followed through on. Analysis of the environment and internal

TABLE 5.5   SWOT Analysis and Strategic Issues From a Strategic Plan of a Public
                Administration Department (Modified)

I. SWOT ANALYSIS

    Strengths: The PA Department has a positive approach to serving its students as well as involvement in professional associations, freedom in decision making, and a sound managerial structure. Classes emphasize hands-on applications that students feel are relevant. The PA program is growing impressively, with an abundance of internships.

    Weaknesses: There are three unfilled positions and high turnover of faculty. The chair is temporary. The faculty should publish more. The department uses too many adjuncts. The student-to-faculty ratio is high, which increases demands made on faculty. The admission standards are minimal; the perception of an "easy" program complicates efforts to raise standards. There are too many meetings as well as considerable travel between branch campuses.

    Opportunities: The three vacant positions should be filled with research active faculty. Curriculum revisions should further shape the program and provide special tracks. Courses in the proposed Ph.D. program should be made available to M.PA. students.

    Threats: There is a pay discrepancy between faculty members as well as inadequate space and resources, insufficient student support for teaching and research, funding limits, competing philosophies among faculty, and sacrifice of quality for quantity.

II. SELECTED STRATEGIC ISSUES

    1. Ensure reaccreditation of the MPA program
    2. Provide support for faculty to increase research productivity
    3. Strengthen ties with the community
    4. Increase diversity among faculty
    5. Update or redesign the public administration curriculum
    6. Pursue additional revenues
    7. Retain faculty, reduce high turnover
    8. Start the Ph.D. program
    9. Identify and fulfill new stakeholder needs

---

capacity culminates in a shared understanding and identification of critical issues. Figure 5.5 shows some elements from a SWOT analysis of an academic department.

The analysis of external and internal conditions is also the basis for formulating a new mission statement. Mission statements are often pro forma, but in some instances the objective of strategic planning actually is the formulation of new missions. A case in point is NASA (the National Aeronautics and Space Administration). During the 1960s, NASA enjoyed widespread support after putting a man on the moon and returning him safely. Since then, NASA has tried to formulate new missions that capture the American imagination and political support in equal measure. This is a daunting challenge by any account. Subsequent missions have been to provide affordable space travel (e.g., through the space shuttle), to establish a permanent space presence by developing a space station, to plan for a Mission to Mars, and increase the Mission to Planet Earth (e.g., through improved Earth observation). These missions have not generated the same level of political support. Arguably, the formulation of a vision as compelling as the first moon mission is too large a task, because the moon mission appealed to a millennia-long human fascination with the moon and responded to an important international crisis that was created by the cold war and Russian success at launching the first satellite *(Sputnik)*. Such conditions are not easily replicated and do not exist at the current time. In the absence of a compelling mission and widespread support, NASA has been unable to undertake grand new missions, and it often finds its management under attack. Box 5.1 discusses NASA's strategic plan. The plan describes a reorganization of NASA around "strategic enterprises," which has yet to fully take hold.

Broadening Commitment

A critical issue is the broadening commitment of organizational groups beyond those of top management. The sense of shared pursuit (and community) must be extended to all affected parts of the organization. In recent years, one approach has been consultation with lower level managers and employees. For example, one strategy is to solicit input from disparate units about the proposed new strategies and to reconsider initial plans based on this additional information. The theory behind this approach is that responsiveness breeds trust and hence cooperation: However, when information is not reflected in subsequent decisions, employees and managers often experience such consultation as manipulation. This situation is somewhat analogous to citizen "participation" in which input is solicited and disregarded by officials (Neuse, 1983). An alternative approach is making units responsible for new missions. In so doing, leaders move beyond consultation to participation. Empowerment increases employee and managerial control over work, provides greater opportunities for making a difference, and creates a stronger sense of ownership. It also allows managers to expend their energy on other matters. Participation sometimes involves conducting strategic planning at lower levels of the organization. That is, for specific tasks, each unit is asked to define its own mission, goals, objectives, and strategies. A strategically important question is how leaders respond to units that do not take up the challenge of participating in the design of their own future.

Strategic planning documents closely resemble those of community-based planning efforts. They contain statements about the mission and guiding values or principles, goals that identify different areas and accomplishments that

BOX 5.1.
NASA's Strategic Plan

NASA's vision is to be "an investment in America's future, by exploring and boldly expanding frontiers in air and space in ways that inspire and serve America, as well as benefit the quality of life on Earth." The NASA mission is to (a) advance and communicate scientific knowledge of the Earth, space, and the solar system; (b) explore, use, and develop space for human enterprise; and (c) research, develop, verify, and transfer advanced aeronautics and space technologies (NASA, 1996).

NASA recognizes changes in its external and internal environments. The external environment has shifted from cold war competition to economic competition and international cooperation as well as responding to domestic budget deficits. However, public support for space exploration remains widespread. The internal environment no longer meets modern management standards. Specifically, NASA does not sufficiently use strategies of privatization, and there is a need to improve relations with contractors, to provide increased accountability for results, to better meet customer needs, and to terminate activities that are no longer relevant.

NASA has five "Strategic Enterprises," each of which contributes to the above missions. Mission to Planet Earth examines the impact of natural and human-induced changes on the global environment. Future goals emphasize the development of technologies for improved measurement of global warming, ozone depletion, and other phenomena. The Aeronautics Enterprise pioneers technologies that increase the safety and productivity of U.S. air transportation. Priorities emphasize research relating to next-generation, high-speed aircraft. The Human Exploration and Development of Space Enterprise examines technologies for exploring and settling space. Its goals are to assemble a Space Station by 2002 and to understand low-gravity processes better. The Space Science Enterprise increases understanding about the origins and workings of the universe. Emphases are to improve the prediction of space weather and to develop new unmanned spacecraft. The Space Technology Enterprise provides access to space and focuses on the development of reusable launchers to complement the Space Shuttle.

NASA's Strategic Plan provides time lines for the above priorities that unfold over time, encompassing the periods 1996-2002, 2003-2009, and 2010-2020. It also discusses how the internal and external conditions, above, affect NASA, for example, through use of international partnerships, privatization, and increased cooperation with contractors. The question is this: How compelling are these programs and the missions?

organizations are seeking, and specific objectives, strategies, and timetables for accomplishment.

A singular frustration, and great source of cynicism, is plans that gather dust. Therefore, strategic planning within organizations requires careful attention to implementation as well. Some causes of "stillbirths" are the lack of resources and inadequate commitment from management, which stifle implementation. To overcome these problems, top management must commit adequate resources and follow-through and ensure that successful outcomes are achieved. Another approach to implementation is assigning managers to pilot projects. For example, a new marketing effort might be implemented on a trial basis by a manager who is willing to take responsibility for it. As discussed in Chapter 4, this strategy has the advantage of creating initial successes and building internal pockets of commitment, prior to dealing with persistent critics.

After initial efforts and implementation by units, gains are sometimes institutionalized in ways that signal approval and normalization of new goals and missions. This can be done in many different ways, such as by changing the formal mission of the public or nonprofit organization, promoting managers who undertake new strategies, creating new departments or raising their status, and so on. Institutionalization is often the last step in strategic planning.

Other Approaches to Strategic Change

Other approaches for setting new strategic directions exist as well. Three commonly used alternative approaches are hiring new managers, using mandates and establishing budget incentives and disincentives, and employing quiet or surreptitious strategies. In comparison with strategic planning, these alternatives have the appeal of simplicity and requiring only a minimum of management time and effort. However, complications frequently occur.

Replacing Managers

A widely used strategy for change is hiring new top-level managers. Agency directors who wish to steer divisions and programs in new directions may replace existing managers. City councils that are disappointed with current management or policy often replace the city manager or chief administrative officer with one who is more attuned to the orientations of the existing council. New managers are apt to follow the directives of their new superiors.

In practice, this magic bullet of hiring seldom works out as intended. New managers require commitment, or at least compliance, from subordinates to implement their new programs. Current employees and managers are usually committed to existing programs from which to derive their raison d'être and power basis in the organization. New managers must instill a similar sense of urgency about the need for change as described above in strategic planning. They need to provide a rationale for change, and find a cadre of managers and employees who are willing to pilot and undertake such efforts.

It is readily observed that some new managers in public and nonprofit organizations do not engage in much broad-based consensus-building. Rather, they often bypass existing decision-making structures and implement changes in a top-down and somewhat autocratic manner. Although they find that some employees and managers embrace their changes, a majority usually experience alienation and frustration, which results in resistance and minimal compliance but little commitment. Such leaders often attempt to remove persistent opponents, such as by giving undesirable assignments. They may also attempt to co-opt others through incentives. Although such managers do win many first battles, subsequent battles are increasingly difficult as managers and employees find ways to avoid participation and, in some instances, sabotage managers' intended outcomes. One reason this pattern occurs so frequently is that managers are not yet mindful of all the relations and conditions, they need to fulfill goals in subsequent years. For example, they may not yet know which managers are critical to their success. Another reason is that they have little formal training and experience with processes of trust-building and strategic planning. Still others may lack the skills for the leadership position in which they are placed.

Thus replacing managers is no guarantee of strategic change. To be successful, new managers will have to build bridges and obtain commitment from others for change. When new managers fail to do so, significant opposition may result. Although heavy-handed tactics may produce initial successes, long-term loss of cooperation, trust, and, ultimately, leadership are likely to stifle subsequent productivity efforts.

Mandates and Budgets

Another approach to strategic change is to reorder priorities through mandates and budget (dis)incentives. For example, federal mandates may cause cities to adopt new municipal recycling programs. Top managers change budget incentives and encourage lower managers to pursue efficiency gains, for example, by allowing them to keep a share of cost savings for a period of time.

The use of mandates and budgets as tools of change is seductive in its "hands-off" approach. The idea is that organizations pursue incentives that are given to them. But in practice the use of mandates and budgets requires considerable follow-up and accountability to ensure that units follow the new guidelines. When organizations perceive that managers do not follow through, little or no change may result. An example is the federal requirement that cities provide Comprehensive Homelessness Assistance Plans (CHAPs) as a condition for receiving federal funds for services for the homeless. Although the intent is to increase community-based efforts and planning in this area, most CHAPs are only a compilation of current efforts (ICMA, 1990). CHAPs fulfill funding requirements but do not further the spirit of the program. A second problem is unintended consequences. The requirement that states get tough on crime has reduced funding for rehabilitation and job training programs in many locales. Instead, more prisons have been built. This, in turn, increases the number of ex-inmates in society who are unable to support themselves, hence increasing both crime and recidivism.

Such problems with the use of mandates and budgets as tools of strategic change suggest that they are often more complex than advocates expect or intend them to be. Education, coalition-building, monitoring, and accountability appear to be necessary, complementary activities when mandates are used: Other organizations must understand how to respond to the mandates and how they will be held accountable. In the absence of such extra efforts, perhaps most budget and mandate strategies are best used for relatively minor changes, namely, those that can readily be accomplished within existing means and that are unlikely to cause much goal displacement.

Quiet Change

Finally, another strategy is to engage in change but not to inform employees and managers of the change. The purpose is to create initial successes while precluding the possibility that powerful opponents thwart initial efforts.

An example is midnight basketball. In many cities, social service agencies recognized that midnight basketball could provide them with access to hard-core, violence-prone youths. They also understood that such programs were likely to generate much public controversy. Thus initial programs were implemented with very little fanfare and discussion. These programs were successful in reaching certain youths and "keeping them out of trouble." Moreover, they quickly built a support network from community leaders and parents. When midnight basketball gained media and political exposure, the support network in many cities ensured its continuance.

However, other examples have less fortunate outcomes. The problem with stealth is that at some point, the effort must come into the open. Thus the use of quiet or surreptitious strategies is tantamount to postponing the inevitable with regard to building broad-based support for proposed efforts. When such support is not forthcoming, the change effort is often halted.

Analytic Techniques

Surveys are frequently used to support the data collection phase of strategic planning. The purpose of these surveys is to identify salient problems facing the community and to involve groups that are frequently left outside the process. For example, surveys among businesses are common elements of strategic planning processes for local economic development. Surveys often focus on (a) the use of programs, services, and so on; (b) the salience of emerging or long-standing issues; (c) evaluation of public and private services; and (d) population characteristics. A typical survey of downtown businesses includes the following questions:

1. Please state the three things you like most about doing business at your present location.
2. Please state the three things you like least about doing business at your present location.
3. Do you have plans for expansion within the next two years? If so, are you considering expansion within this city? If not, why not?
4. What is your overall impression of this city as a place for doing business? What is your overall impression of the downtown area?
5. Do you think this city is good place for residing?
6. How familiar are you with the following business assistance programs? Which have you used? How effective are they? Which services need improvement? What specific recommendations might you make?
7. How often have you had contact with the following public offices during the last year? How do you evaluate the effectiveness of the service you received? How do you evaluate the courtesy you received?
8. What, if anything, can the city do to help your business?

9. What is the nature of your business?

10. How many employees do you have? Full-time? Part-time? How do you rate the quality of your workforce? How do you rate the overall quality of the area workforce?

Surveys among client groups or population target groups are also conducted. For example, a community-based strategic planning effort for neighborhood rehabilitation might ask these questions:

1. Please state the three things you like most about your neighborhood.

2. Please state the three things you like least about your neighborhood.

3. Do you have plans for moving in the next two years? If so, are you considering staying in your present neighborhood? Why or why not?

4. What is your overall impression of this city as a place for living?

5. How familiar are you with the following housing assistance programs? Which have you used? How effective are they?

6. How familiar are you with the following social programs? Which have you used? How effective are they?

7. How familiar are you with the following other programs? Which have you used? How effective are they?

8. How often have you had contact with the following public offices during the last year? How do you evaluate the effectiveness of the service you received? How do you evaluate the courtesy you received?

9. What, if anything, can the city do to improve the quality of your neighborhood? What, if anything, can the city do to assist you in maintaining your home?

10. What is the composition of your household?

Other data collection strategies are also used. Employee surveys are used to identify employee needs, which assist leaders in developing internal strategic plans. Appropriate topics are the need for child/elder care services, education assistance, flextime, health and other benefits, on-the-job training, and so on. Employee surveys should not assess the quality of the work environment and managers in too much detail, because confidentiality is not guaranteed to those who return the surveys. Focus groups are also used. Focus groups provide new understanding about processes, even though the findings are not generalizable. Sometimes panels of experts are used. Client records and performance data help analyze trends in service levels and use rates. These data can be compared across divisions or activities. Area marketing studies suggest trends in the demand for services. To the extent that data or informed hunches are available on other organizations, comparisons can be made.

Another analytic tool is shift-share analysis. Shift-share analysis simply compares ratios, indices, or rates across jurisdictions. For example, birthrates may vary, crime rates per 1,000 population may vary, service use rates may vary, construction and growth rates vary, and so on. These comparisons show similarities and differences among localities. Forecasting is also used. Typical foci are overall population growth (causing need for infrastructure, schools, and services), minority populations (causing a need for bilingual services), population age (causing a need for elder/teen services). Analytically, these forecasts often use trend analysis, although many simply analyze current growth rates from which future trends are implied. Growth rates can also be compared across jurisdictions, providing further understanding about the uniqueness of locales.

Finally, an important skill is the preparation of strategic planning reports. Strategic planning reports often follow the following format:

Title
Letter by the Director or Ranking Elected Official

   I. Introduction (discussing the history, context, and purpose of the effort)

  II. Mandates

 III. Analysis of the environment and internal organization

 IV. Mission or vision statement

  V. Identification of critical issues

 VI. Action Plans (issue areas, goals, objectives, strategies, performance measures)

VII. Implementation plan

Action plans are usually set up according to the following outline, with each issue area listed separately:

GOAL 1

    OBJECTIVE 1.1

        STRATEGY 1.1.1

        STRATEGY 1.1.2

        STRATEGY 1.1.3

         . . .

    OBJECTIVE 1.2

        STRATEGY 1.2.1

                STRATEGY 1.2.2

                . . .

GOAL 2

        OBJECTIVE 2.1

                STRATEGY 2.1.1

                STRATEGY 2.1.2

                STRATEGY 2.1.3

                . . .

        OBJECTIVE 2.2

                STRATEGY 2.2.1

                STRATEGY 2.2.2

                . . .

and so on.

Summary

This chapter discusses productivity improvement through strategic planning and other efforts that shape the missions of public and nonprofit organizations. It examines steps for undertaking community-based strategic planning as well as strategic planning within organizations. It discusses analytic steps as well as processes for building support. The key phases of community-based strategic planning are (a) the decision to initiate a community-based strategic planning process and the selection of a strategic team of leaders; (b) a period of data collection and consensus-building among community leaders; (c) the formulation of missions, visions, priorities, goals, objectives, strategies, performance measures, and target dates of community-based responses; and (d) implementation of recommendations. Key points are the need to create processes that further consensus-building and commitment to implementation. This chapter also discusses other efforts to instill change.

Notes

1. Not all collaborative efforts require broad participation. Collaborations between two or three organizations are often addressed through other means, for example, negotiations that lead to partnerships. However, even in these instances, strategic thinking is required.

2. Some people ask whether voluntary recommendations are sufficient to affect change. Voluntary action is sufficient, because many organizations view new activities as consistent with missions and also because of support from other organizations.

3. Resistance to change is different than regular complaining by employees and managers about the status quo. The latter is often related to processes of bonding and coalition-building and is different than that of accepting the need for change.

References

Berman, E. (1996a). Local government and community-based strategies. *American Review of Public Administration, 26*(1), 71-91.

Berman, E. (1996b). Restoring the bridges of trust: Attitudes of community leaders toward local government. *Public Integrity Annual, 1*(1), 31-39.

Berman, E. (1997). [Survey of cities, social service organization and museums]. Unpublished raw data.

Berman, E., & Werther, W. (1997). Broad-based consensus-building. *International Journal of Public Sector Management, 9*(3), 61-72.

Berman, N., & Stephenson, D. (1996). Grassroots planning supports move to market economy in the Czech Republic. *Economic Development, 10*(4), 7-8.

Bryson, J. (1995). *Strategic planning for public and nonprofit organizations.* San Francisco: Jossey-Bass.

Bryson, J., & Crosby, B. (1992). *Leadership for the common good.* San Francisco: Jossey-Bass.

Chrislip, D., & Larson, C. (1994). *Collaborative leadership: How citizens and civic leaders can make a difference.* San Francisco: Jossey-Bass.

City of Hollywood, Florida, Strategic Planning Task Force. (1994). *Economic development strategic plan.* Hollywood, FL: Author.

Etzioni, A. (1993). *The spirit of community.* New York: Crown.

Fowler, R. (1991). *The dance with community.* Lawrence: University of Kansas Press.

Gardner, J. (1991). *Building community.* Washington, DC: Independent Sector.

Gates, C. (1991). Making a case for collaborative problem solving. *National Civic Review, 80*(1), 113-119.

Giles, M. (1993). The Atlanta Project: A community-based approach to solving urban problems. *National Civic Review, 82*(4), 354-362.

Hay, R. (1990). *Strategic management in non-profit organizations.* New York: Quorum.

Herman, R. (Ed.). (1994). *Handbook of nonprofit leadership and management.* San Francisco: Jossey-Bass.

International City/County Management Association (ICMA). (1990). *Strategies to reduce home-lessness: An MIS report.* Washington, DC: Author.

Kemp, R. (Ed.). (1992). *Strategic planning in local government.* Chicago: American Planning Association.

Michigan Department of Commerce. (1990). *Local strategic planning: A handbook for community leaders.* Lansing: Author.

Mintzberg, H. (1994). *The rise and fall of strategic planning.* New York: Free Press.

National Aeronautics and Space Agency. (1996). *Strategic plan.* Washington, DC: Author.

Neuse, S. (1983). From grass roots to citizen participation: Where we've been and where we are now. *Public Administration Quarterly, 7*(4), 294-309.

Oliver, M. (1995, October 1). Building healthy communities. *Orlando Sentinel,* p. G1.

Ostrom, E. (1993). A communitarian approach to local governance. *National Civic Review, 82*(3), 226-232.

Roberts, N., & Bradley, R. (1991). Stakeholder collaboration and innovation. *Journal of Applied Behavioral Science, 27*(3), 209-227.

Snead, G., & Porter, R. (1996). Restructuring fire and emergency medical services. *Public Management, 78*(2), 8-14.

Thomas, J. (1995). *Public participation in public decisions.* San Francisco: Jossey-Bass.

Vroom, V., & Jago, A. (1988). *The new leadership: Managing participation in organizations.* Englewood Cliffs, NJ: Prentice Hall.

Wheeland, C. (1993). City-wide strategic planning: An evaluation of Rock Hill's empowering the vision. *Public Administration Review, 53*(1), 65-72.

Wood, D., & Gray, B. (1991). Toward a comprehensive theory of collaboration. *Journal of Applied Behavioral Science, 27*(2), 139-162.

6

Partnering and Alignment

▦ Each period in history has its challenges for organizing work. Organizing is the activity of bringing people, resources, and technology together for the purposes of achieving goals and objectives. The challenges of organizing public and nonprofit activities in the 1990s are in large measure driven by demands for achieving more objectives and goals, increasing the efficiency of operations (i.e., doing more with less), and dealing with stagnant resources. For example, nonprofit service providers are expected to serve diverse clienteles and deal with a broad range of problems while maintaining their grants and other funding in an environment of increased competition for resources. In addition, providers are expected to achieve these results with the same (or a smaller) number of staff persons and fewer expenditures for staff positions. This set of conditions prompts the search for new forms of organization.

Three growing responses in the 1990s are partnerships, organizational alignment, and privatization. Partnerships bring organizations together in new ways for meeting mutual needs. They build on the principles of organization discussed in Chapter 2 by coordinating resources to increase the scope of services that are offered. For example, partnerships among local social service agencies often involve the coordination and referral of activities that enable increased specialization in meeting community mental health needs. Partnerships often follow in the wake of community-based strategic planning process. Many social service organizations join together to operate and maintain central food banks. Such partnerships are often very effective, but they also require considerable management.

Organizational alignment also brings people and resources within organizations together in new ways. Alignments are often undertaken to refocus organizations on their missions and to ensure that activities are performed in effective and efficient ways. This often causes organizations to streamline their activities and reduce costs by shedding old functions, reducing the number of departments, and eliminating middle management positions. Alignment increases the efficiency of organizations but requires careful implementation and a process of overcoming resistance. Organizations also seek cost savings through outsourcing and privatization. Through privatization and contracting, organizations avoid responsibility for production and service delivery and enjoy the benefit of reasonably low costs through processes of competition. Privatization has been hotly debated in recent years as an ideological approach to reducing the size of public organizations. Some problems with privatization are reduced flexibility in dealing with situations that are not explicitly contracted for and rapidly rising service costs as initial contracts are renegotiated in subsequent years.

This chapter examines productivity improvement through alternative forms of organizing. Specifically, it discusses strategies for negotiating and maintaining partnerships as well as strategies for undertaking alignment and privatization.

Partnerships

The term *partnership* is often used with a variety of different meanings. Some authors use it philosophically or ideologically to refer to the *roles* of different sectors of society. For example, Salamon (1995) refers to the "partnership" between nonprofit organizations and the federal government in providing for the poor. This partnership is a tacit understanding among leaders about shared responsibilities, specifically, that the federal government supplies funds for services provided by charitable organizations. This understanding, or set of values, shapes policy decisions about the delivery of social services and the relationship of each sector.

By contrast, other authors use the term narrowly to refer to *a family of contractual arrangements that involve open-ended, joint responsibilities for decision making and implementation.* This chapter adopts this latter definition. Typical examples are partnerships among government and nonprofit organizations to create a collective food bank, partnerships among local governments to protect area wildlife and their environment, and collaborations among nonprofit organizations to promote their services. In each instance, decision making and implementation are collective in some aspects. Partnerships require considerable forethought about the roles of each partner. By contrast, contracting for services, subsidization, and privatization are usually not considered partnerships because they involve very little joint decision making. For example, privatization usually means that responsibilities for regulation or production are turned over to the private sector; it does not create joint decision making. It should be noted that a movement exists to establish close linkages with contractors, and, where such relationships exist, they might be called partnerships.[1]

Partnerships are consistent with building network organizations, that is, organizations that are connected by serving a common purpose but that have different owners. Through partnerships, organizations extend their capabilities and build mechanisms for joint decision making and cooperation. Network organizations are attractive because they require relatively few investments or new organizations. The downside is reduced control and increased uncertainty about future capabilities (Hesselbein, 1997).

Purposes of Partnerships

Partnerships fulfill different purposes. Some of the most common purposes involve (a) coordination, (b) policy formulation, (c) funding, and (d) joint service delivery. Many partnerships involve multiple purposes, although some focus on a single purpose.[2]

Coordination. Many public and nonprofit organizations engage in local coalitions, networks, forums, and similar organizations that provide members with a means to coordinate their services. For example, local hospitals are increasingly teaming up with schools, churches, and nonprofit providers to ensure that populations such as pregnant women and infants receive necessary services (Baker et al., 1994). Health insurers and federal programs are eager to provide these services, which prevent more costly services later. Services for the homeless are a particularly good example of the need for coordination, because homeless populations are extremely diverse—involving mentally disabled adults, female-headed families, substance abusers, handicapped persons, and so on— and require comprehensive services that involve health, employment, and housing. Local coalitions of public and private providers that aid the homeless are increasingly common. These coalitions provide coordination for food supplies, emergency shelter needs (blankets, sleeping cots, food and water), primary health care services (including diagnosis of tuberculosis, AIDS/HIV), legal aid, long-term health care (assisted living programs, medical and mental health rehabilitation, family counseling), supplemental income assistance, affordable housing programs, drug and alcohol treatment programs, and so on (Berman, 1996; Harvey, 1993).

Coordination helps organizations, collectively, to provide more comprehensive services without increasing their expenditures or diluting their areas of expertise. To succeed, coordination partnerships such as coalitions and networks often require one or more committed leaders who can maintain the informal, voluntary nature of coordination. These leaders must be able to resist efforts by individual members to engage in policy making that would force upon organizations decisions that they are unwilling to accept or decision-making authority that they are unwilling to transfer to those outside their organization. Such actions are divisive and often lead to distrust and animosity among organizations. Leaders of networks must maintain the raison d'être of coordination and engage in collective decision making that prevents individual members from either abandoning the partnership or forcing their views upon it.

Policy making. Some partnerships are designed for collective decision making among organizations. Sometimes the purpose of these partnerships is also to influence public opinion. The areas of such partnership are often those that concern the "common good," such as environmental, planning, or technology development issues. Such partnerships vary considerably in the degree to which decision-making responsibility is delegated from individual organizations to partnerships. For example, local governments around the Tampa Bay, Florida, area formed a partnership whose purpose is to set policy for protecting wildlife and estuaries. Such planning bodies usually have advisory status, and decisions require ratification by individual members. Consensus is often difficult to reach but can be facilitated by incentives of federal funding or the benefits from collective actions. By contrast, partnerships that engage in implementation are frequently delegated considerable policy-making responsibilities. For example, SEMATECH is a public-private partnership for developing advanced semiconductor manufacturing technology. Its members include firms in the electronics industry and the federal government. Because its members had been struggling to develop state-of-the-art semiconductor manufacturing technology, broad discretion was given to the consortium for defining appropriate technology projects. Individual members are consulted, but none has veto power over its policy decisions.

Joint service delivery. Some partnerships provide joint services. Many orchestras team up with large corporations to promote their concert series as well as to obtain the community involvement of these organizations. For example, EDS Corp. teamed up with the Detroit Symphony Orchestra; EDS not only sponsored the advertising of the DSO but also provided it with a full range of information technology and support for fund-raising, financial management, and marketing services. Arts organizations also team up with neighborhood organizations to increase their exposure in neighborhoods as well as increase access by residents to art. American Express undertook a major advertising campaign whereby it donated 5¢ to nonprofit organizations every time its cards were used. The campaign provided funding for nonprofit organizations and increased the use of the card. Such comarketing arrangements are now increasingly common (Andreasen, 1996; Scheff & Kotler, 1996).

There are many other examples of joint service partnerships as well. For example, the Department of Energy is developing new technologies in collaboration with private companies for cleaning up the DOE's contaminated sites (Sink & Frank, 1996). Both public and private organizations participate in the hope of developing technologies that can be used in other areas as well. Partnerships are also created between law enforcement agencies and neighborhood associations to increase monitoring. Law enforcement personnel frequently assist neighborhood activists and business owners in organizing efforts to better protect their property and increase public safety.

Funding. Other partnerships are financially oriented. These are often found in economic development and housing (Suchman, 1990). In these areas, public and private organizations join together to finance activity that neither can afford separately. In many cities, affordable housing involves financial partnerships of local developers; banks; and local, state, and federal agencies. In these partnerships, local governments often borrow money (through bonds) to undertake infrastructure improvements, which is repaid through higher taxes. They also provide tax incentives for businesses such as supermarkets to locate in these areas. State and federal governments provide subsidies to enable affordable housing. Local developers borrow money to build the houses, which is repaid when the homes are sold or through property management. Such funding collaborations can be quite complex and require considerable trust and persistence.

In recent years, nonprofit organizations have also been playing an important intermediary role in financing the acquisition of land for conservation (Endicott, 1993). These are private lands of great natural value that are acquired by federal and state governments for protection. The problem is that state agencies are often slow to react to opportunities for acquisition. These opportunities occur for different reasons, such as the death or bankruptcy of landowners. In these instances, nonprofit organizations such as Nature Conservancy and the Trust for Public Land provide seed money or bridge loans that enable public agencies to buy the land for conservation.

Making Partnerships Work

Each partnership is different and unique. Yet histories of partnerships suggest the following characteristics in partnerships that are successful, that is, those that achieve objectives that their members think are important.

(1) Create win-win situations. Successful partnerships create win-win situations for their members. As voluntary associations, they otherwise would not form. However, partnerships are seldom the only vehicle for organizations to satisfy their needs, and it is important that the extent to which individual needs are satisfied is sufficient. Members must be willing to continue the partnership after it is formed and is in place. There must be a sense of parity and flexibility to ensure that benefits are fair, proportional to the effort that individual members put into partnership work, and continuously relevant to the missions of organizations. Thus the win-win strategies that are articulated must be periodically revisited and updated, and members must be sensitive to and willing to accommodate the changing needs of organizations. Successful partnerships often plan for ongoing negotiation.[3]

(2) Significant interest. Partnerships work best when all parties have a significant commitment to their success. They cannot be an afterthought. For example, the Department of Energy routinely negotiates partnerships for the commercial development of its technology, which includes microelectronics, software, and materials research. Such negotiations often involve important legal matters of royalties and liabilities. However, for DOE lawyers, technology contracts are not viewed as very important and hence do not always receive high priority. This causes delays and reduces interest by firms (Berman, 1994). Partnerships often work best when they are perceived as central to the mission of all parties. When some partners do not have much commitment, enthusiasm eventually wanes and the commitment to maintaining win-win situations diminishes. Food and blood banks are often examples of enduring partnerships.

(3) Anticipate change. Partnerships are often formed to deal with sudden changes in the environment. For example, health care coalitions often respond to sudden public health changes, such as rising teenage pregnancy, infectious diseases, and malnutrition. Uncertainty in the environment affects ongoing partnerships as well. Successful partnerships anticipate environmental contingencies and develop plans for how these will affect the partnership. In the above example, health care partnerships often plan for further increases in community need, new grant programs to which its members might apply, mergers and changes in its membership, scarcity, or sudden increases in the cost of treatment. The ability to cope with change is a characteristic of successful partnerships. Although partnerships are open-ended, some partnerships plan for their demise when the conditions that gave rise to them cease to exist.

(4) Develop and maintain clear roles and responsibilities. Partnerships build on the diversity of strengths of their members: Different members bring different abilities to partnerships. The well-functioning partnership requires that partners fulfill their commitments. Members must be clear about each other's roles and responsibilities and must establish clear procedures for both formal and informal communication. Timetables, staffing, funding, and liabilities are typically important issues. Staffing involves a considerable commitment on the part of partners, and members are sometimes concerned that other organizations do not commit their best people or that such persons do not have access to decision makers within their organizations. Liabilities are also an important concern. For example, in technology partnerships, a common clause is that members are individually responsible for any litigation that results from the use of technology developed by partnerships; the absence of such a clause would make the risk to other partners unacceptable. Similar issues occur in financial partnerships. Members must be indemnified from the risk that other partners might default on their obligations. Such issues must be identified and resolved.

(5) Skilled leadership. Successful partnerships have leaders who are skilled in negotiating, compromising, and, above all, accomplishing tasks and goals. Leaders know how to balance different interests while maintaining the commitment of partners. Leaders emphasize the importance of building trusting relations among members. This is especially important when members have a history of rivalry or antagonistic relations. For example, leaders of nonprofit organizations sometimes have competitive relations with each other that result from the competition for grants, funding, or membership. Such feelings of

suspicion must be overcome, at least for the purpose of obtaining the goals that are set for the partnership.

Successful partnerships often involve organizations that have a past history of successful participation in partnerships. Such organizations are familiar with the processes and items of negotiation, and they have a clear view of what is possible and how much effort is involved in making partnerships work. They are especially attuned to the reality of different styles and cultures of organizations. Private leaders know that government organizations have lengthy approval processes and that they must allow more time for obtaining the commitment and participation of public organizations. For their participation, they may even have to lobby elected officials. Private leaders of small, collaborative nonprofit organizations know that larger organizations have a more bureaucratic culture and that for-profit organizations are strongly attuned to the bottom line. Leadership is needed to bridge these differences and to create mutual understanding and commitment to the shared purposes of partnerships (Bierenbaum, 1994). These conditions are further examined in Box 6.1.

Managing Negotiations

Establishing partnerships involves negotiation. Negotiations must be constructive, geared toward creating a mutually satisfying partnership. They must be neither hard and antagonistic, as if negotiating with an adversary, nor overly soft and compromising, which may cause one's own goals to be inadequately accomplished. The following principles are recommended (e.g., Muehrcke, 1994):

(1) Prepare. Organizations sometimes fail to prepare adequately for negotiating partnerships (Schwartz, 1994). Preparation requires a priority among acceptable goals, strategies, and conditions. Organizations must know what they want from the proposed partnership and identify concerns that they wish to negotiate. Arguments must be developed that are likely to be persuasive to others. They must do some background investigation on other organizations and anticipate the goals and conditions that other organizations may be seeking. A part of the preparation is also knowing under which conditions organizations will forgo seeking a partnership, for example, when others do not wish to seek important goals. Developing a "best alternative solution" strengthens the negotiation position and protects organizations from getting involved in activities that have too little return. Finally, organizations must ensure that individuals who are

BOX 6.1.
SEMATECH: A Different Kind of Nonprofit

SEMATECH is a nonprofit research and development consortium of U.S. semiconductor manufacturers. SEMATECH was created in 1987 by the U.S. government and leading U.S. firms in response to the growing technological edge of Japanese firms in manufacturing equipment for semiconductors. Such equipment is a sine qua non for manufacturing semiconductors, and advantage in such equipment leads to superior semiconductor design and performance. Until recently, funding for SEMATECH was equally shared between the U.S. Department of Defense and member firms of SEMATECH, with each contributing $100 million per year. However, in recent years, major technological goals have been reached, and public support is currently being phased out. Member firms, including IBM, Hewlett-Packard, Digital Equipment Corporation, Texas Instruments, and Motorola, plan to continue this venture on their own.

Although SEMATECH is somewhat unique because of its size, it shares many factors that contribute to its success. SEMATECH creates a win-win situation by ensuring the Defense Department a U.S. capability in microelectronics manufacturing and by providing lagging producers an opportunity to catch up. The topic is of significant interest to all partners; indeed, for many firms such technology is a matter of survival. SEMATECH operates in a dynamic market and thus research priorities are continuously assessed as a way of dealing with change. Of great importance to SEMATECH is the division of roles among member firms: Firms can choose which projects they wish to participate in, and smaller equipment manufacturers benefit from SEMATECH accomplishments through a separate organization, called SEMI/SEMATECH. The partnership arrangement is sensitive to the need to protect proprietary information of member firms too. Finally, the leadership of SEMATECH is known for its tact and diplomacy in dealing with the many different needs of member firms as well as with Congress, which provides substantial funding for this effort. Other factors contributing to the success of SEMATECH are the magnitude of federal support and the willingness of member firms to contribute their top talent (Berman & Levine, 1996).

Since the inception of SEMATECH, the U.S. share of worldwide semiconductors increased from 39% to 43% following years of decline, and U.S. semiconductor employment increased by 18%, or 45,000 jobs since 1992. Although some analysts argue that these gains are in part due to the problems of Japanese producers, there is agreement that the technological achievements of SEMATECH have helped keep U.S. producers "on track," and that SEMATECH is a model for managing collaborative efforts.

assigned to negotiations are adequately prepared and are able to deal with the arguments that may arise.

(2) Set deadlines and timetables. The purpose of partnerships is accomplishment, and it is a particularly bad indication when negotiations drag on. To ensure expediency, organizations should agree on a timetable for completing their negotiations.

(3) Develop trust. A purpose of negotiation is to build a healthy relationship for subsequent joint activities. Negotiations often start in the absence of trust. There are many things that managers can do to get relations off to a good start. Volunteering to do paperwork and organizing meetings are ways of showing commitment and demonstrating dependability by following up on what was promised. Being understanding about the needs of other organizations and working toward satisfying these needs also builds trust. Relationships are also furthered by being accepting of people, even when there is disagreement with their positions on issues.

(4) Focus on areas of agreement. Partnerships are built on foundations of agreement, not disagreement. Managers must find areas of mutual agreement and therefore create a climate in which brainstorming and exploration can occur to find options of mutual gain. Criteria are agreed upon to evaluate the success of joint efforts. Goals are articulated and emphasized so that they can inspire action to overcome barriers that arise in the course of designing strategies and dealing with concerns. In the process of finding areas of agreement, managers maintain a climate of openness in which members feel free to pursue whatever issues they might have.

(5) Handle disagreements tactfully. The tone and style with which disagreements are dealt with can determine the outcome of negotiations. An important strategy is to respond to positions by identifying interests. It is important to be able to see such interests from someone else's perspective. This helps to avoid the hardening of mutually exclusive positions. When people disagree on positions, then communication stops, coalitions build, perceptions are distorted, and the climate of cooperation rapidly deteriorates. However, when negotiators focus on interests that are served by these positions, it may be possible to identify alternative solutions that serve such interests equally well or better ("I under-

stand that your organization wants to do X to achieve Y, but we cannot do X because . . . However, we can do Z, which also leads to Y. Is doing Z an acceptable alternative to your organization?"). Negotiations that are broken off because of hardened positions often produce a climate that is a barrier to future negotiation.

(6) Summarize agreements and move forward. During negotiations, a variety of different problems and solutions are bandied about. Frequent summaries help keep people on the same page and moving in the same direction. It is also an opportunity to identify any new uncertainties and misunderstandings that may affect the partnership in later stages. Agreements help the process to keep moving forward and are useful in dealing with obstacles that may lie ahead.

Summary

Partnerships exist for a variety of different coordination, policy-making, implementation, and funding purposes. Partnerships help organizations fulfill purposes they are otherwise unable to meet or could meet only at significantly greater expense. Partnerships are a flexible way of organizing such efforts, but they require considerable forethought in planning and negotiating as well as hands-on management of the various relationships. They are increasingly used, however, because they allow organizations to accomplish more without incurring significant new investments.

Privatization

In recent years, privatization and contracting have received renewed interest as tools of productivity improvement. Neither privatization nor contracting involve much joint decision making and implementation, and neither is considered a partnership. Both privatization and contracting help organizations to reduce costs and improve their services by requiring them to compete.

The original purpose of privatization was to reduce of the role of government. During the 1980s, the Reagan administration used privatization to reduce federal regulation of airlines, banking, and other industries as well as support for charitable organizations that provided social services. These efforts aimed to increase efficiency but they seldom produced the gains that were hoped for. For example, banking deregulation led to uncontrolled risk-taking and resulted in costly public bailouts of failed savings and loan institutions. Reducing welfare funding for nonprofit social service organization increased the number of homeless persons and families; private giving did not sufficiently pick up the slack. Although these ideological approaches to privatization have been debunked, the search continues for ways to make public services more effective and efficient, and to use privatization in an accountable way (Johnston, 1996).

In recent years, privatization has come to mean competition by private organizations for public services. The argument is made that if the private sector is more efficient, it should be able to beat public agencies in competition for service delivery. This case was most recently made by defense and space contractors, who face declining federal expenditures in these sectors and who regard privatization as a means for obtaining new contracts. Typical municipal service areas that are subject to increased competition from private sector providers are garbage collection, grass mowing and park maintenance, printing services, fleet operations, building security, snow removal, programs for the elderly, legal services, testing of teacher competence, moving services, and employee training. Under privatization, service standards are set by public organizations and services are paid for by public expenditures (Chi, 1994; McGillicuddy, 1996).

Many public organizations find that they achieve substantial savings through privatization (Savas, 1987). Examples include using for-profit photocopying, cleaning and maintenance, and trash collection services. However, opening up services for competitive bidding does not always result in private provision: Public agencies routinely beat private organizations. One reason in the area of professional services is that top managers and contracted specialists often command much higher salaries in the private sector (Liebowitz, 1995). For example, legal services are increasingly being contracted in by hiring lawyers as public employees. Only exceptional legal needs are contracted out. The threat of job loss also forces public employees to develop new approaches to provide cheaper and better services, and many organizations have avoided privatization by improving their services. Some public organizations that lost their services regained service delivery in subsequent years by making improvements and winning in subsequent bids; this is reverse privatization.

Another rising concern is that private organizations underbid public organizations to obtain the contract but substantially increase prices in subsequent years. This occurs in part because of unrealistic projections, a lack of alternative private providers in many locales, and public organizations that disbanded as a result of privatization. Examples of rapid fee increases are found in some garbage services, cable television services, privatized prison operations, and architectural services. The concern is that privatization is replacing public monopolies with private monopolies. To avoid this situation, many cities *privatize no more than one quarter* of their service effort during any contracting period. This enables public organizations to rebid in subsequent years, and it ensures competition for private providers (Scalar, 1994).

Privatization also involves risks that should be estimated. Public organizations must evaluate the risk of service disruption, poor performance, and legal and financial liability. Although these risks are often small, they must be considered and incorporated into negotiations with vendors. Privatization contracts sometimes initially fail to specify standards for service performance and penalties for underperformance. In this regard, one city experienced dramatic dissatisfaction with its newly privatized garbage collection service, but because it had failed to negotiate penalties for underperformance, the city had very little leverage to increase the contractor's performance short of litigation and the threat of nonrenewal.

The notion of privatization-as-competition can be increased to allow other public agencies to compete for public contracts as well. This practice has been adopted in some European countries where local governments can compete with provinces—which are the equivalent of U.S. state governments—for maintenance of state parks and roads or the printing needs of state agencies. Contracting is also used as a vehicle for accountability, in which higher governments hold lower governments accountable for their performance through "performance contracts." These negotiated contracts contain penalties for targets that are not met. It appears, however, that in a number of cases the legal nature of such contracts and penalties has been successfully contested. Performance contracting between governments has not yet caught on in the United States, in part because it would limit discretionary oversight by the U.S. Congress (Peters, 1996). Also, U.S. governments have other mechanisms to ensure compliance, such as through crossover sanctions. These allow the federal government to withhold funding in a broad range of programs when lower governments fail to perform in any specific program.

Finally, the debate continues about the privatization of entire public functions. For example, the State of Colorado attempted to privatize its University Hospital, but this effort was found to be unconstitutional by the state supreme court: Public organizations cannot abandon their public responsibilities for indigent care and public health, including policy making in these areas. In a subsequent effort, the University Hospital became a public authority, in effect a political subdivision much like a special district or municipality. The University Hospital could, however, privatize operational aspects (Johnston, 1993).

Very little has been written about nonprofit organizations competing success-fully for public sector contracts. Many nonprofit organizations have favorable cost structures due to their use of volunteers. There is also very little known about subcontracting by nonprofits, the equivalent of contracting out by the public sector. One suspects that smaller organizations routinely contract for information, accounting, and cleaning services but that very large nonprofit organizations sometimes have in-house departments that fulfill such operations that could be contracted out.

Restructuring Organizations

In recent years, many organizations have found it necessary to refocus their purposes. Such efforts are strategic in nature, that is, they reflect decisions about core missions and different client groups and needs that public and nonprofit organizations aim to satisfy. After initial strategic decisions have been made, organizations must adapt their structures to align them with their new or reconfigured purposes. This section discusses some of the principal ways in which restructuring occurs as well as its impact on employees.

(1) Consolidating departments. Over time, many organizations increase the number of their departments and divisions. This reflects the continuing addition of new tasks and purposes, and some municipal governments have more than 30 departments. Such a large number of departments complicates communica-tion and oversight. In this situation, reorganization often aims to reduce the number of such departments by merging departments with other units. Focusing on priorities also brings to light activities that are no longer central, and these are often folded into existing structures. By consolidating departments, organi-zations benefit from streamlining budgetary processes and are able to take advantage of economies of scale in administrative services. Consolidation provides organizations with opportunities for cutting back and eliminating unnecessary positions, demoting officials, changing the composition of senior management teams, and altering review and advisory committees. Consolidat-ing departments is also a vehicle for increasing the role of other departments in decision making.

(2) Decentralization. Decentralization is a process of empowering lower man-agers and field offices that provide services directly to clients. The rationale for

delegating decision-making authority and accountability is that units that are closer to their clients have better knowledge of their customers' needs and, when given the means, are better able to provide services than centralized offices. In addition, decentralization reduces the need for middle managers whose purpose is to aggregate and analyze information, make recommendations, and provide coordination. Such functions slow down decision making and add to service costs. Computer technologies enable lower level managers to access the same information and make appropriate decisions.

One challenge of decentralization is to avoid duplication of administrative services and the need for increased coordination. To this end, decentralized units are encouraged to use privatization and competition strategies when needed. They are also given strict ceilings on such expenditures. An example of decentralization is Dade County in South Florida, which includes the City of Miami. Due to immigration and economic growth, Dade County has a rapidly growing population, and an increasing share of the population (53% or about 1 million) now lives in unincorporated areas (Dluhy & Becker, 1996). This growth has caused a need for greater responsiveness to the neighborhoods, which vary greatly in ethnic and economic terms. To this end, Dade County intends to decentralize services by giving district offices greater responsibility for service delivery and decision making in meeting neighborhood needs.

Another challenge of decentralization is to prevent the perversion and corruption of intentions. Segal (1997) describes how the devolution of power in the New York City public school system created opportunities for corruption. Decentralization led to the creation of school boards in each of 31 districts, which were intended to hold principals and other school officials accountable according to the needs of the districts. Instead, the newly elected school board officials used their power to influence hiring and contracting decisions in favor of friends, family, and business partners. Bribery became rampant in some school districts and, in a few instances, sexual favors were exchanged as well. Segal blames the lack of safeguards that prevent corruption for this perverse outcome. Such problems with decentralization occur in organizations as well. Decentralization requires effective work units as well as policies and oversight to ensure that lower units achieve what they are tasked to do.

(3) Downsizing. In many organizations in the 1990s, downsizing is no longer a one-time event but a way of life. This has been the experience in many federal agencies that have experienced successive rounds of downsizing: Between 1993 and 1996, the U.S. federal government cut back 240,000 employees or about 10% of its total workforce. Cutbacks affected all levels of organizations,

especially middle management and headquarter positions (Gore, 1996). Many state governments have also reduced their staff sizes. The purpose of downsizing is often to reduce expenditures *and* improve the alignment of organizations. Organizations try to improve their positioning for future years, and many organizations grow over time in ways that are not directly related to their purposes. Across-the-board cuts do not address the need for realignment and are therefore much criticized. However, in some instances, across-the-board cuts are followed up in subsequent years with targeted growth and spending, which helps organizations grow in the ways that are most needed. Although this addresses some alignment problems, the effective pace of such change is often very slow.

To ensure that organizations are well positioned to meet future challenges, many authors recommend taking a strategic approach to downsizing (Marshall & Yorks, 1994), which, first, addresses goals that organizations seek to pursue in future years and, second, redeploys organizational units and personnel to best meet these goals. In this way, downsizing is seen as organizational redesign. This simple approach is complicated, of course, by the fact that missions are not totally malleable; for example, many public and nonprofit organizations have core missions and stakeholders that must be targeted and that cannot be abandoned. Moreover, the redeployment of staff raises significant issues of layoffs, loss of morale, and litigation. Workforce reductions are hurtful for employees and often demoralize those who are left (Balutis, 1996; Ban, 1997). Indeed, many for-profit organizations experience significant declines in productivity after reorganization and downsizing that are often attributed to the lower morale of remaining workers. In a study of more than 500 firms by the American Management Association, more than 60% failed to show productivity improvement and 80% reported reduced employee morale (American Management Association, 1994).

The redeployment of human resources is perhaps the most critical issue in downsizing. Some large for-profit organizations have resolved the redeployment issue by dismissing all employees and requiring each employee to reapply for specific, new positions. The loss of staff morale is to some extent managed by consistently and persistently communicating management's intent and involving employees and managers in decision making. Many employees and managers participate in their own downsizing, in part because it allows them to better position themselves in subsequent hiring. Also, the 25-50-25 rule, described in Chapter 4, suggests that many employees will see value in the realignment. Communication, participation, goal-setting, and emphasis of competency and purpose over organizational politics are widely viewed as keys to successful downsizing. Managers expend considerable effort communicating the need for downsizing. Organizations further reduce the loss of morale by operating according to a swift time schedule and providing employees who remain with adequate training and team-building for their new jobs (Marks, 1994). They must also deal with the fears of remaining employees that they might be the next casualties of downsizing.

Downsizing requires a strategy for minimizing employee pain (and hence litigation). Public and nonprofit organizations can sometimes avoid total layoff and selective rehiring by using other strategies of reducing overtime, providing furloughs, getting employees to accept cuts in pay, job sharing, converting full-time to part-time positions, encouraging early retirement, and using hiring freezes to promote staff reduction by natural attrition. These strategies reduce the speed of downsizing but, unlike the environments of many for-profit organizations, the pace of change in the environments of many public organizations is somewhat slower, which may justify a somewhat different and less radical strategy. Of course, a problem with lengthier downsizing processes is that morale may suffer for a longer period and managers will need to make ongoing efforts to communicate and ensure participation.

Although the emphasis in downsizing should be on the remaining employees, managers nevertheless expend considerable efforts in dealing with layoffs. It has been estimated that in the early 1990s, each federal government termination cost about $9,500 in severance pay alone (Liebman & McCarthy, 1993). By contrast, the cost of "job bridging" or helping workers to find employment in another organization is estimated at $2,000 to $3,000 per worker in the United States. Job bridging (or outplacement) is the activity of helping employees to classify their skills, identify vacancies, and prepare them to succeed in job interviews while providing counseling for dealing with life and family issues. In addition to employment and financial concerns, layoff involves a loss of identity and purpose. This causes grieving and hence going through stages of denial, anger, sadness, and realization. Many organizations are moving toward outplacement strategies. In general, both remaining and separating employees feel better off when assistance exists that deals with these various issues (Cipolla & Goodwin, 1995).

Analytical Techniques

Analytical techniques for partnering and alignment help managers to choose among competing approaches, to decide whether they or their partner or their organization is ready to proceed with a given approach, and to assess the outcomes of particular strategy. Analytical techniques usually involve checklists. The following is a checklist that helps to determine the viability of partnerships:

Is This Partnership Right for Me?

I. Our Priorities

Is participation the most cost-effective way of accomplishing our mission?

Which alternative approaches have been explored?

Which alternative partnerships have been considered?

On the basis of which criteria is this partnership the best approach?

How will our mission be affected if the partnership fails to perform as expected?

What remedy would be required to correct failure of the partnership?

Can we afford the cost and implications of such failure?

Are we willing to provide adequate resources, personnel, and technology to the partnership as is expected of us?

What is our commitment to the partnership in future years?

II. The Other Organization(s)

Do we know the missions of the partner organization(s)?

Do we understand how the partnership fits into their missions?

Do we understand why other organizations do not fulfill the goals of the partnership themselves?

Do we understand why the other organizations are committed to this partnership rather than to some other partnership or approach?

What is the evidence of their commitment to the partnership today and in the future?

Do we understand how to work with the other organizations? Do we understand their frequency of interaction and communication style?

Do we have procedures for admitting other organizations into the partnership?

III. Process for Accomplishment

Is there a timetable for accomplishment?

Have we discussed and agreed upon the requirements for each step along the way?

Have we agreed upon criteria for success?

Have we discussed how often we will meet to review progress of the partnership toward goals?

Have we agreed on how we will deal with midcourse corrections?

Have we agreed on how success and accomplishment might affect the future of the partnership?

IV. Procedures for Contingencies and Termination

Is there a process in place for dealing with disagreements?

Have we agreed on how we will deal with deviations from goals and success?

Are there preestablished conditions under which the partnership should be terminated?

Have we agreed on how we will deal with other organizations' nonperformance, for example, their lack in contributing resources, personnel, or technology?

Are we legally protected from actions by partners and by the partnership?

What property rights, if any, does the partnership create, and what responsibilities are implied by these rights?

Can we continue the partnership with other organizations if one or more partners pull out?

Can partnerships be created with subsets of members of the current partnership?

Are organizations required to give advance warning of their intent to leave the partnership?

Are future managers bound by this agreement?

Checklist for Downsizing

The following questions are consistent with the framework discussed in Chapter 2.

I. External Stakeholders

Which groups of external stakeholders does the new mission aim to satisfy? Will the organization be able to meet the needs of each group adequately? By what measure will we assess stakeholder satisfaction after the downsizing?

Will the new organization be able to deliver world-class services? What strategy is in place for continuous improvement?

Will the new organization draw adequate support from external stakeholders? What strategy is in place to ensure stakeholder support?

II. Organization

Is the new mission clear and consistent with the needs of external stakeholders?

Are all responsibilities identified to accomplish the mission? Is support provided for those units that have this responsibility?

Are all responsibilities assigned? How will units be held accountable for their results? How will performance be measured?

Are decision-making structures consistent with the focus of the new organization? Are new advisory groups needed?

Are units using the most cost-effective form of organizing to fulfill their responsibilities? Are they using contracting and partnering strategies?

Have managers of reorganized units developed a structure for clear communication and accountability? How will they deal with malperformance?

III. Employees

Are we using strategies to avoid layoffs such as early/phased retirement, buyouts, natural attrition, relocation/reassignment, and part-time/job sharing?

Are employees adequately and repeatedly informed about the need for downsizing? Do they know when and how it occurs? Did we get their (union) input into the development of downsizing procedures? Are salary reductions an option for avoiding layoffs?

Are we using fair procedures for selecting those who will be laid off?

Are we giving maximum assistance to those who will be laid off: job search assistance, financial assistance, psychological counseling, support in meeting family needs (e.g., continuation of health insurance, day care, other benefits)?

Are we giving maximum support to remaining workers to help adjust to their new situation and increased job insecurity? Is training provided for new job skills? Are managers trained to deal with adjustment issues? Will a survey be undertaken to identify new employee needs?

IV. Projects and Programs

Which operations are affected by the downsizing? How are they affected? Do we have a strategy for deciding which projects and program will receive additional funding to deal with the effects of downsizing?

Are timetables and resources reevaluated regarding the feasibility of existing projects and programs?

How does the downsizing affect existing investment plans for technology?

Summary

This chapter discusses strategies for improving productivity through organizational structures. Partnerships are increasingly used. Partnerships increase capabilities of organizations and enable public and nonprofit organizations to address myriad community problems better. Different purposes of partnerships are discussed as well as strategies for negotiating and managing partnerships. Managers should seek to create win-win situations, ensure significant interest by participating organizations, anticipate change, develop clear roles and responsibilities, and exercise appropriate leadership. In addition, this chapter discusses organizational realignment and the critical issue of managing remaining employees after downsizing. Finally, this chapter draws attention to privatization strategies as a means of productivity improvement through increased competition.

Notes

1. Joint ventures also involve collective decision making and implementation but they are usually undertaken for specific projects that are have a start date and a finish date. By contrast, partnerships involve open-ended commitments.

2. Another way of classifying partnerships is according to the sectors of participants: There are public-public, public-private, and private-private partnerships.

3. Pulling out of partnerships does not signal failure; it may be that individual needs have changed and are no longer being met by the partnership.

References

American Management Association (AMA). (1994). *Survey on downsizing.* New York: Author.

Andreasen, A. (1996). Profit for nonprofits: Find a corporate partner. *Harvard Business Review, 74*(12), 47-59.

Baker, E., Melton, R., Stange, P., Fields, M., Koplan, J., Guerra, F., & Satcher, D. (1994). Health reform and the health of the public: Forging community health partnerships. *Journal of the American Medical Association, 272*(16), 1276-1282.

Balutis, A. (1996, June 29-July 3). *Surviving dismantlement: Has downsizing become a way of life.* Paper presented at the American Society for Public Administration national conference, Atlanta, GA.

Ban, C. (1997). The challenges of cutback management. In C. Ban & N. Riccucci (Eds.), *Public personnel management* (pp. 269-280). New York: Longman.

Berman, E. (1994). Technology transfer and the federal laboratories. *Policy Studies Journal, 22*(2), 338-348.

Berman, E. (1996). Local government and community-based strategies. *American Review of Public Administration, 26*(1), 71-91.

Berman, E., & Levine, A. (1996). Cooperation hones competitive edge. *Forum for Applied Research and Public Policy, 11*(3), 54-59.

Bierenbaum, A. (1994). Building coalitions: Lessons from the field of disability. *Nonprofit World, 12*(2), 39-42.

Chi, K. (1994, July 23-27). *Privatization in state government: Trends and issues.* Paper presented at the American Society for Public Administration national conference, Kansas City, MO.

Cipolla, F., & Goodwin, L. (1995). Effective downsizing: Lessons learned. *Public Manager, 24*(3), 23-25.

Endicott, E. (1993). *Land conservation through public/private partnerships.* Washington, DC: Island.

Gore, A. (1996). *The best kept secrets in government.* New York: Random House.

Harvey, L. (1993). Public-private-nonprofit partnerships for breaking welfare dependency. *National Civic Review, 82*(2), 16-25.

Hesselbein, F. (Ed.). (1997). *The organization of the future.* San Francisco: Jossey-Bass.

Johnston, V. (1993, July 17-21). *Entrepreneurial government: Privatization's contributions toward re-inventing partnerships for progress.* Paper presented at the American Association for Public Administration national conference, San Francisco.

Johnston, V. (1996). Optimizing productivity through privatization and entrepreneurial management. *Policy Studies Journal, 24*(3), 444-463.

Liebman, H., & McCarthy, S. (1993). Job bridging: Downsizing without RIFs. *Public Manager, 22*(3), 25-27.

Liebowitz, B. (1995, March 10). Privatizing public hospitals just doesn't work. *New York Times,* p. 14.

Marks, M. (1994). *From turmoil to triumph.* New York: Lexington.

Marshall, R., & Yorks, L. (1994). Planning for a restructured, revitalized organization. *Sloan Management Review, 35*(3), 81-91.

McGillicuddy, J. (1996). A blueprint for privatization and competition. *Public Manager, 78*(11), 8-13.

Muehrcke, J. (1994). Ingredients for collaboration success. *Nonprofit World, 12*(4), 48.

Peters, G. (1996, August). *Contracts as a tool for public managers: Their surprising absence in North America.* Paper presented at the annual meeting of the European Group on Public Administration, Budapest, Hungary.

Salamon, L. (1995). *Partners in public service: Government-nonprofit relations in the modern welfare state.* Baltimore, MD: Johns Hopkins University Press.

Savas, E. (1987). *Privatization: The key to better government.* Chatham, NJ: Chatham House.

Scalar, E. (1994). Public service privatization: Ideology or economics? *Dissent, 41*(3), 329-337.

Scheff, J., & Kotler, P. (1996). How the arts can prosper through strategic collaborations. *Harvard Business Review, 74*(1), 52-62.

Schwartz, A. (1994). Creative collaborations: The art of negotiating. *Nonprofit World, 12*(4), 34-38.

Segal, L. (1997). The pitfalls of political decentralization and proposals for reform: The case of New York City Public Schools. *Public Administration Review, 57*(2), 141-149.

Sink, C., & Frank, C. (1996). Department of Energy forges partnerships for environmental cleanup. *Forum for Applied Research and Public Policy, 11*(3), 65-69.

Suchman, D. (1990). *Public/private housing partnerships.* Washington, DC: Urban Land Institute.

7

The Quality Paradigm

The sad truth is that excellence makes people nervous.
Shane Alexander

The current period in productivity improvement is characterized by the emergence of the "quality paradigm." The objectives of the quality paradigm are to increase the orientations of managers and organizations toward meeting customer needs and to develop effective and efficient strategies in this regard (Berman & West, 1997; Hunt, 1993; Kennedy, 1991; West, 1995). Total Quality Management (TQM) is associated with the early development of the quality paradigm, which began during the late 1980s and, in some public and nonprofit organizations, is still continuing today. TQM emphasizes meeting customer needs through a comprehensive strategy that encompasses empowerment, process analysis and improvement, customer service, partnering, and benchmarking. However, organizations that have implemented TQM have often done so by focusing on only one or two components, notably, quality circles and customer orientation. According to Berman and West (1995), only 11% of cities had a commitment to a broad range of TQM activities in 1993, but 70% of cities monitored customer satisfaction and 35% used benchmarking. Likewise, a study by the General Accounting Office (1993) found that 68% of all federal units had some familiarity with TQM but that few had made comprehensive efforts.

At the present time, in the late 1990s, TQM is regarded more as a management philosophy than an all-encompassing single strategy. The present midphase of the quality paradigm emphasizes *TQM as philosophy, called the quality paradigm, that encompasses diverse quality improvement strategies such as customer orientation, reengineering, continuous improvement, empowerment, and benchmarking.* Each strategy advances the customer orientation and quality improvement in some way and is implemented separately from the others. Although some strategies are not wholly new, such as empowerment, all have been rethought in recent years. The quality paradigm thus provides many strategies whose implementation is currently under way and will likely take many years to complete.

The core of values of the quality paradigm is very similar to those of TQM, namely, to (a) identify, meet, and exceed the needs of customers (and other stakeholders); (b) strive to produce services right the first time (i.e., reduce errors, which upset stakeholders and cause rework and increased costs); (c) use systematic analysis to evaluate and improve service delivery; and (d) consistently support workers in their efforts to improve quality and meet customer needs (Rosander, 1989). In this regard, the quality paradigm invites managers to think broadly about customer service and needs, and to develop innovative approaches to improve service delivery (Van Wart, 1996). Managers lead, empower, assess, and partner (LEAP) with employees to provide better service. Employees are given more latitude and are held accountable for producing outcomes, not mere effort. Team-based efforts are more often used. By contrast, traditional management is viewed as punitive and unimaginative in its emphasis on conformity and compliance, directing and controlling.

The breadth of quality strategies implies that applications of the quality paradigm vary greatly. Applications include improving marketing of social services, responding more quickly to citizen telephone inquiries, adopting one-stop "shopping" programs in city hall, reducing the time and cost of purchasing in government, improving emergency response time, or developing new program measures. TQM often involves many small changes that add up to big improvements. This chapter discusses three distinctive quality strategies: customer service, reengineering, and analytical techniques for continuous improvement. Other strategies of TQM are discussed elsewhere in this book: Measurement and benchmarking are discussed in Chapter 3 and empowerment is discussed in Chapter 10.

History. The origins of quality management can be traced to Word War II, when production demanded higher levels of performance, reliability, and timeliness.

Defective radios, tanks, artillery, and aircraft posed a clear and present danger. During this period, engineers built on previous time-motion studies, quality control practices, and mass production experiences to improve quality. After World War II, U.S. manufacturers switched back to earlier peacetime production practices. The engineers who created higher quality standards found employment in Japan, rebuilding its factories. U.S. practices were absorbed by Japanese engineers and further improved. Among the U.S. engineers in Japan was W. Edwards Deming, who in the1980s would become an outspoken advocate for U.S. quality improvement. By the mid-1970s, improvements in Japanese cars and electronic products made them competitive with designs of U.S. producers. American executives, concerned about loss of market share, studied these then-Japanese approaches. Many strategies were adopted, first as quality circles (groups of employees who study opportunities for process and product improvement) and later as TQM. As quality improved among U.S. multinational corporations, other sectors of the U.S. economy became interested as well. By the end of the 1980s, TQM had spread through many large and medium-size companies, and by the mid-1990s, it had made inroads into many governments and hospitals. The federal government contributed to the diffusion of TQM through its prestigious Baldridge Quality Award program (Connors, 1992). By most accounts, nonprofit organizations, universities, and some local governments are now among the last vestiges of society to increase their customer orientation and adopt strategies associated with TQM. Many other organizations are improving their initial TQM efforts. This continuing interest in TQM is reflected by continuing sales of books on this topic. Some books have repackaged elements (e.g., as "high-performance organizations"), whereas other books focus on specific management techniques.

Is Quality Possible?

Conditions for Success

As with many new productivity efforts, quality improvement has drawn praise as well as criticism. Quality improvement efforts require leadership to assess, organize, and encourage improvement and are built on a foundation of trust. Both leadership and trust are sometimes in short supply. The following are some general lessons that have been learned since the introduction of TQM.

(1) Implement quality improvement strategies in manageable pieces. As mentioned before, early TQM efforts often implemented all five strategies simultaneously: empowerment, benchmarking, customer service orientation, reengineering, and continuous improvement. Such comprehensive efforts demanded too much change in too short a period; and current efforts introduce change through one strategy at a time. Because many strategies have overlapping characteristics, such as customer orientation, individual responsibility, and results orientation, the piecemeal approach reinforces these important values. For example, measurement is part of benchmarking, reengineering, continuous improvement, and even customer service. Most quality improvement strategies can be successfully implemented in about nine months, but it often takes up to five years of repetition and diffusion to produce enduring changes in values and attitudes. This is, in part, because managers and employees are hesitant to give up existing orientations and habits to which they are accustomed (Patten, 1995).

(2) All quality improvement strategies require top management support—most require leadership too. Managers play different roles in implementing quality improvement. Leadership is required to overcome obstacles, devise implementation strategies, legitimate change, and lead by example. Support is required of those who implement quality improvement, for example, by providing adequate resources and legitimation. Although leadership by top managers is highly recommended for quality improvement efforts, top leaders sometimes fail to follow through, which causes quality implementation efforts to flounder. Some causes of the lack of top management leadership are turnover (e.g., incoming leaders don't support TQM or other quality improvement efforts that they view as leftovers from the old guard), gamesmanship (leaders want to appear forward-looking but do not have a commitment to quality), incompetence (leaders are committed to the quality paradigm but understand neither its application nor its implementation), and other competing priorities such as fund-raising or putting out fires. The lack of top management leadership suggests that sometimes lower managers must lead. For example, organizationwide restructuring through reengineering often requires top management leadership, but divisionwide use of customer service requires only middle management leadership and top management support of middle managers. The distinction between leadership and support is increasingly being developed as new quality strategies are developed. It should be noted that although most authors advocate wholesale organizational change, the lack of top management leadership implies that this is not always possible (Brown, Hitchcock, & Willard, 1994).[1]

(3) Quality efforts must match quality readiness. An important challenge for all managers is to identify specific improvement strategies that their organizations are able to support. When organizations are deeply rooted in traditional, authoritarian management practices that emphasize hierarchy and following orders, lower managers may be able to implement only a few quality strategies, if any. Such mangers face an uphill and possibly unwise battle when top managers do not fully support quality improvement. By contrast, managers in more open organizations are often encouraged to use a broad range of quality strategies. *Managers must identify the limits of support for their improvement efforts.* In many organizations, support for quality is increasing as organizations increase their responsiveness to customers and adopt new ways of improving efficiency.

(4) Appointed officials and elected officials/board members play different roles. The quality paradigm has little appeal as a political instrument; politicians only give lip service to quality improvement (Halachmi, 1995). Although quality strategies can help implement policy in a more flexible and effective manner, and may inform policy making of client preferences, it is not a tool of politics. Similar criticisms about overselling are made in nonprofit organizations: Although support from board members is required, it is seldom a tool of board activity. The limited appeal helps draw the line between elected and appointed officials: As a management philosophy, the quality paradigm and its associated strategies require only support (i.e., sanctioning) from elected officials, for example, to legitimate the effort, to prevent end runs by employees, and to ensure adequate resources.

(5) Quality is a change effort, not a program. The quality paradigm requires revising goals and expectations and adopting new work processes and standards. The measure of success in implementing quality strategies is the extent that functions, such as budgeting, and processes, such as strategic planning, *integrate* quality and especially a customer orientation into their approaches. Quality improvement should *not* be implemented as a program with separate staff and resources. Introducing TQM and other quality efforts as programs causes conflict with existing expectations and departments. Often, the latter win out, causing the demise of separate, program-based quality efforts.

(6) Quality strategies do not address crises. Organizations frequently find themselves embroiled in battles for survival: the need to obtain new grants, to fend off politically inspired attacks, to reduce expenditures immediately, or to deal with the threat of litigation. These immediate needs require responses that

the quality paradigm is not designed to provide. The quality paradigm is a management philosophy that aims to prevent such problems. For example, through a customer orientation, it aims to achieve long-term stakeholder support and it uses continuous improvement to improve efficiency and effectiveness. Such strategies eliminate many sources of short-term needs. Quality improvement strategies are not very useful for putting out fires. Rather, managers will need to use emergency teams, political persuasion, and other strategies to deal with short-term concerns.

(7) Quality improvement produces some short-term results, too. Although most benefits of the quality paradigm increase over time, many of its strategies produce some benefits immediately. Indeed, successful implementation often depends on demonstrating some immediate results. For example, continuous improvement efforts identify and ameliorate immediate concerns about errors and unresponsiveness.

(8) Quality requires additional resources—but not many. Quality improvement requires some additional resources, but mostly for training and rewards. A criticism of current training is that it often increases awareness but fails to provide sufficient application. Recent advances in training suggest that it should be tailored to specific problems that employees face, and that training should be delivered when employees need it. This reduces unnecessary training and increases its effectiveness (Bedwell, 1993; Miller, 1995). Some training can also be provided by supervisors themselves. Rewards increasingly include acknowledgment, being asked to participate on key teams, becoming eligible for training, and receiving additional comp time. Such rewards require relatively few resources. Thus the level of additional resources for quality improvement is modest. However, customer service may require investments in physical infrastructure (office appearance, information technology) as organizations strive to improve their services.

Increasing Customer Orientation

A distinctive objective of the quality paradigm in TQM is increasing the customer orientation. Since the introduction of TQM, a customer orientation has been implemented in many different organizations, and many public and non-profit organizations now collect some data on client satisfaction. Customer orientation rests on four pillars: (a) defining the customer, (b) identifying customer needs and service objectives, (c) achieving customer-oriented behavior and service, and (d) assessing customer satisfaction.

Defining the Customer

The first step in customer orientation is identifying who the customers are. Public and nonprofit organizations have multiple customers. *External customers* are defined as people who do not work for the organization but who come in contact with it: Clients, representatives of other organizations, and citizens are common external customers. Examples of clients are people who receive social services, use library services, or make informational requests of agencies. In the public sector, many clients are *involuntary,* such as business owners who are subject to regulation, drivers who are issued traffic violation citations, and prison inmates. Such clients have needs, too, such as inmates who require increased job skills to find postrelease employment. Meeting these needs can greatly improve program outcomes. Most clients of nonprofit organizations are voluntary, although not those who, for example, are required to make use of counseling services.

Citizens are also customers of public organizations, specifically in their roles of taxpayers, residents, or voters. Citizens sometimes also feel that they have a stake in nonprofit organizations, such as the United Way or local hospitals, that play important community roles. Of particular interest are representatives of other organizations and lawmakers: Most organizations depend on other organizations to fulfill their goals, and it is important that they establish good working relations with them. Lawmakers are also important, especially for nonprofit organizations in securing grants. In sum, organizations have various external customers who are defined by the roles that people play as they come into contact with them. The first step in increasing customer orientation is to identify different stakeholder groups. Usually, three or four groups of key external customers are identified that are especially important to the organization.

Internal customers are people who work inside the organization. Internal customers too are defined by the roles that people play. When employees are recipients of services, they are customers. For example, when they make a purchasing request, they are customers of the purchasing department. However, when employees provide a service, they are dealing with customers. Customer-oriented organizations are easily recognized by how they make employees feel: as customers of internal transactions or as an annoyance to other departments.[2] A key step in TQM is identifying customers and prioritizing those that have been neglected or otherwise require significant improvement in service delivery.

Defining Customer Needs
and Service Objectives

The concept of a customer orientation or service includes, at a minimum, identifying what customers want and giving it to them. A common problem is that managers fail to ask customers about their needs. Instead, they mistakenly assume that they know their customers' needs and priorities. For example, police districts frequently measure their productivity by the number of arrests, citations, and investigations that are cleared. Increases in these measures reflect *unsafety* and seldom reflect citizen priorities for *safety*. When asked, citizens often identify adequate street lighting as an important priority. A customer orientation for police departments means that they must ensure adequate street lighting, often through collaboration with public works departments. Likewise, hospitals often fail to adequately ascertain patients' priorities and need for feeling that they are being cared for, for receiving effective services, and for having convenient services. Many hospital services are not convenient, nor do they make patients feel cared for. The failure to ask customers about their needs is a persistent and serious problem in many organizations.

Therefore, a key activity in developing a customer orientation is bringing customers into contact with mangers and employees. The latter must often hear from customers what they value: Hearing and seeing is believing. A public works manager might believe that he or she is oriented toward serving the needs of citizens, but does the department seek citizen input in deciding when roadwork that makes a key road inaccessible will be conducted? In this regard, organizations sometimes face contradictory needs. For example, as involuntary clients, citizens may feel that traffic regulations are too strict when they are being issued a citation, but as neighborhood residents, they may also feel that enforcement should be more strict. Public organizations must resolve these contradictions. For example, local police might increase speed enforcement activities in neighborhoods rather than on main roads and explain to motorists who are issued citations in residential neighborhoods the importance of maintaining low speeds to ensure the safety of children and others. The fact that different needs must be balanced does not reduce the need for identifying customer needs and trying to meet them.

However, not all needs are verbalized, and unarticulated needs must be identified too. For example, customers of social services may not know the agency can provide transportation to and from work, and thus fail to request transportation. While customer input is important, professional input is important, too. In addition, customers may have unarticulated *dissatisfiers;* for example, they may not complain about the office appearance, but cluttered spaces and uncomfortable chairs add to their dissatisfaction. According to Carter (1993), few dissatisfied customers inform an organization that they are unhappy. Focus groups help bring to light unarticulated needs and dissatisfiers. An important assessment objective is also to identify *new* customer needs. In other instances, organizations must go to where customers use their services to better understand how they can improve them. Recently, U.S. custom officials in Miami traveled to Colombia to better understand how drug smugglers use flowers and produce to transport their goods. Direct observation led to new opportunities for drug interdiction.

Although much emphasis is placed on meeting the needs of external customers, many employees and managers work in settings in which they seldom come into contact with external customers. In these instances, managers must focus on the needs of their important internal customers. For example, human resource departments serve a multitude of internal customers whose needs should be identified. In some instances, offices have a single internal customer, such as a policy analysis group that serves an agency director. In this instance, understanding the director's needs is of obvious importance.

A quality dictum is to *exceed* customer expectations, not only meet them. Service objectives build on a thorough understanding of customer needs. In this regard, it is necessary to establish standards for service objectives. Generally, quality standards concern *performance* (the extent to which outcomes are achieved), *conformance* (the extent to which predetermined standards are met), *reliability* (i.e., dependability), *accuracy,* and *timeliness.* Additional dimensions of quality include *serviceability,* having a *range of features,* and *good aesthetics,* although these are typically used in connection with products rather than services. Quality requires professional judgment because stakeholders may not know all the standards that should be met. Figure 7.1 shows customer service standards for answering telephone inquiries from external customers.

Finally, Whiteley and Hessan (1996) note that services should also be commensurate with the nature of customer relations. For example, many customer relations are very short term, transaction oriented, and uninvolved, such as counter requests and telephone inquiries. In these situations, customers increasingly expect that employees will deal with their requests in a *courteous and effective* manner. By contrast, partnerships are complex and enduring. Customers expect courtesy as well as a higher level of effectiveness that includes active involvement and knowledge of the activities of customers as well. Professional expertise is necessary to maintain effectiveness. Other relations

TABLE 7.1 Service Standards for External Customers

Any external customer doing business with city employees can expect the following:

- Phones to be answered on four rings
- To be given a time when the person being called will be available if he or she is not available at the time of the call
- The call to be forwarded to the appropriate department if an incorrect department is called first
- The call to be returned within 24 hours
- That if he or she does not speak English, an employee will be available to communicate with him or her using the AT&T multilanguage line
- The person who puts them on hold will be conscientious of the call on hold
- When an employee is away from his or her desk, calls are forwarded to another staff member
- All persons will be at their workstations at their scheduled time and ready to assist the public
- Food consumption and grooming will be kept from public view
- City staff to be at scheduled meetings on time
- Requested printed information to be distributed within 24 hours
- Information requests requiring research to be answered within five days
- To be acknowledged immediately in a professional and courteous manner when approaching the front counter
- To receive accurate information from city staff
- An employee to call ahead before directing to another city department to ensure that the referral is appropriate

---

SOURCE: Based on material from the City of Escondido, 1990.

involve little technical knowledge but a commitment to a long-lasting relationship, or vice versa. For example, relationship-oriented interactions involve little information but require an in-depth familiarity with the client. Regulators often need in-depth knowledge of the businesses they are regulating, and although they may provide advice for solving code violations, most do not view themselves as business partners. Organizations need to think through the nature of their customer relationships.

Achieving Customer-Oriented Behavior

All customer relations require employee behavior that is both courteous *and* effective. This requires that the following habits and practices are emphasized (Leland & Bailey, 1995; McClendon, 1992):

- Being on time
- Following up on what was said or promised

- Never overpromising
- Going the extra mile
- Giving options (but not so many as to confuse the customer)
- Treating customers as if they are the most important aspect of the job
- Making eye contact and smiling a lot
- Seeing disappointments from the customer's point of view

These habits are *not* window dressing but help form productive relationships by showing respect (such as by being on time), integrity (following up), commitment to the relationship (going the extra mile, treating customers as important), effectiveness (delivering what was promised, showing optimism by smiling), and the ability to relate (seeing things from the customer's point of view), while avoiding some things that upset relationships (creating disappointments, being insensitive to disappointments, and avoiding eye contact, which suggests suspicion).

Good customer-oriented behavior is especially important when public officials and nonprofit providers are confronted with customer requests that they cannot meet. There are many ways to make customers into enemies. Some bad responses are as follows: "No" (without further explanation), "I can't do that," "Come back tomorrow" (in the hope that the customer won't come back), and "It's against our policy or the law." These responses create anger, because customers' expectations of having their problems solved are dashed and, importantly, ignored and disrespected. These responses are aggravated by body language signifying withdrawal and by insisting on having the last word. Rather, officials should focus on the underlying problem and reach agreement with the customer on some alternative course of action ("I'm sorry that we can't do that this way, but we can do this. Would that help?"). This approach is especially important when dealing with customers for whom nothing is satisfactory and adequate ("I understand that you feel that way, but . . .").

Training and commitment are keys to developing good habits. As discussed in Chapter 4, the rule of three means that employees will take requests for improving their customer orientation seriously only when management makes repeated requests and shows its commitment to improving when dealing with customers and employees as well. Improving habits is no small feat, and it should be treated as an important new challenge. The rule of seven implies the need for training and coaching. Employees must know (a) what specific values and behaviors are expected from them and (b) what behaviors are inappropriate. Because habits are, by definition, ingrained, it takes much training and practice to modify them. Rewards and incentives for new behaviors signal organizational

---

BOX 7.1.
From Planning to Service

Many organizations adopt customer service training activities following their strategic planning. This is the case, for example, in Orange County, Florida, which launched a community-based strategic planning effort called "Citizens First!" in April 1995. This planning effort aimed to get citizens more involved in their community and to ensure that agencies put the needs and values of citizens first (Denhardt, 1997). Agencies examined opportunities to empower citizens to take greater responsibility for their communities as well as to provide better service to citizens and clients.

Two years after initiating the "Citizens First!" effort, Orange County is now planning to undertake countywide customer service training called "Customer Service Partnerships" (Orange County, 1997). This training helps employees to understand their role in the "Citizens First!" effort, to create service partnerships with citizens and clients, and to build customer commitment and support for services. It provides employees with tools to better resolve service problems, deal with conflict resolution, and improve service recovery. Behaviors such as dependability, responsiveness, courtesy, resourcefulness, flexibility, and communication are examined. Advanced training is provided for all supervisory and management staff to coach employees in the delivery of quality customer service. It also provides examples of service performance measurement and evaluation techniques.

---

commitment, and training is sometimes conducted in team settings in which employees receive frequent feedback, for example, through the use of videos. It is also important to note that people vary with regard to the degree that they are people oriented: Some people may never excel at customer relations, but everybody is capable of arresting habits that cause customer relations problems. Box 7.1 discusses a further example of customer service training.

Assessing Customer Satisfaction

The final step in customer service is assessing and monitoring customer satisfaction. Some organizations undertake customer surveys but fail to rethink their service objectives from the perspective of customer needs. This is, of course, a serious shortcoming in developing a customer orientation. Assessing stakeholder satisfaction is also a key aspect of performance measurement. Whereas administrative data are used to determine outputs, customer surveys are usually needed to determine satisfaction with *outcomes* (Chapter 3). The ultimate measure of the success of public safety efforts is whether citizens feel safer.

Two frequent assessment strategies are to use customer complaints and self-administered customer satisfaction surveys. However, both are often invalid. For example, a large number of complaints may indicate customer service problems (which should be immediately addressed), but most customers do not file complaints when they are dissatisfied. *Customer complaint logs underestimate dissatisfaction and do not measure satisfaction.* Self-administered surveys often rely on self-selection such as when customers take surveys from a waiting room table or when surveys are sent to all customers (e.g., when enclosed in utility bills). Both approaches to implementation produce respondents who are seldom representative of the customer base; in the latter case, because the response rate is often very low, this raises concerns about nonresponse bias.

Strategies for implementing surveys are discussed in Chapter 3, along with standards for assessing the quality of survey research. Managers must be sure to draw a *representative sample* from their customer base and to ensure high response rates. For example, when a list of customers is available, managers should draw a random sample from this list. When no such list is available, they should choose random days and times to interview their customers. Organizations are increasingly using telephone or in-person surveys to ensure *high response rates.* Customers seldom take time to return mail surveys in adequate numbers, even when repeated mailings are used.

Survey responses of external customer satisfaction are often analyzed according to subsets of customers, such as those who recently had contact with the organization or those who no longer use the services of the organization. Demographic subsets are also used, such as ethnic minorities, the elderly, single mothers, and people who are poor. The problem of biased questions is well known and should be avoided: Questions should be clear and not leading. However, the problem of biased response scales is important, too. For example, the following scale has four positive categories and only one negative category: Outstanding/Very Good/Satisfactory/Fair/Poor. When combining the first four categories, organizations often report high levels of customer satisfaction because very few respondents check the single negative category (Poor). Such practices are deceitful. Unbiased scales should be used, such as Likert scales. For example, the question, "How do you rate the overall level of our services?" should be followed by the following scale: Very Good/Good/Somewhat Good/No Opinion/Somewhat Poor/Poor/Very Poor (see Chapter 3). It is generally recommended that questions and scales should set high standards of excellence so that there is room for improvement in performance. Table 7.2 lists some generic customer service questions. Likewise, questions can be designed to assess employee satisfaction with internal service.

In addition to surveys, managers also assess customer satisfaction through direct observation. Although friendliness and courtesy are hard to measure, elements such as smiling, eye contact, and good grooming are readily observed as well as the willingness of employees to help clients solve their problems. Organizations also use ghost clients (who are anonymous raters posing as clients) to make direct observations, but employees are frequently adept at identifying such persons. Videos are also used. Many public spaces already use videos for security purposes, and these can be upgraded. Videos are used in subsequent training sessions to assess both good and bad behaviors. Teams are then used to discuss the results of these videos as well as customer surveys and progress in customer satisfaction ratings.

Reengineering

Although increasing customer orientation is essential to improving service quality, customer service is an incremental process that seldom changes the way in which an organization or department thinks about delivering its services. By contrast, reengineering takes a radical view; it examines the *entire* process of service delivery (Champy & Hammer, 1993). Reengineering is a comprehensive approach to organizing. There are two types of reengineering efforts: organizationwide and process specific. The former is associated with massive reorganization efforts in which entire departments are restructured, assigned different responsibilities, or eliminated. This is discussed in Chapter 6. Process-specific reengineering focuses on making work processes more efficient, effective, and timely. Although it is a micro-level activity, it frequently cuts across departments. This section focuses on the latter and discusses key principles and implementation strategies.

Organize Around Outcomes, Not Efforts or Tasks

Customers want results, not efforts. People want to be served quickly, effectively, now. They do not want to wait on the phone or be transferred to different departments. They don't care that officials are serving other people and that they have to wait their turn: They want to be served *now*. To satisfy this

TABLE 7.2 External Customer Service Questions

How often do you use the following services?
How familiar are you with the following services?
Which services are the most important to you?
Please rate your level of satisfaction with the following services.
Which of the following programs would you like to see added to our efforts?
Which existing services should be increased?
How do our services compare with those of other organizations with which you are familiar?
Please rate the following characteristics about our programs with which you are familiar.
What are the three things you like best about our programs?
Which three things do you like least about our programs?
During which hours are you most likely to use the following services?
To what extent do services meet your needs?
To what extent does program staff try to fit our services to your needs?
On average, how courteous is program staff?
On average, how effective is program staff?
How do you rate the appearance of our office?
How did you learn of our programs?
Do you get adequate information about our services?
On average, how long did it take for staff to get back to you regarding your request?
Would you like to have more input into how we choose our services?
Would you like to have more input into how we deliver our services?

Please state your sex, race, approximate age, occupation, and so on, to assist with further analysis.

need, organizations are rethinking the way they are organized. Traditionally, many organizations and work processes have been organized around functional specializations, for example, as departments of finance, zoning, accounting, or health inspections. Separate departments help organizations to obtain necessary skills, but they also produce bureau pathologies: Requests for services fall between the cracks of departments; requests are shuffled between departments, which causes delays; and departments are often unable or unwilling to solve customer needs that don't fit exactly into departmental categories. Quality suffers as a result. A key principle of process reengineering is to organize around results and outcomes rather than efforts, tasks, or departments: Work should be structured so that each person (or unit) performs as many tasks as possible to reduce the number of times that work is "handed off." Every time that work is handed off, the potential for error, delays, and in-fighting increases.

Three strategies are used to minimize this problem: First, single departments are required to take responsibility for satisfying customer requests, even when they must coordinate with other departments. For example, many organizations now provide a *single point of contact* between customers and organizations. Employees who fulfill such positions (e.g., one-stop shopping) are assigned responsibility for fulfilling customer requests and are given the authority to secure the provision of services. They are also often cross-trained in different disciplines to ensure that they have adequate technical knowledge. Second, teams made up of employees from different departments are made responsible for fulfilling customer requests. For example, in health care organizations, members of different departments are assigned to teams that meet the different care needs of clients such as for rehabilitation and social services (Linden, 1994b; McAdoo & Pynes, 1995). Third, individual employees are cross-trained to handle more tasks, thereby reducing the need to hand off tasks. However, when very different skills are needed to fulfill such tasks, teams of employees must be used.

This principle has guided, at an organizational level, many state welfare reform efforts in the 1990s. States such as Florida devolved responsibilities from central offices to local offices so that the latter better meet community needs for family services, drug abuse treatments, child day care training, child medical services, and so on. Prior to the change, field offices collected requests that were processed in central offices, and services were assigned to local units. This created delays and many errors. Specific requests, which required services tailored to client needs, caused further delays. Organizing around outcomes created field offices that are composed of multidisciplinary teams assigned responsibilities for their individual communities. Although devolution is not complete in Florida, it allows local offices to better connect with the needs of the community, even though some specialized services and administrative functions are still provided centrally. There is also further evidence that in state welfare agencies that embraced TQM, delegation has been more frequent and efforts to improve the quality and timeliness of services have been more pervasive and effective (Berman, 1995).

It is widely recommended that organizations engage in reengineering only after they have established their commitment to a strategic purpose, because reengineered work processes involve a commitment that is locked in. Frequent changes reduce commitment on the part of employees and managers that is disrupted at considerable psychological and motivational expense. It should be noted that organizing around outcomes and results rather than efforts and tasks does not (thus far) imply that functional departments are likely to disappear. Functional departments help ensure necessary skills for the organization. But reducing the number of times that work gets handed off does help focus on who the customer is and what the customer wants.

Reducing Steps and Using Parallel Processes

Further gains are made by reducing the number of steps that are required to achieve an outcome. These improvements are in addition to those that result from reducing the number of times that work is handed off. The first step for reducing the number of steps is obtaining a thorough understanding of the work process. Process flowcharting is used for this purpose. Process flowcharts require little specialized knowledge. The left column of Figure 7.1 shows an existing process for reimbursing staff travel. Many organizations require multiple approvals from different offices. The symbols are used to identify activities and facilitate later comparison with other processes. The chart shows involvement from three offices, namely, the department that is requesting the reimbursement, the budget office, and the accounting department.

Reducing the number of steps often implies delegation of authority. Many processes are delayed because of people checking the work of other people. Gore estimates that one third of the federal workforce in Washington, D.C., is assigned duties involving checking someone else's work (Gore, 1996). A first step in reducing the number of steps is to eliminate red tape by delegating authority to people to check their own work; this reduces delays caused by handing off work, and it also speeds up improvements. A key to delegation is to ensure that accountability is provided after the fact, such as through documentation and customer satisfaction. A second step in reducing the number of steps is delegating authority to those using the services. Specifically, budgeting, purchasing, and contracting decisions should be delegated to work units rather than to separate departments. This, too, reduces steps and delays. The result of such delegations is shortened work processes. The revised reimbursement process, shown in the right column of Figure 7.1, increases the authority of the office manager and speeds up the payment process. This reduces transactions among departments as well as "signing off" procedures.

The time and quality of work is also improved by conducting work in *parallel* fashion (Stalk & Hout, 1990). For example, health assessments sometimes include a range of both physical tests and laboratory work. By conducting tests in parallel (i.e., simultaneously), final results are available sooner. Likewise, it

ACTIVITY: Travel Reimbursement
OM = Office Manager
BO = Budget Office
AD = Accounting Department

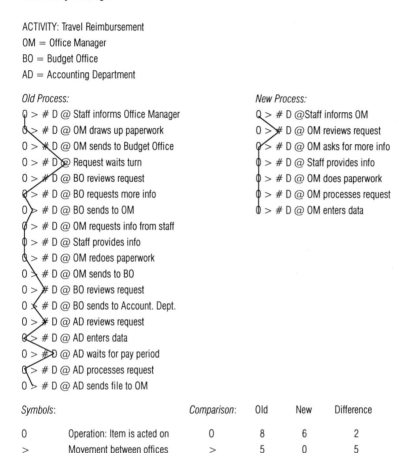

Old Process:

0 > # D @ Staff informs Office Manager
0 > # D @ OM draws up paperwork
0 > # D @ OM sends to Budget Office
0 > # D @ Request waits turn
0 > # D @ BO reviews request
0 > # D @ BO requests more info
0 > # D @ BO sends to OM
0 > # D @ OM requests info from staff
0 > # D @ Staff provides info
0 > # D @ OM redoes paperwork
0 > # D @ OM sends to BO
0 > # D @ BO reviews request
0 > # D @ BO sends to Account. Dept.
0 > # D @ AD reviews request
0 > # D @ AD enters data
0 > # D @ AD waits for pay period
0 > # D @ AD processes request
0 > # D @ AD sends file to OM

New Process:

0 > # D @ Staff informs OM
0 > # D @ OM reviews request
0 > # D @ OM asks for more info
0 > # D @ Staff provides info
0 > # D @ OM does paperwork
0 > # D @ OM processes request
0 > # D @ OM enters data

Symbols:		*Comparison:*	Old	New	Difference
0	Operation: Item is acted on	0	8	6	2
>	Movement between offices	>	5	0	5
#	Review or quality control	#	3	1	2
D	Delay or Interruption	D	2	0	2
@	Storage: Item not acted on	@	0	0	0
		Total Steps:	18	7	11

Figure 7.1. Process Flowchart

takes less time to check the background of several job candidates simultaneously rather than sequentially. Roadwork is completed more quickly when different tasks are completed in parallel fashion. It is often recommended that organizations reengineer their work process so that required steps that do not add value to customer satisfaction, such as mandatory background checks, insurance verification, check-in procedures, and so on, are conducted in parallel fashion with other steps that do add value to the customer (Linden, 1994a).

Make Better Use of Information
and Information Technology

Another reengineering principle is to improve the use and acquisition of information. First, managers should ask how providing information to others helps speed up and improve decision making. For example, when customers know ahead of time any documentation that agencies need to process their requests, they can plan to obtain such information and avoid unnecessary delays and frustration. When vendors know what agencies are looking for in their requests for proposals (e.g., low purchase price or low lifetime operating costs), they can prepare better proposals. When citizens know that roadwork will likely cause delays, they can plan to take alternate routes. Knowing how long roadwork will take, and the purposes that are served by it, also helps reduce frustration. People often make better decisions when they are given timely and accurate information in a user-friendly way.

Second, information should be gathered only once and made available to all who may have a need for it. In this regard, the use of information technology is increasingly a necessity. Integration of databases across departments reduces the need for duplication of input. It allows employees to quickly see the status of clients or projects in other departments as well as to communicate about clients or projects in an efficient and more timely manner. Information technology can help make integrated information more readily available. It can also provide clients with one-stop access to their files. Internet access increases transactions that do not require support staff. Such integrated systems are increasingly used in hospitals, universities, and social service agencies where customers engage in multiple activities, in different departments. The use of information technology speeds up transactions and allows customers to conduct transactions at their convenience. Information technology is discussed further in Chapter 9.

Finally, information is also relevant to feedback and improvement. When managers and employees receive timely feedback, they may be able to make adjustments in a more timely manner. Performance measurement systems that provide ongoing measurement of activities, outputs, and outcomes assist in this improvement effort. Data are typically provided about cycle times, waiting periods, errors, efficiency, and outcomes (Bogan & English, 1994; Hyde, 1995). A reengineering principle is that processes should include efficient and efficient feedback information. Techniques for using such information are discussed below.

A Note on Implementation

Reengineering often involves top management leadership because of changes in work processes that affect relations among departments, the functions of departments, and the skills and abilities of employees. These changes are often radical. Reengineering efforts follow the comprehensive implementation strategies discussed in Chapter 4 (Berry, 1990; Burke, 1992). The first step is to increase awareness among senior managers that fundamental review of work processes is necessary. Measures of effectiveness, frequent customer feedback procedures, and competitive processes used by other organizations are employed to make this case. The second step is to assemble a senior-level advisory group to study existing work processes and gather ideas from employees and middle managers about possible improvements. These study efforts frequently use process flowcharting to better understand existing work processes.

The third step is to create a pilot project team that consists of motivated employees and managers who will be affected by changes. This group further refines the suggested change, implements the proposed change on a trial or mock basis (e.g., through role-playing), and develops operational plans for both the reengineered process and the transition. Mock trials help specify the requirements of reengineered work processes and identify bugs and sources of errors. Transition planning is also used and involves the development of information technologies, employee training programs, policies, and procedures for reassigning employees. Of particular importance is the pilot development of *cross-training*. Cross-training involves employees' learning the skills of multiple, related positions. Cross-training is critical to the success one-stop shopping efforts, and it also speeds up parallel work efforts, reduces errors by decreasing the number of times that work is handled, and decreases unnecessary delays and underuse of costly specialists. However, cross-training often creates confusion because of changes in employee time schedules and performance expectations. For this reason, cross-training should also first be tried on a small-scale, pilot basis.

The fourth step is actual implementation. Communication is key. Managers need to explain to employees why changes are necessary as well as how employees will be assisted in making adjustments and, in some cases, finding a new job in the organization. Preparatory steps include infrastructure adjustments such as counters for one-stop shopping programs and rerouting of computer cables as well as training and development (cross-training as well, for example, in customer service). Actual implementation involves using reengineered work processes for the first time. This is a short but sometimes crisis-laden period: Although some problems are anticipated due to the successful pilot effort, many unexpected events and situations will still occur. The follow-through period is characterized by integrating new situations into work processes and settling down into new routines. Team leaders fulfill counseling roles during this phase; the development of new teams is a period of transition that induces anxiety. This is usually punctuated by the development of new procedure and training manuals. The final phase is institutionalization and normalization of work processes.

Analytical Techniques
for Continuous Improvement

Continuous improvement is both *a management philosophy and a set of analytic tools* to identify problems and monitor progress. As a management philosophy, continuous improvement (CI) is based on the belief that almost any process can be improved and that it is virtuous to do so. Improvement is consistent with providing better service and using organizational resources more effectively and efficiently. Although different authors vary somewhat in their approaches, CI usually involves the following four steps of problem solving (Milakovich, 1995): (a) identifying the problem, (b) analyzing causes, (c) planning and undertaking corrective action, and (d) monitoring and evaluating results.

Identifying the Problem

CI assumes the existence of improvement opportunities. TQM strategies use employees to identify problems as well as improvement efforts: Unit employees are often keenly aware of work process problems and may have suggestions for improvement. Quality circles consist of unit employees who engage in a collaborative effort to identify which problem they wish to address. Brainstorming and group discussion are techniques that are used for this purpose. Internal assessments are also complemented by surveys or focus groups of internal and external customers to provide additional perspectives.

In most organizations, there is no shortage of problems to be addressed. The problem therefore is to prioritize among competing problems. A tendency exists to work on very large problems, but these may involve issues that are beyond the sphere of influence of the unit. Quality circles should work on those problems that they can affect. The following criteria are commonly used to select problems: (a) The problem can be addressed and resolved by the group; (b) the level of effort appears to be feasible given time, resources, and authority; and (c) resolution of the problem, if possible, would have a large impact. The first two criteria are screening criteria (pass/no pass), whereas the latter requires assessing the consequence of the problem.

Impact analysis is an analytical technique that can help prioritize problems. It requires that units assign points to the following questions:

1. What percentage of our customers are affected by the problem?
   Scale: 3 = > 75%; 2 = 40%-75%; 1 = 10%-39%; 0 = < 10%

2. How important is the impact of the problem on customers, on average?
   Scale: 3 = critical, 2 = important, 1 = somewhat important, 0 = not important

3. How often does the problem occur?
   Scale: 3 = very often, 2 = often, 1 = from time to time, 0 = seldom

The scores that are assigned to the responses of each question are added up. This technique helps identify the most important problems. In some instances, additional data are available that support these assessments, such as the number of client complaints or problems over time; the nature or type of complaints; or the problems by location, service type, service period, or customer or employee category. However, additional considerations may be necessary to sort out the top problems, for example, consistency with other improvements or planning efforts.

Another approach for determining the magnitude of problems is the *cost of poor quality.* This analytic approach has two major steps: First, a process flowchart is designed similar to that shown in Figure 7.1 and the cost of each step is determined. Often, smaller steps are combined into larger ones for the purpose of determining costs. Second, errors and other quality problems (such as delays, overwork, rework) are identified for each step, and the cost of correcting each error is determined. Often, the cost of correcting errors is substantial in relation to the overall cost, and in most cases the cost of errors justifies further efforts to find ways to prevent errors. In this regard, Kline (1995) notes that although prevention requires resources, experience suggests that for every $1 of prevention, about $10 of problems are avoided.

Analyzing Causes of the Problem

Often, problems that are identified are, upon further analysis, but symptoms or consequences of the processes that give rise to them. For example, the "problem" of customer complaints is actually the consequence of work processes

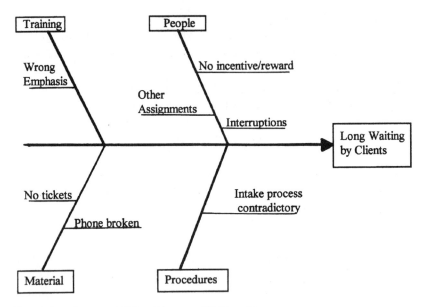

Figure 7.2. Cause-and-Effect Diagram ("Fishbone")

that give rise to dissatisfaction. This second step aims to identify such consequences and work processes. For example, customer complaints about inaccurate billing may reflect poor communication between departments, clerical errors in data input or processing, unauthorized access to computers by employees (resulting in unforeseen errors), and bills that are not sent on time. Mapping the work process is essential to tracing the source of errors. Work processes reveal steps that may give rise to problems as well as steps that may be missing; for example, long waiting periods for customers may reflect a lack of scheduling as a needed step.

An analytical tool that helps identify causes of incomplete or "wrong" steps is a cause-and-effect or fishbone diagram (Koehler & Pankowski, 1996). This is a brainstorming tool that helps focus on problems of training, people, material, and procedures that cause the faulty work process to occur. The causes of errors are identified on the diagonals such that the resulting figure resembles a fishbone. Figure 7.2 shows an example of a fishbone diagram. This figure shows that interruptions are one of several causes of long waits.

Regardless of whether a fishbone diagram is used, after the causes of faulty work process steps have been identified, it is necessary to identify those that will be addressed. It is a common experience that although problems have many

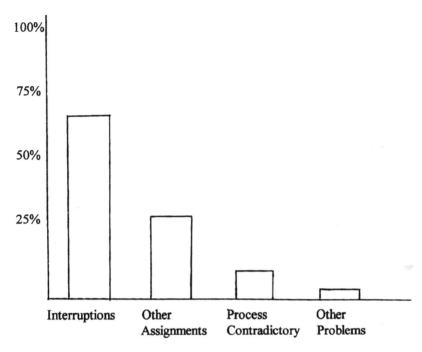

Figure 7.3. Frequency Chart ("Pareto")

causes, some causes occur more often or are of greater significance. It is important to direct efforts to those causes that are most important. Although managers may deselect those that are of minor importance, they must address those causes that greatly contribute to the faulty work process. An analytical technique to help identify such causes is a frequency chart that displays the frequency of each in descending order; thus frequently occurring causes are readily observed from this chart (see Figure 7.3). In TQM, such charts are also called "Pareto" charts, named after the Italian economist who noted that in many countries 80% of the wealth was held by only 20% of the population. Likewise, in many work processes, a few problems often account for the majority of reasons for poor quality. In practice, such data are not always available or are very costly to gather. Although managers should seek out empirical data, in some instances managers will have to rely on their hunches and those of employees. Managers must then select important causes by asking employees and managers to rank them individually and subsequently determine the sum of their rankings.

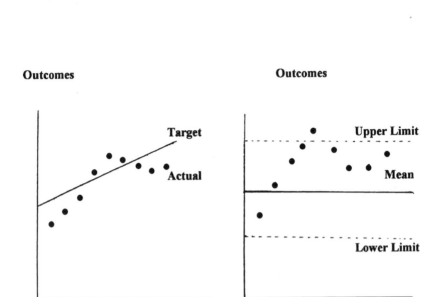

Figure 7.4. Time-Series and Control Charts

Plan, Implement, and Monitor Corrective Action

The purpose of corrective action is to try to *eliminate* the causes at hand. This usually involves process reengineering, discussed above. When the faulty step is reengineered out of existence, the causes may disappear (assuming they are not part of other work processes too). When this is not possible, the objective may be to greatly reduce the frequency of the cause. In any event, the performance of the new process must be monitored. Standards for improvement should be set, for example, at monthly or quarterly intervals. At these intervals, actual performance is compared against these standards. Actual performance can be presented graphically using a time series or control chart, as shown in Figure 7.4. It is common to analyze deviations from these preset standards, shown as target outcomes (time series) and upper or lower limits (control chart).[3] Variations are sometimes discussed in terms of "special causes" and "normal variations."

BOX 7.2.
Analytical Tools in Action

Performance measurement is increasingly used by public and nonprofit organizations to identify levels of accomplishment and, through quality management, to set numerical goals for future improvement. Among local governments, the City of Phoenix, Arizona, is widely regarded as a leader: Almost all of its departments use some form of performance measurement. Results are compared across time periods and with other cities. Such measurement also strengthens communication with citizens and clients who wish to know how well public and nonprofit organizations are doing (Fairbanks, 1996).

Public and nonprofit organizations have numerous opportunities for continuous improvement. For example, many universities use student feedback to evaluate and improve their student services. Benchmarks are set for student use of and satisfaction with career placement services. In this regard, job placement is important to the ability of private universities to command high tuition rates. Performance measurement is also used to evaluate services such as parking, registration, and enrollment, as well as teaching quality. Standards are set for each, and targets set for annual improvement. Standards are even set for improvement itself. To assist in these efforts, services are tracked and performance data are made available on a monthly basis. Organizations also conduct numerous surveys and focus groups to better understand the causes of satisfaction. The results of such efforts are displayed as Pareto charts.

However, top management leadership is critical to the success of such efforts. Units may set targets that are low and thus readily satisfied. They may also resist publishing results of their client or citizen surveys. Some units may even alter the results of their performance measures to buy time for necessary improvements. Overall, tools of continuous improvement have no inherent value other than the way in which they are used by managers to improve productivity. Therefore, to show commitment to improvement, some public and nonprofit organizations are now tying manager compensation to department performance. In these instances, cost-of-living adjustments often fall short of actual inflation and managers depend on merit pay increases. Leadership is also shown by making continuous improvement part

---

Normal variations are random variations that occur as part of processes. "Special causes" are nonrandom variations that suggest unfavorable patterns or frequent outliers. These variations require further study and improvement, using the tools mentioned above. The study of variations is especially important in such activities as administrative error rates, response time of emergency medical services, and errors made by air traffic control systems.

Implementation requires that employees assume responsibility for tasks that are either assigned or volunteered. The scope of tasks varies depending on the extent of reengineering that is required. Some extensive efforts may use time lines or Gantt charts to ensure that efforts are undertaken and completed. It is recommended that members of quality circles, when used, communicate on a regular basis about their progress. This shows commitment by managers and creates opportunities to monitor progress, such as through time charts, and to deal with unanticipated obstacles. Box 7.2 discusses performance measurement and leadership in connection with these analytical techniques.

Summary

This chapter discusses the quality paradigm in productivity improvement. The quality paradigm emphasizes a customer orientation and encompasses various strategies such as customer empowerment, benchmarking, a customer service orientation, reengineering, and continuous improvement; this chapter discusses the latter three strategies. A customer orientation focuses services on the needs of specific customers, ensures customer-oriented behavior, and measures customer satisfaction. Reengineering aims to reduce unresponsiveness by redesigning how services are produced and delivered. Continuous improvement is a philosophy and strategy for identifying and correcting problems of work processes that cause poor quality and customer dissatisfaction. All three strategies emphasize the importance of monitoring improvement through measurement. This chapter also discusses the importance of implementation.

Notes

1. Wholesale change efforts sometimes follow incremental or isolated change in different units. Also, wholesale change strategies often experience "uneven" progress by different units, causing some units to be ahead of the curve.

2. When top management provides support for change to the lower levels of the organization, top management becomes the customer of these lower units. A challenge is to get top managers to see themselves in this "servant leadership" role.

3. When more than 20 observations are available, upper and lower critical limits are easily found by calculating the standard deviation of the data. Observations that lie within two standard deviations from the mean are usually not considered outliers. When fewer than 20 observations

are available, the analyst must consult control chart tables, which are found in books that discuss quality tools and measurements (e.g., Rosander, 1989, p. 498).

References

Bedwell, R. (1993). Total Quality Management: Making the decision. *Nonprofit World, 11*(3), 29-31.

Berman, E. (1995). Implementing TQM in state welfare agencies. *Administration in Social Work, 19*(1), 55-72.

Berman, E., & West, J. (1995). Municipal commitment to Total Quality Management. *Public Administration Review, 55*(1), 57-66.

Berman, E., & West, J. (1997). Total Quality Management in local government. In J. Gargan (Ed.), *Handbook of local government administration* (pp. 213-238). New York: Marcel Dekker.

Berry, T. (1990). *Managing the total quality transformation.* New York: McGraw-Hill.

Bogan, C., & English, M. (1994). *Benchmarking for best practices.* New York: McGraw-Hill.

Brown, M., Hitchcock, D., & Willard, M. (1994). *Why TQM fails and what to do about it.* Chicago: Irwin.

Burke, W. (1992). *Organization development.* Reading, MA: Addison-Wesley.

Carter, M. (1993). How to be a role model in the quest for quality. *Nonprofit World, 11*(5), 30-34.

Champy, J., & Hammer, M. (1993). *Reengineering the corporation.* London: Nicholas Brealy.

Connors, T. (1992). Avoiding "quality shock": Nonprofits and the National Quality Award. *Nonprofit World, 10*(4), 25-28.

Denhardt, R. (1997). Local governments learn to put citizens first. *PA Times, 20*(2), 1-2.

Fairbanks, F. (1996). Managing for results. *Public Management, 78*(1), 12-15.

General Accounting Office. (1993). *Quality management: Survey of federal organizations.* Washington, DC: Government Printing Office.

Gore, A. (1996). *The best kept secrets in government.* New York: Random House.

Halachmi, A. (1995). Is TQM ready for the public sector? In A. Halachmi & G. Bouckaert (Eds.), *Public productivity through quality and strategic management* (pp. 257-270). Washington, DC: IOS Press.

Hunt, V. (1993). *Quality management for government.* Milwaukee, WI: Quality Press.

Hyde, A. (1995). A primer on process reengineering. *Public Manager, 24*(1), 55-68.

Kennedy, L. (1991). *Quality management in the nonprofit world.* San Francisco: Jossey-Bass.

Koehler, J., & Pankowski, J. (1996). *Continual improvement in government: Tools and methods.* Delray Beach, FL: St. Lucie Press.

Kline, J. (1995). Quality tools are applicable to local government. In J. West (Ed.), *Quality management today* (pp. 120-132). Washington, DC: International City/County Management Association.

Leland, K., & Bailey, K. (1995). *Customer service for dummies.* Foster City, CA: IDG.

Linden, R. (1994a). *MIS report: Re-engineering local government.* Washington, DC: International City/County Management Association.

Linden, R. (1994b). Reengineering to capture the customer's voice. *Public Manager, 23*(2), 47-50.

McAdoo, S., & Pynes, J. (1995). Reinventing mental health service delivery: One nonprofit's experience. *Public Administration Quarterly, 19*(3), 367-374.

McClendon, B. (1992). *Customer service in local government.* Chicago: American Planning Association.

Milakovich, M. (1995). *Improving service quality: Achieving high performance in the public and private sectors.* Delray Beach, FL: St. Lucie Press.

Miller, G. (1995). Reengineering: Forty useful hints. *Hospital Material Management Quarterly, 17*(2), 37-46.

Patten, T. (1995). Beyond systems: The politics of managing in a TQM environment. In J. West (Ed.), *Quality management today.* Washington, DC: ICMA.

Rosander, A. (1989). *The quest for quality in services.* Milwaukee, WI: Quality Press

Stalk, G., & Hout, T. (1990). *Competing against time.* New York: Free Press.

Van Wart, M. (1996). Reinventing in the public sector: The critical role of value restructuring. *Public Administration Quarterly, 20*(4), 456-478.

West, J. (1995). *Quality management today.* Washington, DC: International City/County Management Association.

Whiteley, R., & Hessan, D. (1996). *Customer-centered growth.* Reading, MA: Addison-Wesley.

8

Improving Efficiency

▓▓▓▓ Through efficiency improvements, public and nonprofit organizations are able to build more roads per tax dollar, serve more clients per staff person, oversee more inmates with less staff, and manage organizations with lower overhead costs. Efficiency strategies help organizations by addressing such problems as rising service demands, budget shortfalls, and competition from alternative service providers. *Efficiency* is defined as the ratio of outcomes or outputs to inputs. Stakeholders expect organizations to increase their efficiency, and organizations are sometimes compared on the basis of their efficiency. Some public and nonprofit organizations are also touted as models of efficiency, and managers increase their reputations by ensuring that their organizations are among the most efficient.

A wide range of efficiency strategies exist. Ayres and Kettinger (1983) state that organizations can improve their efficiency by achieving (a) lower costs and greater outcomes, (b) lower costs and the same level of outcomes, (c) increased outcomes with the same costs, (d) higher costs and even greater outcomes, and (e) a decrease in outcomes that is matched by an even greater decrease in costs. For example, using fewer caseworkers to treat more clients exemplifies the first strategy, and using information technology is often an example of the fourth strategy. This chapter examines efforts to increase efficiency by reducing costs, increasing revenues, and improving the effectiveness of resources to produce efficiency gains. Numerous examples and applications are included.

It bears repeating that efficiency is but one of several values of productivity improvement. Managers must balance efficiency with effectiveness, without which managers may fail to satisfy their stakeholders. This problem is further exacerbated when workload measures are substituted for outcome measures, for example, when school systems pursue increased teacher workloads at the expense of student graduation rates. Nonetheless, efficiency is also important, and managers must continuously strive to increase it. Stakeholders expect efficiency improvements. The following strategies, in conjunction with those of reengineering (Chapter 7), are increasingly a staple of management practice.

Decreasing Costs, Raising Revenues

Efficiency gains are often pursued by reducing costs. Substituting resources with less costly ones, while maintaining outcomes, increases the ratio of outcomes to inputs and hence efficiency. The analysis of costs is therefore an important subject of productivity. Important cost-reducing strategies include using volunteers and clients in service delivery, and reducing other costs such as rent, equipment, and fringe benefits.

Using Volunteers, Interns, and Clients

Personnel costs often constitute more than 60% of program expenditures, and the use of volunteers, interns, and clients in service delivery reduces personnel costs. A distinctive characteristic of nonprofit organizations is their use of volunteers as ushers in museums, as caregivers in hospitals, as coordinators for local chapters of the humane society, and so on. Many governments also use volunteers. For example, libraries and parks services have active volunteer programs, and police departments too are using volunteers for clerical tasks, victim assistance, surveillance, and graffiti eradication (Liddell, 1995; Markwood, 1994). It is estimated that about 100 million Americans donate their time each year for volunteer activities: Three quarters of all volunteered time, about 16 billion hours, is undertaken in organizations, and the estimated market value of this time is $170 million. About 70% of these volunteer efforts are undertaken in nonprofit organizations (Brudney, 1994).

The use of volunteers requires a careful management plan. Organizations should have cogent reasons for using volunteers. Cost substitution is a key reason, but other goals include building bridges with community groups, obtaining access to skilled support, and increasing service delivery by using volunteers to leverage current funds (Connors, 1995; Coolsen, 1992). Volunteers are often used for tasks that are incidental or performed periodically rather than those that are undertaken frequently or daily: Because they are not paid, volunteers often have other commitments and are seldom available for tasks that must be performed on a continuous basis. Typical activities for which volunteers might be used are activities that require either very low skills or skills that are not found within the organization. For example, people require relatively few skills and little training to be ushers or support staff in social or community events. Professionals also volunteer their services, such as lawyers who donate their services to provide local coalitions for the homeless or builders who donate their professional expertise to Habitat for the Humanity projects.

Volunteers must be budgeted for; they are not a free resource. Volunteers often require considerable recruitment, training, and development as well as the resolution of cost-reimbursement and liability issues. In some instances, volunteers receive nonsalary benefits such as those who join the Peace Corps or AmeriCorps. Volunteers require training and orientation on organizational workplace policies (such as regarding sexual harassment and use of property), evaluation and grievance procedures, and benefits and absenteeism policies, as applicable. Recruiting volunteers also requires considerable effort. Although some organizations have a plethora of people who want to volunteer their time, in many instances staff must be appointed to obtain the "right" volunteers. Once accepted, management must find meaningful tasks for them or risk that they leave the organization. Directive and punitive management styles may cause volunteers to quit and should be avoided. Volunteers must also receive feedback regarding their efforts (demonstrating that their contributions are taken seriously) and be guided to help improve them when necessary. Thus volunteers are indeed not a free resource.

A second strategy for reducing labor costs is using interns, who differ from volunteers in that they are typically seeking an opportunity to prove themselves, to obtain a quality learning experience, and to improve their marketability at the end of the internship. Many seek to be hired by the organization that is providing them with the internship opportunity. Internships are also different than volunteering in that they are closed-ended commitments. Organizations benefit from interns because they are inexpensive (requiring a stipend or nothing), usually highly motivated, and skilled (albeit inexperienced), and they provide organizations with an opportunity to observe a candidate carefully without making employment commitments. However, organizations misuse interns when they fail to support the learning and employment objectives of interns, such as when interns are only used for menial tasks and are not offered any prospect of employment. Organizations benefit from developing a quality internship program that meets their needs as well as those of interns (Pierson, 1992).

Third, organizations are increasingly involving their program clients in service delivery. Public and nonprofit organizations reduce costs by creating "partnerships" with their clients, that is, requiring clients to assume some responsibilities for the services that they receive. For example, food processing plants are increasingly required to provide to regulators with more timely and accurate safety data as well as detailed documentation of their self-inspections; professional sports organizations are asked to bear the costs of their own public safety; developers are asked to work with government officials to prepare impact assessments; and so on. Public and nonprofit organizations must explain to their clients the rationale for their increased involvement and the specific roles and activities that they are expected to fulfill. For example, food processing companies may be required to develop more detailed risk management plans and to guarantee the payment of costs that are associated with emergencies involving their products or services: They, rather than government, become responsible for sorting out liability issues.

Finally, many organizations are also using temporary workers to fill emergency needs. Such workers are seldom cheap, but they do eliminate the need for hiring full-time staff that might be underused in subsequent periods. They also allow employers an opportunity to better screen employees before hiring them. A variety of other strategies include using part-time employees (who may require fewer benefits) and staff that is "on loan" from other agencies, organizations, or units.

Audit, Audit, Audit

Organizations incur a wide range of expenses and need an annual plan for examining their costs at different intervals. For example, rents should be examined annually (three to six months prior to lease renewal); employee benefits and office equipment expenditures should be examined biannually (but in different months); phone expenses are monitored on a quarterly basis; and so on. Managers need to develop and execute a plan for improving their cost structures.

Employee compensation and benefits. Total compensation includes salary, health care benefits, tuition reimbursement, retirement contributions, vacation and sick leave, and child/elder care support as well as performance incentives and other bonuses. Organizations undertake different strategies to control these costs. First, in recent years, many organizations have reduced the rate of accelerating health care benefits by switching from traditional health care indemnity programs to those of managed health care. These programs achieve considerable cost savings while, in some instances, only slightly reducing coverage but significantly increasing copayments and deductibles. Many public and nonprofit organizations find it profitable to use benefits consultants who monitor health insurance trends and identify less costly alternatives while ensuring competitive and attractive employee benefits. Second, organizations also review other benefits such as tuition and continuing education programs. Some organizations limit total tuition costs rather the number of classes that employees can be reimbursed for. This discourages the use of more costly private universities. Third, to reduce salary costs, organizations are increasingly using merit-based salary adjustments rather than providing full cost-of-living adjustments. Market-based adjustments are made from time to time when salary levels fall markedly behind those of labor markets for specific job classifications. Organizations also encourage hiring recent graduates rather than more costly experienced staff. However, organizations must balance these cost-reduction strategies with the need to maintain competitive pay and benefits structures that attract and retain quality employees. These cost-reduction practices are also more difficult in public organizations that have collective bargaining practices (Cayer, 1997).

Rent. Many office leases contain clauses that cause lease payments to increase over time. Managers should periodically review lease costs based on a comparative analysis of similar properties in the area. Such analyses are often provided by commercial real estate agents. Managers should also familiarize themselves with local regulations that may exempt landlords from part of their real estate taxes when a significant part of buildings are occupied by nonprofit organizations. Awareness of such regulations increases the bargaining power of nonprofit organizations in lease negotiations. Finally, nonprofit organizations should consider ownership rather than office rental: Because nonprofit organizations are unable to raise money by issuing equity investments, real estate is an important asset against which business loans can be secured (Ries & Alstadler, 1994).

Equipment. Organizations often must choose between leasing or buying office equipment and furniture. These decisions require careful analysis, especially because leasing and maintenance terms change over time. The following is a lease/buy analysis involving a photocopier:

Annual cost to lease ($273.69 × 12 months =):	$3,284.28
Annual maintenance cost ($165.00 × 12 months =):	$1,980.00
Annualized purchase cost (purchase price of $2,040, 3 years in service, 10% interest, and no salvage value =):[1]	$820.31
Savings from purchasing	$483.97

Despite cost savings from purchasing, continuing increases in service contracts and improvements in leasing terms (such as providing new-model machines each year) make leases more attractive. Lease terms frequently change and managers need to periodically review previous lease/buy decisions. Computers are an increasingly important equipment cost. The average lifetime of computers in the recent past has been about 2.5 years, and new models are increasingly necessary to operate newer software. This suggests that public and nonprofit organizations should budget these costs as operating rather than capital expenses.

Organizations should also consider the full-life cost of equipment rather than the bid or purchase price. The full-life cost of equipment includes (a) the expected lifetime and salvage value of equipment; (b) maintenance and repair costs; (c) energy costs (which often exceed the purchase price of such items as lightbulbs, motors, and cooling devices); and (d) failure costs, that is, the impact of equipment failure on other items and operations. When full costs are figured into the acquisition decision, the purchase price is sometimes not the determining factor.

Operating expenses. Energy, phone, and mailing costs are substantial in many public and nonprofit organizations. Managers frequently audit these costs and achieve many cost savings. First, many local utilities now provide free energy audits and may be able to suggest savings on current equipment. Second, phone companies often change their rate structures, and periodic research may suggest advantages from changing long distance and cellular carriers as well as Internet access providers. Third, many public and nonprofit organizations reduce their mailing expenditures by using bulk mail and postcards. They also use mail meters and companies that specialize in providing mailing lists. Fourth, costs can also be reduced by borrowing or pooling resources with other organizations, such as warehousing and transportation services. Fifth, computer maintenance costs are increasingly important. Although many organizations employ in-house technicians to provide support, others are finding cost-effective ways to contract for and pool this resource.

Sixth, organizations need to review their insurance costs too. The lack of adequate insurance is a major liability that can offset potential savings. Organizations require different types of insurance. General liability insurance covers most bodily injury and property damage claims, but managers must ensure that such insurance includes volunteers, too. Liability insurance usually excludes damage that is caused by the use of vehicles. Automobile insurance must be purchased separately for organization-owned cars, and many organizations require their employees to carry their own automobile insurance. Board and director's insurance is necessary to protect board members against the consequences of litigation filed against their organization. Umbrella insurance fills gaps in coverage, such as lawsuits that concern various forms of wrongdoing. In general, the insurance market is volatile and periodic reexamination of rates and coverage can provide substantial cost savings.[2]

Raising Revenues

Three frequent alternative revenue strategies are (a) fund-raising, (b) enterprise (including fees for service and licensing), and (c) obtaining grants. By seeking alternative revenues, public and nonprofit organizations increase the leverage (or efficiency) of traditional income sources.[3]

Fund-raising. In social service organizations, private donations often constitute 20% to 40% of total revenue, and many nonprofit organizations have well-developed fund-raising programs. Successful fund-raising efforts help meet the matching requirements of funding agencies and often signal that the organization and its programs are well understood and accepted in a community. By contrast, unsuccessful fund-raising efforts imply that programs and services have little support in the community. Although organizations undertake fund-raising to increase their revenue, successful fund-raising is usually premised on the ability of the organization to satisfy important values or needs of donors. Donors give so as to show their support to organizations. For example, university presidents spend considerable time explaining the purpose and relationship of their institution to community and business needs. Donors usually start by giving small amounts and, as they become more comfortable with the organization's accomplishments, may make larger gifts.

Fund-raising involves a broad range of activities. Activities such as mass mailings or telethons often result in many small gifts. Most such pledges are under $100, but some are larger. The efficiency of telethons depends in large measure on the extent to which individuals have given in prior years: It is less costly to obtain pledges from those who have given in the past. A strategic reason for conducting telethons is the recruitment of future donors. Depending on various factors, the fund-raising cost per dollar raised through mail and phone campaigns is often $0.75 to $1.25 for first-time donors and about $0.25 to .$0.40 for repeat mail and phone donors, hence justifying the high cost of acquiring first-time donors (Smith, 1994). Special events such as galas often target donors who have given previously at special events or during telethons. Those who are good prospects for $100 to $1,000 donations are targeted. Annual galas are often followed by capital campaigns and other special fund-raising projects. These help accommodate a large number of donors. Large gifts are usually made to organizations with which donors have long-term relations or affinity. Such individuals are identified and attended to by organizational leaders. According to Fogal (1994), the efficiency of special events and large gifts is about $.20 to $.50 per dollar raised, and many social service organizations that raise $160,000 annually can expect to receive 60% of their total donations from gifts that are greater than $500.

In sum, fund-raising requires considerable leadership, management, and coordination. Leaders must set annual goals, develop a vision for donors, and commit resources to a range of fund-raising efforts. Fund-raising is a rewarding but long-term strategy (Rushkin, 1995; Wagner, 1992).

Enterprise. Public and nonprofit organizations are increasingly engaged in new forms of enterprise. Fee-for-service arrangements are increasingly common, such as requiring citizens to pay for garbage collection or passport applications or requiring businesses to pay for the cost of their inspections and licenses. These "cost-recovery" practices allow general revenues to stretch further. The ability to charge fees for services is, of course, in part contingent on the willingness of clients to pay for services, the ability to collect payments, and, for public organizations, the impact on low-income groups. Many organizations are also raising money through cause-related marketing and licensing. As discussed in Chapter 5, many arts organizations now market themselves through large corporations, that pay for advertisements and often contribute large donations. Large corporations benefit by affiliating themselves with socially valued causes. In other instances, organizations license their names or logos for commercial products, or engage in sales of merchandise. Examples include the New York Metropolitan Museum of Art as well as most major universities, which now sell "official" T-shirts, coffee cups, beach towels, pens, and so forth. It is important to note that although nonprofit organizations are generally exempt from taxation, they may be taxed for profits that the Internal Revenue Service deems are derived from unrelated business. This is also the case when public and nonprofit organizations engage in business partnerships or develop revenue-raising subsidiaries (Burgers & van Vleuten, 1992).

Grants. Grants remain a key source of funding for nonprofit organizations. They are also becoming increasingly important for many state and local governments as they attempt to meet rising demands with stagnant revenues. For example, the federal government's Enterprise Zone grant program for rehabilitation and development of blighted areas has attracted substantial response from local governments. Because many grants and contracts are payments for specific services or accomplishments, the credibility of nonprofit agencies to perform is key to successfully obtaining grants. Although credibility is somewhat addressed through staff qualifications, experience, previous success, and detailed plans, long-term familiarity between grantee and grantor is also important: Successful leaders often engage in visible community leadership and continuing dialogue with granting agencies, often through the advocacy of board members. Such dialogue helps both sides better understand each other's needs and may result in requests for proposals (RFPs) that are tailored to specific capabilities. In recent years, a growing problem has also been that many fixed cost grants fail to cover actual program costs. This causes a need for raising matching funds as well as pursing other cost-reduction and efficiency increasing strategies, which are also discussed below.

Increasing Efficiency

Whereas the above strategies aim to reduce costs and increase revenues other strategies aim to increase the efficiency of resources. These strategies are variously called industrial engineering, operations research, and management science approaches to productivity improvement. As discussed in Chapter 1, these approaches were first developed in the early 1900s as principles of scientific management and industrial engineering, and were further developed as operations research (OR) during World War II and thereafter for solving a variety of defense and business problems related to inventory, scheduling, and transportation. Some approaches were also applied later to complex social problems, such as studies that evaluate the impact of pollution, population growth, resource scarcity, and other conditions involving the global ecosystem and human survival. Many of these approaches are no longer new, but they continue to have widespread application: For example, work-flow analysis is currently used in reengineering (Chapter 7). Some applications require the use of computers for simulation and estimation, and this section discusses those that require computer-based analysis as well as those that do not (Levin, Rubin, Stinson, & Gardner, 1989; Starr, 1996).

Operations research tools solve well-structured problems, and managers must think creatively about how situations or problems in their organizations relate to the range of problems that are relevant to different tools. Many OR techniques also make assumptions that require "what-if" analyses without which their validity is rightfully questioned. OR techniques should be used by managers as tools that help force open and structure discussions, rather than as those that dictate a particular course of action, which these do not (Keys, 1995). It should be noted that some tools associated with Chapters 7 (quality and reengineering) and 9 (project management) are also considered to be a part of operations research, but they are not discussed here.

Task Analysis

Many efficiency techniques were first developed to deal with factory work processes in the early 1990s. Researchers studied in great detail the tasks that workers performed. From these early studies, principles were derived for increasing the efficiency of repetitive work processes. Some important principles of work design are as follows (Haynes, 1980):

- Work should be conveniently located within arc of forearm motions.
- Work tools should be easy to find and within range.
- Disparate tasks should be combined into separate lots.
- Distractions should be minimized.
- Motion patterns should be varied to reduce muscle stress.
- Good working conditions should be maintained (good lighting, minimal noise, etc.).
- Employees should avoid lifting heavy objects; they should slide objects instead.
- Employees should avoid physical exertion, for example, by minimizing upper arm motions.

These basic principles are still applicable today. For example, employees should have printers conveniently located so they do not have to leave their work area; frequently used files should be well organized and kept within range; different jobs should done at different times (e.g., travel vouchers done only twice each week); lighting should be adequate; and employees should avoid injury by taking sensible precautions such as using movers to move heavy objects and adopting good work posture. Managers can improve the efficiency of repetitive tasks by applying the above principles. Often, workers are well aware of inefficiencies that affect them and they welcome improvement: For example, many employees readily prefer personal ink jets rather than central laser jets as printing devices so that they do not need to stand up and leave their work area each time they need to print a computer file. Doing so is tiring as well as distracting.[4]

Another problem is that employees frequently travel to central printers, filing cabinets, and other spaces. Two main strategies for minimizing travel time are (a) bringing destinations and those who frequent them most closer together and (b) bundling activities that involve travel so that these activities require fewer trips. Although the cost of office travel is often minimal for individual employees, the aggregate cost is often significant. For example, many offices have only one photocopier per floor. Assume that the average, one-way travel time between workstations and the photocopier is 20 seconds. When 25 people travel to the copier on average five times each day, the total travel time is $(25 \times 5 \times 20 \times 2 =)$ 5,000 seconds or 1.39 hours per day. This is equivalent to $(1.39 \times 5 \times 52 =)$ 361 hours per year, or about \$4,514 per floor per year (assuming about \$12.50 per hour average total compensation per worker). This cost is greater than the annual lease price calculated above. In many offices, a small number of people use the machine most, for example, assistants and office managers. Savings are possible by relocating the photocopiers closer to them. These savings are further increased by moving machines away from extremely disadvantageous locations such as corner offices and by bundling photocopying needs into fewer trips. (This finding also demonstrates the utility of fully specifying and calculating all costs.)

Other travel examples involve the location of nurses' stations in hospitals and trips to equipment storage sheds. Of particular interest is the increased use of case management systems in large hospitals. When nurses or social workers are assigned to inpatients, they must follow them through the different units that they traverse: intake, surgery, postsurgery, various floors such as oncology and infectious diseases, and rehabilitation. In large, campus-style hospital complexes, this requires enormous travel time, which includes waiting for elevators. The above calculations are then used to assess the cost of such proposed care. Also important is travel time outside offices. Organizations increasingly use dispatchers to coordinate employee travel for health inspections, police patrols, park repair and maintenance activities, and social service home visits. By coordinating the travel needs of different employees, it is often possible to greatly diminish this expense.

Task analysis usually involves repetitive tasks. The efficiency of repetitive, multitask jobs is also increased by applying work-flow analysis and process reengineering, discussed in Chapter 7. However, these techniques are seldom used for nonrepetitive tasks because the cost of analysis seldom justifies the efficiency gains. The efficiency of nonrepetitive tasks is increased in a variety of ways, including project management, which is discussed in Chapter 9.

Staffing Analysis

Work staffing is often an important productivity issue. When employees are assigned to several unrelated tasks, they may be unable to focus sufficiently on each task, and thus commit errors or fail to meet expectations for quality (Haynes, 1980). When several employees are assigned to do the same task, they may get in each other's way: This increases the need for coordination and the management of personal style differences. When employees are assigned to do tasks that lesser qualified employees can undertake, efficiency suffers because tasks can be accomplished more cheaply. Staffing analysis provides objective data for addressing these issues. Although it seldom conclusively "proves" the existence of such problems, it does help structure discussion (Ammons, 1991).

The first step of staffing analysis is to identify jobs that units need to fulfill. For example, museum marketing and public relations departments undertake regular mailings to a wide range of patrons about upcoming events. They also conduct fund-raising special events, such as preopening shows of exhibitions or special, black-tie gala performances of opera and other performing arts. In addition, they conduct surveys of visitors and are responsible for the design and distribution of posters and advertisements of upcoming events. These tasks are identified, as shown in Figure 8.1.

The second step is to identify employees who are involved in these jobs and to identify the amount of time that each person spends on these jobs, that is, a distribution of time for each activity in which he or she is involved. Such data are not usually available, unless staff are accustomed to filling out detailed work/time reports. Rather, such data are estimated through conversations with staff. These data are entered in the Staffing Analysis Table. The third step is to determine how much time is spent by the collective unit on each job.

At this point, several potential problems of staffing may be suggested. First, it may become apparent that some tasks do not have the involvement of those

TABLE 8.1 Staffing Analysis: Museum Marketing Department

Activity	Total	Director	Staff 1	Staff 2	Staff 3	Assistant
Fund-raising						
Direct mail	8.0	0.5	0.5			7.0
Special events	15.0	3.0	6.0	3.0		3.0
Patrons	3.0	0.5	2.5			
Corporate	6.0			6.0		
Survey						
Visitors	4.0					4.0
Citizens, other	0.0					
Graphics						
Design	4.0			4.0		
Production	5.0			4.0		1.0
Media relations						
Promotion	14.0		5.0		9.0	
Advertisement	8.5		5.5		2.0	1.0
Database						
List management	5.5		0.5			5.0
Education	2.0			2.0		
Other	16.0	15.0	1.0			
Leave	4.0	2.0		2.0		
Total Staff	95.0	21.0	21.0	21.0	11.0	21.0

NOTE: Estimated days per month (21 working days).

who should be involved. For example, from Table 8.1, it is apparent that no staff persons are involved with the survey effort: Is the assistant appropriately qualified to undertake the survey? If so few people are involved, how well are the data being used? Second, tasks with which many persons have limited involvement might be a concern, especially those that might be better conducted by a few persons who focus on this activity. For example, maintaining client records is often best undertaken by a limited number of staff to avoid data entry errors. Third, excessive dependence on individual employees is also a problem. For example, when client records are maintained by only a single person, the absence of that person could frustrate many other operations. Fourth, staffing analysis can also be used to identify tasks that are being inadequately pursued. Table 8.1 shows that very little effort is undertaken to inform the community about the museum through education.

A dynamic form of staffing analysis is *demand analysis.* Many public and nonprofit organizations face service demands and workloads that vary by time

of day, day of the week, month of the year, or location. For example, student enrollment applications peak between December and March; patient care requires more nursing services in the early morning than any other part of the day; and police calls are often geographically concentrated in poorer parts of cities. These variations in service demand frequently cause high levels of employee stress and customer complaints. Uneven service demand is principally dealt with through three strategies: (a) reallocating staff to ensure that staffing levels meet peak demands; (b) requiring clients to schedule appointments with staff at specific times, locations, or dates when service demands are low and staff are available; and (c) using information technology and mail-in strategies to reduce the need for face-to-face or telephone interactions. The latter strategy is used in student registration, driver license renewals, and doctors' offices.

In its simplest form, demand analysis only requires measuring the level of service demand at different hours, days, months, or locations. A bar chart of service demand is made for people who ask for services. Such bar charts resemble Figure 7.3 in Chapter 7. In some instances, the nature of their request is tracked too. Managers are often surprised to find that the volume of peak-hour demand is as high as it is, and providing these data is an important step toward creating awareness about the magnitude of the problem. Although some managers resist addressing uneven demands because they fear that it will require additional overtime or hiring, the purpose of demand analysis is to resolve such problems through the above strategies, and doing so may reduce the need for already existing overtime.

Efficiency Analysis

The purpose of efficiency or optimization analysis is to increase the cost-effectiveness of services. For example, park services assess the efficiency of lawn mowing; police departments calculate the efficiency of interdictions; health care clinics, the cost of immunizations; and so forth. Such workload ratios are sometimes compared against other organizations or as a trend over time. For example, the National Recreation and Park Association publishes labor standards for maintaining lawns and sports fields (Ammons, 1996). Optimization analyses are also conducted with regard to output and outcomes rather than workloads. For example, orchestras calculate the efficiency of recruiting new season subscribers and patrons; police departments calculate the efficiency of obtaining convictions and the value of confiscated properties; and hospitals examine the cost of settling litigation. Other examples of efficiency measures

BOX 8.1.
Efficiency Analysis

There are many different ways to perform efficiency analyses. Most follow the following steps: (a) Identify costs and activities or outcomes, (b) estimate the efficiency of the entire activity or outcome, (c) estimate the efficiency of incremental increases of activities or outcomes, and (d) evaluate the impact of varying one or more assumptions in the analysis.

For example, assume that an orchestra has a 3% ticket sales rate for 2,000 direct mailings to patrons. On average, each ticket sale nets $20.00 and the costs for the first 2,000 mailings are 31¢ postage and 10¢ printing for each mailing, a one-time charge of $350.00 for offset costs, and 8 hours of professional staff time at $12.50 per hour (some volunteers are used too). An easy calculation shows that it is cost-effective to undertake the mailing: Revenues are $(0.03 * 2,000 * \$20 =)$ $1,200 and exceed the costs of $(\$0.31 * 2,000 + \$350 + 8 * \$12.50 =)$ $1,070.00. The net profit is $130.00.

Encouraged by this result, the director wants to know how many further mailings should be undertaken. That is, the number of mailings at which revenues equal costs, or the breakeven point. Assume that for each subsequent 1,000 mailings, only 2 additional hours of staff time are required because the mailing process is already in place. Also assume that for each subsequent 1,000 mailings, ticket sales decrease by 30%, as these represent buyers who are less likely to purchase tickets. Revenues for 3,000 mailings are $1,200 plus $(0.03 0.7 * 1,000 * \$20 =)$ $420, or $1,620. Costs are now $1,070 plus $(\$0.31 * 1,000 + 2 * \$12.50 =)$ $360, or $1,430. The net profit on 3,000 mailings is $190. The director continues this calculation for the next 1,000, and then smaller increments, until the breakeven point is found at about 4,800 mailings. At this number of mailings, 104 tickets are sold and revenues are $2,080 .

Such calculations are readily undertaken on a spreadsheet but can be done by hand too. The advantage of the computer is readily seen when the director wishes to assess the impact of changing assumptions, such as the marginal rate of ticket sales. What if additional tickets sales decrease by 50% instead of 30%? Such questions help in understanding the sensitivity of such analyses. In this case, 3,300 mailings should be undertaken and 77 tickets will be sold, which will generate $1,540 in sales. This what-if analysis is useful because it suggests that under various assumptions, slightly fewer than 100 tickets can be sold.

Finally, the analysis can also be used to determine the number of mailings for which profit is maximized, rather than sales: Profit reaches a maximum of $190 for 3,000 mailings, assuming a 30% decline on sales from subsequent mailings. At this level, 81 tickets will be sold.

are discussed in Chapter 3. Efficiency analyses are used to evaluate as well as to help determine courses of action. For example, when deciding how many additional marketing letters to mail out, a museum can examine its previous returns to estimate a breakeven point for sending out more (see Box 8.1).

Efficiency analysis is related to cost-benefit and cost-effectiveness analysis. However, the latter is usually quite comprehensive and aims to assess all costs and benefits. Cost-benefit analyses are sometimes requested when proposing new investments or initiatives (Gramlich, 1981). Different cost-benefit applications, such as those in social services, environmental management, and road construction have different standards and conventions for measuring costs and benefits. For example, benefits are often undervalued in social service programs because quality-of-life increases are hard to quantify in dollars. Although policy makers often look to cost-benefit and cost-effectiveness studies to provide a "bottom line," such studies are often controversial because (a) it is seldom possible to identify and quantify all direct and indirect costs and benefits, and (b) the decision to undertake activities includes other values such as effectiveness and equity. Thus cost-benefit analysis is usually only one tool in the game of obtaining approval. Perhaps the greatest utility of such studies is the systematic identification of all costs and benefits as well as an initial assessment of whether, under conservative estimates, estimable benefits are likely to be greater than estimable costs. Kee (1994) discusses a cost-benefit analysis of the Job Corps program.

Both efficiency and cost-benefit analyses are ideally suited for "what-if" analysis, that is, (a) changes in initial conditions and assumptions and (b) assessment of consequences. Indeed, cost-benefit analyses are best presented with an analysis of the effect of different assumptions, such as those about inflation factors, income growth projections, recidivism, and so forth. Likewise, efficiency analyses often involve assumptions about growth rates and so on that can be evaluated (see Box 8.1). Comparative efficiency analyses should also take into account factors that vary between organizations; for example, the cost of maintaining lawns varies in different parts of the country due to labor costs, seasonal variations, the amount of rainfall, and the need for fertilizers and pesticides. Although precise data on such conditions are usually unavailable, analysts and managers can often agree on a range of estimates that are acceptable. What-if analysis helps defuse concern about the robustness of data and assumptions by examining the effect of different assumptions.

Finally, efficiency analysis can also be used to take distributional considerations into account. For example, assume that data are available about park maintenance costs, use rates, and area incomes. Assume furthermore that the

Park Department is experiencing a budget shortfall and cost savings must be made. Efficiency analysis can suggest a way of distributing the budget shortfall so that high-use parks and those in low-income areas suffer least. After accounting for critical maintenance activities, the remaining shortfall is budgeted according to the weighted sum of priorities, as follows:

	Use Ranking	Area Income	Total Ranking	Share of Shortfall
	(1 = high)	(1 = lowest)		
Park North	1	3	4	4/20 = 20%
Park South	2	1	3	3/20 = 15%
Park East	4	4	8	8/20 = 40%
Park West	3	2	5	5/20 = 25%
			20	

Of course, in practice, actual use and income data might be used. Also, what-if analysis might be used by adding a third criterion or by weighting the criteria. For example, if park usage is rated twice as much as area income, the relative budget shortfall allocations of the four parks become, respectively, 17%, 17%, 40%, and 27%. These are very small differences in comparison with those above and usefully inform decision making.

Linear Programming

Linear programming is an operations research tool that aims to allocate resources and activities when certain goals must be achieved and constraints must be taken into account. Although many activities of public and nonprofit organizations can be described this way, linear programming is limited to those situations in which goals, activities, and constraints can be quantitatively described and in which the relations between these goals, activities, and constraints can be described in quantitative terms as well. Linear programming requires well-structured problems. The following three examples illustrate various kinds of problems that linear programming is appropriate for. First, a city is trying to meet the pollution standards that its incinerators not generate more than a certain amount of sulfur dioxide and particulates. Each incinerator has a different emission profile and capacity. What is the best combination of usage that minimizes pollution and meets the city's needs?

BOX 8.2.
Linear Programming Example

The following example of linear programming is solved using the Excel program. An Air Force logistics officer has to transport 850 plans from the United States to the Pacific. Currently, 500 planes are stationed at Minot AFB and 350 at Offutt AFB. Of these 850 places, 200 must go to Kadena, 150 to Guam, 400 to Osan, and 100 to Hickham. The cost of transporting each plane is shown below. How can the officer transport these planes at least cost?

The first step is constructing a spreadsheet for these data. Although there are different ways of doing this, one approach is shown below. The cells that make up the rectangle E14 through F17 are only zeros; they contain no formulas. Cell G14 contains a formula that is the sum of F14 and E14, that is, the number of planes transferred to Kadena; prior to the analysis, this number is zero. Cells G15 through G17 contain similar formulas. Likewise, Cells E18 and E19 identify the number of planes transferred from Minot and Offutt AFBs, respectively. Cell A22 calculates the total cost of the transfer operating, using the formula shown; the final solution will have to minimize this value.

The next step is to identify various constraints. Cells H14 through H17 identify the number of planes that must be transferred to each of the bases. These values must equal the number of planes that are actually transferred, which are to be calculated in Cells G14 through G17. Likewise, Cells E19 and F19 show the number of planes that are currently available at Minot and Offutt AFBs. The actual number of planes that are transferred off these bases cannot exceed these values.

Excel-Solver finds the solution. It prompts the user to identify the target cell (A22, to be minimized), the cells to be changed (E13 through F17), and the constraints, which are as follows: G14 = H14, G15 = H15, G16 = H16, G17 = H17, E18 ≤ E19, F18 ≤ F19, as well as E14:F17 ≥ 0 and A22 ≥ 0. The solution generated by Excel shows that the minimum transfer cost is $590,000, for which 100 planes are transferred from Minot to Kadena, 400 planes from Minot to Osan, 100 planes from Offutt to Kadena, 150 planes from Offutt to Guam, and 100 planes from Offutt to Hickham. This is the cheapest way of accomplishing the transfer objective.

(Box 8.2 continues on p. 205)

A second example is adapted from the Air Force (Meier & Brudney, 1993). A logistics officer has to transport 850 planes from two U.S. airbases to four bases in the Pacific. The cost of transporting each plane is known from its current base to each of the four bases, as well as the number of planes that must be delivered to each of the four bases. Linear programming is appropriate because

BOX 8.2.
(Continued)

	A	B	C	D	E	F	G	H	
10									
11	Cost of each plane transfer:				Number of planes transferred:				
12	TO:	FROM:						CONSTRAINT:	
13		MINOT	OFFUTT		MINOT	OFFUTT	TOTAL:		
14	KADENA	$600	$900		0	0	0	200	
15	GUAM	$700	$600		0	0	0	150	
16	OSAN	$800	$1,100		0	0	0	400	
17	HICKAM	$400	$300		0	0	0	100	
18				TOTAL	0	0			
19				CONSTR:	500	350			
20									
21	TOTAL COSTS:								
22	0	$\rightarrow$	+ e14 × 14 + e15 × b15 + e16 × b16 + e17 × b17 + f14 × c14 + f16 × c16 + f17 × c17						

the objective (minimizing expenditures), transportation costs, and constraints are known in quantifiable terms. A third example is taken from a hospital: What is the optimum number of different surgeries that can be scheduled, given the profitability of each type of surgery and the limited capacity of different wards to process and handle patients?

In practice, linear programming has a narrow range of applications but has important uses within that range. Most applications require the use of a computer, and some problems can be solved using Excel spreadsheets (Person, 1993). The Excel user creates a spreadsheet that identifies the relationships among activities, goals, and constraints in quantitative terms. Excel prompts the user to indicate which cells are constraints (i.e, cells that cannot exceed certain values), which cells are variable (i.e., to be changed such as incineration volumes or planes transferred among bases), and which cells are to be maximized or minimized, such as transportation costs, which are called target cells. Excel solves both linear and nonlinear relations. The Air Force transfer problem is shown in Box 8.2.

An important concept in linear programming is the "shadow price." In solving the above problems, some constraints are binding; that is, they impose solutions because these resources are being exhausted or fully used. For example, incinerators cannot produce more than their capacity. The optimal solution will show that some incinerators should be operated at full capacity. These are binding constraints, but not all incinerators will be operated at maximum capacity. The shadow price is defined as the effect on the goal of relaxing a constraint by one unit, for example, the effect on pollution of operating an incinerator by one unit more. This information is important in the event that the city needs to increase its incineration activity. In practice, the shadow price is found by changing the initial constraint by one unit and reestimating the solution.

Site location is a frequent problem in public organizations. For example, fire stations often must find the best location that minimizes emergency response time, and parks departments must identify the best central storage and maintenance facility that minimizes travel time. Although sophisticated computer programs are available for this purpose, one hand-calculation method is the *grid method*. This approach requires the following steps. First, managers identify the map coordinates of each location to which trips are made, and the "horizontal" and "vertical" distances are noted. Second, managers multiply these distances by the frequency of trips to each location. For example, if the coordinates of a location are "2, 3" and three trips are taken to this location, the respective values are 6 (horizontal) and 9 (vertical). Alternatively, managers can identify the number of clients served at each location. Third, all of the horizontal distances are added and divided by the total number of trips. Vertical distances are treated in the same manner. The resulting set of coordinates is the site location that minimizes travel. These calculations are as follows:

Site	X	Y	Number of Trips	Weighted X	Weighted Y
A	1	4	5	5	20
B	2	2	4	8	8
C	4	3	1	4	3
D	5	1	6	30	6
E	1	1	2	2	2
Total:			18	49	39

Ideal X Coordinate: (49/18 =) 2.7
Ideal Y Coordinate: (39/18 =) 2.2

Queuing and Inventory Problems

A frequent complaint in public organizations is long waits in service lines for driver's license renewals, post office services, business licenses, homestead tax exemptions, tollbooths, zoning and building applications, and marriage licenses. Nonprofit organizations sometimes also face long lines, especially in health care clinics and for ticket sales. Although mail and telephone requests reduce the need for personal service, a need exists for estimating the correct number of service clerks.

Queuing models estimate the average wait time of customers. Such models require knowledge about the average service time and arrival rate of clients. Queuing models vary with regard to the number of servers, whether clients are served in phases by subsequent servers (e.g., first waiting for a receptionist, who directs clients to appropriate servers, which causes further waits); whether queue lines are limited in length (e.g., service is closed when more than 50 clients are waiting); whether clients arrive in a probabilistic manner (although clients arrive at an average rate, simultaneous arrivals may cause excessive waiting); whether there are maximum waits that may not be exceeded (such as for the availability of emergency response teams); and whether servers can be added if needed.

Inventory models are analytically similar to queuing models but optimize stock levels rather than minimize service delays. All inventory models make assumptions about stock levels and requests for stock. Additional requirements concern the frequency of requests and the average amount of each type of request, as well as requirements about any maximum or minimum acceptable inventory levels and delays due to reordering (i.e., lead time). Inventory models also vary with regard to the probabilistic nature of inventory requests (although requests are made at an average rate, simultaneous requests may cause sudden shortages) and whether monitoring of the current stock level is ongoing or periodic. Thus there are similarities between queuing and inventory models.

A variety of operations research software analyzes queues and inventories. However, "canned" models do not always serve specific applications, and spreadsheets must then be used. The strategy for designing spreadsheets is to start at time $t = 0$, and calculate the queue/inventory consequence for the first and subsequent interactions. For example, assume a simple model with two servers and an average service time of 5 minutes. The average arrival time of clients is 3 minutes, but it varies in a random way. The first client arrives at $t = 0$ and is helped by server one. There is no wait. The second client arrives at $t = 3$ and is immediately helped by server two. Again, there is no wait. The third client arrives at $t = 4$, almost immediately following the second client. This client will have to wait 1 minute to be helped by server one. The fourth client arrives at t = 8. This client can be immediately helped by server two. Each event is analyzed in this manner. The repetitive nature of the calculation suggests that it is adaptable for spreadsheet analysis (see Stokey & Zeckhauser, 1978).

Summary

This chapter examines a wide range of strategies for increasing the efficiency of public and nonprofit organizations. It examines strategies to reduce costs by using volunteers, interns, and clients, as well as strategies that are based on auditing expenses of rent, equipment, fringe benefits, and other expenses. Alternative revenue-enhancing strategies are also discussed, as well as various industrial engineering and operations research strategies. The latter include (a) task analysis, (b) staffing and demand analysis, (c) efficiency or optimization analysis, (d) linear programming, and (e) queuing and inventory analysis. This chapter provides numerous examples of the application of these techniques to public and nonprofit organizations.

Notes

1. The annualized cost is calculated as the purchase prices times $[i * (1 + i)^n]/[(1 + i)^n - 1]$, where i = interest rate and n = number of periods. For $i = 10\%$ and $n = 3$, the factor is 0.402. This formula coverts a single payment to an annual cost. The annualized cost is also calculated on most hand calculators that perform financial operations. In this case, the future value is zero, the present value is $2,040, the interest is 10%, and the number of periods is three; the computer calculates the required payment.

2. Organizations need to protect themselves against litigation. This requires that they have stated employment policies, provide adequate training, conduct safety programs, and have a range of processes to provide timely feedback to employees, among other safe employment practices.

3. Alternative revenues increase the efficiency (or leverage) of taxes. This notion is admittedly problematic, because increased revenues may shift costs from one group to another without increasing service efficiency.

4. Asking workers to identify and prioritize improvements is both an efficient and a consultative manner of data collection. By contrast, requiring employees to complete forms on their activities or using direct observation of their time-motion activities is often experienced as demeaning because it suggests that workers are unaware or unable to evaluate their own motions or problems. Quality circles involve employees and managers documenting and tracking work processes in a collaborative manner (Chapter 7).

References

Ammons, D. (1991). *Administrative analysis for local government: Practical application of selected techniques.* Athens, GA: Carl Vinson Institute of Government.

Ammons, D. (1996). *Municipal benchmarks.* Thousand Oaks, CA: Sage.

Ayres, Q., & Kettinger, W. (1983). Information technology and models of governmental productivity. *Public Administration Review, 43*(6), 561-566.

Brudney, J. (1994). Designing and managing volunteer programs. In R. Herman (Ed.), *Handbook of nonprofit leadership* (pp. 279-302). San Francisco: Jossey-Bass.

Burgers, M., & van Vleuten, R. (1992). The pros and cons of corporate sponsorship. In International Council of Museums, *Marketing the arts* (pp. 29-36). Paris: ICOM.

Cayer, N. (1997). Issues in compensation and benefits. In C. Ban & N. Riccucci (Eds.), *Public personnel management* (pp. 221-236). New York: Longman.

Connors, T. (1995). *The volunteer management handbook.* New York: John Wiley.

Coolsen, P. (1992). Six keys to strong volunteer networks. *Nonprofit World, 10*(6), 22-24.

Fogal, R. (1994). Designing and managing the fundraising program. In R. Herman (Ed.), *Handbook of nonprofit leadership* (pp. 369-381). San Francisco: Jossey-Bass.

Gramlich. E. (1981). *Benefit-cost analysis of government programs.* Englewood Cliffs, NJ: Prentice Hall.

Haynes, P. (1980). Industrial engineering techniques. In G. Washnis (Ed.), *Productivity improvement handbook for state and local government* (pp. 204-236). New York: John Wiley.

Kee, J. (1994). Benefit-cost analysis in program evaluation. In J. Wholey, H. Hatry, & K. Newcomer (Eds.), *Handbook of practical program evaluation* (pp. 456-487). San Francisco: Jossey-Bass.

Keys, P. (Ed.). (1995). *Understanding the process of operational research.* New York: John Wiley.

Levin, R., Rubin, D., Stinson, J., & Gardner, E. (1989). *Quantitative approaches to management.* New York: McGraw-Hill.

Liddell, R. (1995). Volunteers help shoulder the load. *FBI Law Enforcement Bulletin, 64*(8), 21-26.

Markwood, S. (1994). Volunteers in local government: Partners in service. *Public Management, 76*(4), 6-10.

Meier, K., & Brudney, J. (1993). *Applied statistics for public administration.* Belmont, CA: Wadsworth.

Monks, J. (1996). *Operations management.* New York: McGraw-Hill.

Person, R. (1993). *Using Excel.* Indianapolis, IN: Que Corporation.

Pierson, J. (1992). Effective local government internships. *Public Management, 74*(2), 16-19.

Ries, R., & Alstadler, E. (1994). Thirteen ways to cut costs. *Nonprofit World, 12*(4), 44-46.

Rushkin, K. (1995). *Grantwriting, fundraising and partnerships that work.* Thousand Oaks, CA: Corwin.

Smith, W. (1994). *The complete guide to nonprofit management.* New York: John Wiley.

Starr, K. (1996). *Operations research: A systems approach.* Danvers, MA: Boyd & Fraser.

Stokey, E., & Zeckhauser, R. (1978). *A primer for policy analysis.* New York: Norton.

Wagner, L. (1992). Fundraising research: Prospecting for gold. *Fund Raising Management, 5*(10), 36-43.

CHAPTER

9

Managing Information Technology Systems

Information technology is ubiquitous in many public and nonprofit organizations. Nearly all public and nonprofit organizations have computers that are routinely used by administrative staff, managers, and others. Information technology (IT) enables managers and employees to accomplish more and increase their effectiveness by using more—and frequently better—information. For example, police officers who use IT for database searches report greater arrest rates and more cases cleared than those who do not use computers (Swain & White, 1992). The most frequent applications of IT are for word processing, budget applications, and electronic communication (Norris & Kraemer, 1996; Society for Nonprofit Organizations, 1996). The management challenge of IT is to ensure that existing applications are used and maintained in productive ways and that new IT applications are identified. IT management requires well-defined productivity goals and also strategies for overcoming such frequent problems as runaway costs, inadequate funding, wrong hardware/software choices, software "glitches," managers who are inadequately informed about IT capabilities, employees who are fearful of losing their jobs, and frustrating service calls by IT professionals. Such challenges complicate the productive use of IT (Kraemer, 1996; Pinto, 1994).

Although these problems occur in the public and private sectors alike, there are some differences as well. First, some public agencies with very specialized missions have substantial investments in tailored IT applications; these agencies often find it difficult to develop upgrades in the present era of tight constraints. Some examples of this problem are the air traffic control systems of the U.S. Federal Aviation Administration and many state social service agencies that have specialized programs for tracking millions of applicants, dealing with myriad eligibility rules, and identifying fraud and abuse (Gurwitt, 1996). Second, other public agencies are oriented toward the development of new technologies such as defense, space, health, and environmental agencies. These agencies are often leaders in IT and expend considerable energy in managing new IT efforts. For example, the U.S. National Science Foundation pioneered electronic communications among universities in the 1980s, called Bitnet—the forerunner of the Internet. Third, nonprofit agencies face some different constraints. Their missions often do not require much IT, and they are often unable to afford adequate investments in IT. Consequently, many lag behind public and for-profit organizations. Public agencies that are not technology oriented sometimes suffer additional challenges of red tape and a lack of leadership and interest by senior managers in IT (Cats-Baril & Thompson, 1995).

This chapter examines productivity applications of IT as well as organizational structures and planning processes for increasing the productivity of IT. It also discusses strategic IT issues, such as concerns about data security and the need for a recovery management plan. The section concludes with processes for introducing new IT projects as well as evaluating the productivity of the IT function itself.

Some authors distinguish between information management and IT management (Buckholtz, 1995). Whereas the former is concerned with ensuring adequate information for decision making, IT management is concerned with the implementation of information technology. A main concern of information management is obtaining relevant information in a timely manner and interpreting vague and inconsistent information in a meaningful way. In this regard, IT is but one of several sources of information. Many IT applications focus on transactions and data processing, which result in databases that aid strategic decisions and improve operational decision making in air traffic control, tax collection, enrollment forecasting, and other services. Although an IT management objective is to improve the relevance of IT for decision making, goals and justifications for IT investments frequently go beyond this concern. Applications such as electronic toll collection and school enrollment enable public and nonprofit organizations to serve their customers more quickly, more cheaply, and frequently better.

Managing Information
Technology for Productivity

During the past decade, IT has evolved in many public and nonprofit organizations as a separate organizational function that requires its own organization, planning, and evaluation processes. What was once the activity of enthusiastic hobbyists is now staffed by managers and employees with appropriate professional and technical credentials. The present challenge is to ensure that the IT function is managed in efficient and effective ways as well.

Objectives of Information Technology

Managers need to develop a strategic perspective about the use of IT. The potential of IT exceeds conventional applications such as word processing, budgeting, and communication (including the Internet). Information technology affects, for example, how organizations get their work done and how they interact with stakeholders. Some IT objectives are as follows:

- Increasing the speed of transactions and operations
- Reducing the cost of transactions and operations
- Improving the accuracy and reliability of operations
- Increasing interactions among stakeholders inside and outside organizations
- Increasing the use of external databases for improving operations (e.g., use of fingerprint files)
- Providing employees and managers with ongoing feedback regarding their performance (for example, weekly progress reports)
- Providing expert systems for analysis of special or complex problems
- Facilitating interactions among teams of employees and managers at different locations
- Enabling stakeholders and employees to communicate with each other from remote locations

At a minimum, managers need to be familiar with the range of applications that is used in their line of work. For example, state-of-the-art IT applications in transportation include electronic toll collections, automatic license plate readers (to identify those violating toll collection and speeding regulations), speed monitoring equipment connected to driver's license information systems, traffic management systems (e.g., to regulate traffic lights and direct traffic), and electronic communications between transportation departments and contractors responsible for maintenance and improvements. Other applications include ramp metering, incidence response systems, travel information systems, and fleet management systems (Johnson, 1996). Different functions in public and nonprofit organizations have different IT applications. State-of-the-art IT systems in correction departments are very different. These emphasize automated, labor-saving security systems, integrated inmate management records, management, and linkages with other law enforcement offices.

Some applications are driven by technological developments, and creative managers find new ways to apply these advanced developments to the objectives of their organizations. User-friendly, multimedia, and Internet applications are increasingly common, and some clients access organizations through their televisions rather than computers (Moura, 1996). These applications increase the range of clients and citizens who can electronically communicate with organizations. Voice recognition systems and virtual reality applications will continue to improve and become affordable. At the same time, existing applications will continue to proliferate such as Geographic Information Systems (GIS) and artificial intelligence/expert systems that are used in emergency management (e.g., for chemical spills). These applications make productivity improvements available to a broader range of public and nonprofit organizations. Clearly, managers have many opportunities to improve their organizations through the use of IT. Box 9.1 discusses further applications.

Planning for IT

In recent years, planning for IT has become an important vehicle for increasing the productivity of information technology. IT must be planned at several levels. At the executive level, organizationwide strategic planning helps link IT to the overall strategy of public and nonprofit organizations. IT units are increasingly directed by a chief information officer (CIO) or vice president for information technology (VP-IT). Their specific responsibilities include the following (Cats-Baril & Thompson, 1997; Gurwitt, 1996; Stephens, 1995):

1. Developing a comprehensive IT strategy
2. Determining policies, procedures, and standards for IT
3. Evaluating and acquiring major IT products and systems
4. Ensuring coordination among IT units and between IT and the rest of the organization
5. Educating top managers and others about uses and developments in IT
6. Staffing and overseeing the general operations of IT programs

BOX 9.1.
Applications of IT

The basic applications of IT are (a) to support operations, (b) to improve management decision making, and (c) to advance strategic goals of organizations.

Supporting operations. IT supports operations through (a) office automation; (b) transaction processing; (c) monitoring and using databases that are specific to such units as police, human resources, parks and recreation, marketing, and budgeting; and (d) the deployment of expert systems. The principal goals of office automation (which involves desktop publishing, e-mail, video conferencing, and multimedia communications) and transaction processing (e.g., through automatic toll collections, electronic order processing, and the use of smart cards) are to increase productivity by reducing costs and increasing speed. This also improves customer service. An example of monitoring by personnel departments is keeping track of employee skills, training activities, performance evaluations, benefits, and compensation. This also provides a database that can be used to match employees to specific needs. Similarly, marketing departments often maintain records of customers that are used to provide a database and trend analysis of repeat customers. Some tracking and database applications are very large, such as the FBI fingerprint files. Operations are also supported through expert systems (also known as decision support systems) that help employees with complex operational problems, such as those in emergency management dealing with environmental disasters and medical challenges. IT gives field personnel ready access to expert information (Cats-Baril & Thompson, 1997; O'Brien, 1996).

Management decision making. IT also helps improve management decision making through (a) periodic reports, (b) special analyses, and (c) group decision-making software. Managers often use databases to produce periodic reports of transactions and tracking information. These reports evaluate workloads, budgets, effectiveness, efficiency, absenteeism, requests, and complaints over time. They also help managers solve management problems. For example, managers of nursing homes must periodically determine how much they should spend on marketing to ensure an adequate occupation rate of their beds. The future of performance measurement is in distributed, on-time reports through Management Information Systems (MIS). In New York City, police supervisors receive weekly reports of crime in their areas that support fast and frequent improvements. Other tools are complex, such as traffic management models that optimize increasing traffic flows. Of recent interest is groupware that helps groups of managers to brainstorm on problems in a structured way with real-time feedback, at the same or different locations. Electronic group decision-making processes can be conducted simultaneously or over several time periods (Bohan & Beaulieu, 1993).

BOX 9.1.
(Continued)

Advancing strategic goals. IT applications also advance and shape strategic goals. For example, to empower citizens and clients, zoning and planning departments can electronically provide information about zoning changes to contractors, and they can develop systems for plans to be submitted electronically as well. To improve neighborhood safety, some law enforcement agencies now use Internet "home pages" to make available information about incidents in the community and actions that residents can take to better protect themselves. While these applications also improve operations and management, they also address strategic goals. Managers also use IT to advance productivity improvement strategies, for example, by using IT to reengineer processes. By requiring units to reengineer using IT, managers advance both IT and productivity improvement in their organizations.

Although small organizations do not always have formal CIO positions, these functions must nevertheless be carried out. By participating in different planning activities of organizations, including strategic planning, CIOs, or employees who fulfill these functions, contribute IT opportunities that shape organizational goals and objectives (Stephens, 1995). For example, the need to improve business licensing processes may cause CIOs to suggest implementing new databases and electronic access to departments. CIOs may also suggest solutions for improving employee productivity or linking customers and other stakeholders with organizations.

The basic organization of IT involves the CIO function, central IT units, and technical, user-support services. Central IT staff often manage central computing operations, such as for financial accounting and operations management, and they are also responsible for the development and implementation of system changes. These efforts often consume a majority of IT manpower resources, and productivity in such operations requires careful management and planning. Planning involves such questions as the following (Silk, 1991): How well are we meeting the organization's current IT needs? Which needs are likely to grow over time? What are some alternative ways in which we might meet these needs? Which of these alternatives is best to aim for? Which new strategies must be developed and implemented? What are the critical success factors? Which performance indicators should be used to assess progress toward objectives?

Increasingly, IT units use advisory councils of other managers that involve user departments in such processes. Typically, such advisory councils meet on a monthly basis; they are discussed further below.

Central IT units also assist user departments in *their* planning for IT. The productivity of organizations requires that they periodically plan to adopt new IT systems such as wide area networks, electronic communication systems with clients, the use of new computers and their programming, and the development of new databases and information for operations and management. Although such systems should be linked to the productivity goals of different units, often managers invest in new IT without full consideration of their strategic needs. For example, capacities are upgraded that do not take advantage of automation opportunities. Central IT can assist users by providing input to answer the following questions: What information technologies are needed for core activities? Why do existing information technologies need to be replaced? How will new IT improve current goals and objectives? How does the proposed investment affect future goals and priorities? What is the cost of the new information technology, and how is it justified? Does the cost include peripheral expenses such as additional hardware, software, staff training, consulting or service calls, as well as infrastructure adjustments? What is the total lifetime cost of the capability? For how long will the new capability be used before it is replaced? What is the implementation plan?

Central IT units also help end users in their need for technical support. This support often involves (a) training in systems (e.g., using E-mail or the Unix operating systems), (b) assistance in installing new hardware and software (e.g., added memory, new e-mail software), and (c) providing emergency assistance in dealing with system crashes, data recovery, and viruses. Central IT units need to work with user departments to plan for these needs. Some IT organizations also use planning procedures or advisory groups to help them better plan for meeting the technical needs of users. These are discussed below, along with a survey instrument for assessing user needs.

Measuring IT Productivity

In recent years, public and nonprofit organizations have made large investments in information technology. Consequently, many managers are now beginning to ponder the effectiveness of these investments. Many find it difficult to evaluate the returns on their IT investments and to justify the costs of prospective investments. According to Willcocks (1993), the difficulty of measuring benefits and costs is a major constraint in making IT investments in both the public and the private sectors, including for-profit organizations.

The multifaceted and strategic nature of IT projects suggests that narrow, rate-of-return analyses are not always appropriate (Remenyi, Money, & Twite, 1993). Efficiency analyses are usually only appropriate for investments in operations in which the main purpose is to automate functions that result in cost savings. Examples include applications that automate the handling of citizen inquiries. In such cases, personnel savings can be compared with IT costs. Research shows that organizations that set formal targets for returns on such investments are more likely to produce high rates of return (Kearney, 1990). However, even in these instances, it is often a challenge to assess the full cost of IT investments: Hardware and software often constitute only 25%-40% of total costs; other costs include training, purchasing, installation, maintenance, conversion, modification, and consulting. A further challenge is to estimate a realistic range of probable outcomes (Strock & Atkins, 1989).

Cost-benefit analyses (CBA) must identify the full range of costs and benefits. CBA should be based on a three-year time frame; longer periods are seldom justified in view of IT developments. Costs are usually divided into (a) acquisition costs (hardware, software, installation, training, and purchasing), (b) initial start-up costs (training and support, troubleshooting, running old and new systems simultaneously), and (c) monthly maintenance costs thereafter. Costs are usually discounted at about 10%.[1] Benefits include (a) reduction in personnel costs, (b) release of office space, (c) increases in unit efficiency (over and above those implied by the reduction of labor costs), and (d) a reduced error rate (assessed as the cost of correcting errors). Intangible benefits such as improved information for decision making are noted, but analysts may find it difficult to assign monetary value to such benefits. However, underestimating benefits adds to the credibility of CBA because it addresses concerns of "rosy scenarios" and "wishful thinking" by those who perform CBA.

Strategic and managerial IT investments often aim to improve customer service, improve decision-making capabilities, and increase employee skills. The evaluation of such projects requires more balanced, multifaceted analysis. Willcocks (1993) suggests combining a financial perspective with criteria of customer satisfaction, innovation, and performance enhancement, and a strategic perspective that focuses on making core functions competitive. Such assessment measures are shown in Table 9.1 and are used as the foundation for performance standards for IT projects. For example, IT investments that aim to improve managerial decision making might be evaluated on the basis of whether

TABLE 9.1 Assessment Criteria for IT Projects

Customer Satisfaction:
　　Customer demand for project
　　Projected customer use
　　Customer ability to use IT project
　　Timeliness of IT project
　　Integration with other user systems
　　Service responsiveness

Performance Improvement:
　　Increases speed of operations or decision making
　　Increases output
　　Reduces costs
　　Reduces errors
　　Improves quality of output
　　Provides more/better information for decision making
　　Provides more timely information for decision making

Core Function Enhancement:
　　Improves information for managerial decision making
　　Meets minimum industry requirements
　　Increases number of clients (increases program size)
　　Is consistent with strategic purpose of the organization
　　Expands core functions into new areas or applications
　　Makes the core function more competitive

Financial Management:
　　Return on investment (total returns/total outlays)
　　Net present value (present value of future, net cash flows)
　　Payback method (time required for breakeven)
　　Rate of return (discount rate at which future outlays equal returns)

---

they concern core functions, the likely impact on productivity, and the extent to which managers find that they provide useful information.

Managers may also wish to evaluate the IT function as a whole (Thierauff, 1994). General assessments focus on (a) the qualifications and leadership of IT managers; (b) whether IT departments have adequate strategic and operations plans; (c) consultation and support by user departments for IT plans and activities; (d) the use of quality standards and tools in IT operations; (e) the use of project planning for systems development and implementation; (f) the development of performance appraisal standards for MIS personnel; (g) the use of appropriate controls to ensure reliability of data operations and networks; (h) training, positive evaluation, and capabilities of MIS personnel fulfilling technical support; (i) the existence of appropriate disaster recovery plans; and (j) appropriate security and control procedures.

A Note on Organization

Although organizational IT structures greatly vary, most distinguish among responsibilities for (a) executive functions (CIOs), (b) system development, (c) system operations, (d) data management, (e) data communication, and (f) technical support. These responsibilities require separate skills, and large organizations often organize these functions as separate units within IT units. Small IT units often combine these responsibilities as part of the assignments of individual employees and managers. For example, very small IT units may have one person who is both the CIO and the systems development manager, another who does operations and management, and a third staff person who is responsible for both user support and communications.

An important productivity issue in the organization of information technology is the extent of decentralization. With the use of PCs and local area networks (LANs) has come a need for new central IT functions to train and support local users. Although local units enjoy autonomy in their purchasing decisions, a recent problem is the need for standardization and central decision making: For example, decentralized purchasing is uneconomical because organizations fail to take advantage of economies of scale. Norris and Kraemer (1996) also find that cities with central computing systems are more automated than those that only have PC systems. This reflects the input of information technology knowledge by central IT units. Andersen (1995) finds that national coordination of IT increases automation. In the United States, the National Institutes of Health have established national databases for cancer research that are used by researchers at all levels of government, and in Sweden, national oversight of information technology has increased municipal automation and citizen access efforts. A recent study of central IT agencies in different countries finds that a majority are responsible for policy making, security, intergovernmental relations, strategic planning, oversight, and setting data and telecommunication standards (Ady, 1995).

Another problem is achieving effective control over central IT units. Most IT units are headed by IT directors such as chief information officers (CIOs) who report directly to the head of the organization. This structure ensures technical expertise and the development of IT policies, but it does not ensure that IT activities are aligned with the needs of user departments. End users frequently complain about inadequate service by central IT staff. In addition, CIOs often emphasize technical over financial criteria in making their information technology investment plans. Advisory councils of end users help overcome these problems by ensuring that they are composed of managers of user departments as well as finance directors. This arrangement is frequently better than making IT units a part of end-user departments because the latter may lack necessary coordination among different end-user systems as well as expertise for IT policy development. It is also better than placing IT units under the control of finance directors, who often emphasize financial criteria and may be too conservative in undertaking strategic rather than operational IT investments. Finally, organizations also exert control over IT units by influencing their personnel hiring and evaluation practices. For example, by influencing personnel hiring criteria, they can improve the quality of technical support as well as the development of future IT priorities.

Strategic IT Issues

The present management of IT involves the resolution of issues that have gained strategic importance in recent years. These issues concern contracting out, disaster recovery programs, user service, security, and governance. Effectively dealing with these issues is of considerable importance for increasing productivity and client satisfaction with IT.

Contracting Out

Many public and nonprofit organizations use vendors to satisfy their IT needs for hardware and software upgrades, installation and maintenance of area networks, staff training, expert solutions, data management (e.g., payroll and accounting), and general consultation about technology and available options. The current market for state and local government IT is about $34.5 billion annually.[2] Many managers tell "horror stories" about much-ballyhooed software that failed to perform, such as payroll software that calculated wrong deductions or consultants who overpromised and were absent when their systems failed. As noted by Norris and Kraemer (1996): "Many (municipal governments) have learned to their sorrow that the small software services firms with which they contract for custom development lack the market and staying power to improve upon or even support their products beyond the first few years" (p. 569). Such problems suggest that choosing a vendor and consultant must be done carefully and with objectivity.

Choosing a vendor begins with a needs assessment that should be based on multiple users and experts. The outcome of a needs assessment is usually a specification of technical attributes as well as service and maintenance require-

TABLE 9.2 Evaluation Criteria for IT Contractors

Project Criteria:
For which project components is the price lowest?
Is the proposed hardware proven and reliable?
Is the proposed software dependable and adequate?
Are upgrades included?
Is the proposed level of service and maintenance adequate?
Are the proposed levels of training adequate?
Are the emergency and recovery plans adequate?
Does the proposed project interface well with other systems?
Is proposed project staff technically adequate?
Do the expressed warranties address our concerns?
Does the contractor guarantee performance and price?
What provisions exist to renegotiate the contract?

Contractor Criteria:
What are the technical and business reputations of the contractor?
What is the contractor's past performance in this area?
Does the contractor have technical and financial resources to deal with unforeseen problems?
Is the proposed project within the main business of the contractor?
Is the contractor financially stable?
Is the contractor facing major litigation?
Is the contractor easy to access?
If the contractor performs, are we likely to continue with this contractor?

---

ments. Globerman and Vining (1996) write that outsourcing problems often occur when required products or services are complex, when they require large investments by the contractee, and when there are few competing providers. To overcome these problems, specifications should be biased toward standard rather than custom-made products and services, competition among multiple contractors, and requirements that vendors share in capital investments. The latter is important, because contractors who incur few capital costs have little at stake. Bid specifications should also include attention to the need for emergency support, technology upgrades, the financial security of contractors, and provisions for dealing with escalating costs. Table 9.2 provides criteria for evaluating vendor proposals.

Overall, the selection of bid proposals is but the first step in the negotiation process. Most proposals require further specification. For example, system maintenance contracts require great detail with regard to software development and enhancement, purchasing procedures, the expertise of service personnel, staff training, and responsibilities with regard to system reliability and security. Warranties must be spelled out: For example, are hardware services provided on site, by the contractor, or by the factory? If they are not provided on site, who is responsible for shipment? Will temporary devices be provided? Within what time frame will repairs be made? Managers must carefully plan for manifold contingencies and negotiate these with contractors. They must also be familiar with the tactics of bid negotiation. For example, managers attain negotiating leverage by ensuring competition among contractors, by subjecting contracts to future rebidding, and by deferring payment until major parts of the project are completed to the contractee's satisfaction.

Disaster Recovery

During the 1990s, many public and nonprofit organizations experienced problems with the reliability of their information technology systems. IT systems often fail, and the consequences of such failures are sometimes catastrophic. At a minimum, data files may be lost, such as those concerning recent transactions or invoices that have not yet been paid. More ominously, when air traffic computer systems failed in Miami, Florida, in the mid-1990s, commercial jetliners on multiple occasions flew for several minutes with only voice guidance from traffic controllers. Although no disasters occurred, these events prompted the Federal Aviation Administration to speed up its computer disaster recovery efforts. Although the causes of IT failures are not always known, many analysts attribute computer failures to the increased complexity of computer systems and software that cause small bugs to come into play. In other instances, human errors and sabotage cause networks to fail, most dramatically in the 1995 bombing of the federal building in Oklahoma City.

Disaster recovery plans must begin with a thorough understanding of the organization's core operations and how IT failures affect these functions. First, data must be identified that are critical to the functioning of public and nonprofit organizations. Second, managers must assess the likelihood of such data becoming unavailable due to IT failure and measures that can be undertaken to reduce the possibility of failure. For example, failures are reduced by using software that is known to be reliable. In organizations with distributed, interrelated local area networks (LANs), critical data are less likely to be permanently lost when they are shared across networks; however, many public organizations still use central computers and other organizations do not have linked LANs that share data on a permanent basis.

Disaster recovery options depend to a large extent on the relationship between losses and system downtime. For example, when several hours can be allowed for disaster recovery, it may be possible to shut down the entire system and restart it. Backup tapes can then be directly loaded. A critical issue then is the frequency of making backup tapes, the time needed to reboot the system, and the reliability of software that may have caused the system failure. Some public and nonprofit organizations also maintain software copies that are simplified, known to be error-free, and used until existing software has been carefully examined. Alternatively, organizations have arrangements with other LANs or providers to temporarily use those systems. In other instances, very little downtime can be tolerated, such as in nuclear power facilities, air traffic control, subway and other rail systems, and strategic weapon systems. These disaster recovery plans rely on concurrent systems that run parallel with existing systems. These backup systems are automatically switched over when needed. This more expensive solution is justified because of the high cost of system failure (Thierauff, 1994).

Service to Users

The explosion of end-user computing has increased the demand for technical service. However, people who are hired by IT units often lack the communication skills that are necessary to effectively interact with end users. Unresponsiveness and poor social interactions cause great client dissatisfaction: As noted in Chapter 2, technical skills alone are insufficient to ensure effectiveness. Yet, end-user satisfaction with well-functioning technical support is of strategic importance to IT efforts (Danziger, Kraemer, Dunkle, & King, 1993). Many IT units now train their staff to deal with end users. Such training efforts acknowledge the technical proclivity of their staff but emphasize familiarity with frequent end-user problems and the need for prompt, courteous, and effective responses. Staff also learn to communicate with end users with minimal jargon to further understanding.

Technical staff must often learn to first address end-user needs and then attempt necessary technical work. Prompt attention to user needs is critical because many users are under pressures to perform. As a practical matter, many IT units now have extra PCs with frequently used software. When equipment failure occurs, these PCs are readily used as temporary loaners to employees. This addresses users' need for performance and it provides IT units with the necessary time to fix the problem at hand. IT units also plan for LAN failures and have backup plans to reboot systems with minimal loss of existing data.

In addition to effectively handling service requests, IT units must plan and evaluate their technical support. Some units periodically visit end users to inquire about their current or future needs, apart from service calls. CIOs must encourage other departments to speak frankly about the service that they are receiving. CIOs should also adopt performance standards for technical service,

TABLE 9.3 Technical Support User Satisfaction Survey Questions

Technical Support Services:

How often have you called our office for technical support during the last three months? Approximately how often have you contacted us during the last year?

Do you normally contact us by phone, E-mail, written request, or dropping by?

How satisfied are you with our handling of your initial response?

If we had to come out to your office to examine the problem, on average, how satisfied are you with the speed with which we did so?

On average, how satisfied are you with our ability to promptly solve your problem?

In the event that we did not immediately solve your problem, how satisfied are you with the final result? What did you like? What did you not like?

Please rate us according to how courteous we are.

Please rate us according to how prompt we are.

Please rate us according to how knowledgeable we are.

Are you looking forward to interacting with us again?

Purchasing Needs:

Are you planning to purchase any new software or hardware in the near future? If so, what?

Do you feel that you might benefit from assistance in your purchasing effort?

Would you welcome us assisting you in matters concerning your service contract?

Would you like us to install your system or software for you?

Would you like us to show you how to make basic use of your system?

Training Needs:

Have you received training from us before? If yes, how satisfied are you with the training? What training did you receive? What did you like most? What did you not like?

Was the training that you received timely? Was the training responsive to your needs? Did it solve your problem?

Was the technical specialist courteous?

Was support available for follow-up questions?

Would you recommend our training efforts to any other departments?

Do you have any needs for computer, network, or software training? If so, which specific needs are they?

Do you have a need for computer-based training relating to your job performance?

for example, returning phone calls within four hours and providing operational machines within one working day. IT units must also strive to delight their end users in other ways, for example, by making available free software to end users who might not be familiar with it. An example of a technical user survey is provided in Table 9.3.

Governance

In recent years, many public organizations have explored using e-mail and the Internet for direct communication with their citizens and program clients. Three strategies for electronic communication are increased access to databases (e.g., library catalogues or real estate taxes), increased dissemination of electronic information through, for example, bulletin boards, and two-way E-mail services that allow exchanges between citizens and officials. Although cities that experimented with this new technology in the early 1990s such as Santa Monica and Irvine (both in California) often invested in their own e-mail technology, most cities are now using the Internet. Although no data are available regarding the number of government "home pages," it is believed that this number is rapidly increasing. The use of home pages and e-mail exchanges in government also raises the possibility of using the Internet for up-to-date citizen polling. Such use is referred to as "teledemocracy."

Teledemocracy has its proponents and opponents. Arguments in favor of teledemocracy include instant communication and the possibility of broader participation, such as by those who do not regularly participate in voting and other citizen input processes. Teledemocracy gives people who are handicapped, shy, or stutter a bias-free, electronic arena in which to express their views. An obvious argument against teledemocracy is that it discriminates against those who do not own computers. Although studies find that families with school-age children are increasingly likely to have a computer, poor and older residents are less likely to have a computer with a modem. Another argument against teledemocracy is that, at the present time, very few people participate in this form of communication. Elected officials are also wary of using telecommunication for fear of stirring up uncontrolled discussion and the loss of deniability (Conte, 1995; Guthrie & Dutton, 1992). This suggests that at the present time, the practice of teledemocracy still lies in the future. Perhaps when computers are as widespread and as frequently used as telephones, public organizations will rely on electronic, jurisdictionwide information to solicit debate and input. In the interim, public organizations can work toward teledemocracy by developing interactive processes and making these available as alternatives to standard forms of communication, interaction, and voting.

Governance issues are also sometimes involved in ensuring that local communities have state-of-the-art telecommunication services. Local governments must sometimes provide telecommunication infrastructure when private firms fail to make these investments, as sometimes happens in small communities and rural areas. Even large cities such as Tacoma, Washington, have found private investment lagging. In response, some public utilities are now extending their fiber optic networks to businesses and residents. Although critics contend that this is tantamount to unfair competition by subsidized, public enterprises, the need for modern infrastructure and services is an important, pragmatic argument in allowing these entities to provide these services (Healey, 1997).

Security

Security remains an important IT issue. Access, data integrity, and the protection of information assets are important, because public and nonprofit organizations increasingly rely on their information systems for operations and decision making and because IT systems are increasingly subject to the threat of sophisticated viruses, hackers, and sabotage. Many organizations have horror stories of stolen computer files, lost data, and compromised systems. In one case, a Tampa, Florida, department of health and human services office lost a confidential file on AIDS patients in the community, which later surfaced after it had been sold to several people at a nightclub.

Access to IT systems is often limited through the use of passwords that grant access to specific data and program libraries. Site verification and ID devices can be used to further ensure the identity of computer users. Beyond these procedures, data encryption strategies protect public and nonprofit organizations from unauthorized eavesdropping over transmission lines. Computer viruses are programs that corrupt other programs and data files, and are considered a main threat to IT systems. Organizations protect themselves against computer viruses by scanning all diskettes and backup tapes. Data integrity is further increased by training users in correct data input procedures, verifying new data, periodically checking data files for errors, and employing built-in checks of data accuracy. Through these procedures, managers increase their IT security and minimize the likelihood of losses in productivity.

While many security systems minimize unauthorized access and use, citizens have the right to know about information on them that is kept in the records of public agencies. Individuals must be able to find out which data are in their records, and how these data are used. They have the right to prevent agency use of their information for purposes other than those for which data are collected. Agencies must provide citizens access to their files so that they can become familiar with their data. These basic rights are part of the Privacy Act of 1974, which has been upheld in subsequent legislation and many court rulings (Andersen & Dawes, 1991).

Managing IT Projects

Information technology projects are often a source of major frustration. From large-scale implementation projects to seemingly minor tasks such as license renewals, information technology is often associated with delays, cost overruns, and end users who feel that their needs are being served inadequately. As IT continues to proliferate, so too do complaints about information technology systems and IT professionals. Managing IT projects well is therefore imperative to both IT and non-IT managers alike. This section discusses productivity through project management as applied to information technology.

A basic element of project management is that projects must be evaluated with regard to *cost, quality, and time.* A key objective of project management is to ensure that projects are on time, are within budget, perform at or above specifications, and also achieve customer satisfaction. Projects must be planned, executed, and completed with these ends in mind (Frame, 1994; Haynes, 1989).

Critical Success Factors

Many studies have examined the characteristics of both failed and successful information technology projects. Pinto (1994) provides a review of such studies and finds that although technical problems and limitations are important, other barriers are poor top management support, unmotivated teams, leadership problems, conflicting objectives, and deficient procedures. These findings are replicated in many different settings and for different project phases. Such findings suggest that management matters. For example, although technical problems can surface at any time, the lack of planning and leadership may cause such problems to be detected late in the project, without there having been adequate foresight to develop contingency strategies.[3]

Based on such studies, Pinto (1994) suggests that managers should adopt the following practices. First, IT managers should keep the project mission and specific objectives in the forefront at all times. Projects usually experience myriad pressures that cause delays or changes to specifications. Managers must guard the initial specifications and purposes to ensure that organizational politics and ad hoc considerations do not cause projects to fail to meet essential objectives. Second, project managers must consult with clients and users early in the process. Their input is essential for specifying quality, time, and cost objectives, as well as critical user needs that the project must satisfy. It is often very costly to modify specifications in late stages to incorporate user parameters. Third, managers should also stay in touch with clients throughout the project. Doing so allows for client input and for trying out new ideas or deviations from contract specifications on clients. Involving clients also helps bridge the gap between contract specification and final product.

Fourth, IT managers must ensure that IT technology works. Many projects involve great creativity to ensure that applications work as contractually agreed upon. Managers must plan to put their applications through rigorous testing to ensure that clients do not experience failure during warranty periods. Fifth, managers must set and maintain project parameters. A tendency exists to allow for time and cost "creep" as managers and employees deal with unexpected problems. Managers must insist that, despite unanticipated problems, project parameters remain intact. Sixth, managers must select the right people for the team. This involves ensuring technical competence as well as the ability of employees to work well together and with others so they can interact effectively with clients and other organizations whose support is needed. Work units should not exceed team people: A rule of project management is that any project requiring more than 10 people will never get done; when more people are needed, managers should consider using two or more small teams. Seventh, all projects must have top management support. This helps overcome threats to authority and to the budget, and may facilitate overcoming bureaucratic red tape. Eight, managers must anticipate the possibility of failure and deal with it. Managers need a variety of contingency plans to deal with unanticipated complications. For example, key people get sick, small tasks may have to be further subdivided and potentially cause delays, and essential liaison persons get transferred (Fried, 1995).

These critical success factors are shared by many authors and validated by many projects. For example, although most Geographic Information Systems (GIS) have brought many benefits to departments, in one city, one such system was implemented and maintained by central IT staff. Users had to schedule time with central IT staff to use the GIS and they also incurred costs associated with travel to the central IT site. These inconveniences suggest that the system was not implemented with adequate user input, and, indeed, the system failed to be used as had been projected.

Project Management Tools

A variety of analytical tools exists that help managers to improve the management and hence the productivity of projects. These project management tools are generic and can be applied to IT projects, as discussed below.

The planning phase of IT projects requires that managers specify quality, cost, and time parameters of the projects. It is very difficult to estimate the time and cost of large projects at the initial stages of idea conception because many details and complexities are not well understood until the project is well under way. According to Fried (1995), initial estimates of projects are often off by 50%, and this is only reduced to 30% upon specification of technical and user require-ments. A basic rule is that estimates gain in accuracy as IT projects progress.

User surveys and need assessments are used to determine user needs. Pinto (1994) suggests undertaking a *client analysis* that encompasses the following aspects: (a) identification of client needs and relation to clients' business or other objectives; (b) alternative strategies for satisfying client needs and selection of appropriate strategy; (c) tolerance of clients for accepting deviations from quality, cost, and time specifications; (d) opportunities for client to influence project specifications at different stages of the project; (e) responsibilities of the client in project development; and (f) support within the client's organization for the project. Written client analyses help managers avoid "specification creep," that is, changes by users and others in specifications in late project stages or in other ways that significantly affect costs and time. Some estimates show that specification creep can cause IT project costs to increase by 35%. Client analyses also help to ensure continuance in the face of personnel turnover.

After project specifications have been determined, managers need to identify the necessary steps for completing the project. Most projects can be described as a series of smaller tasks; understanding and identifying these tasks is a first step toward effective project management. A Work Breakdown Structure iden-tifies these steps and is shown in Table 9.4 for installing a LAN.

The next steps are assigning responsibility and estimating the cost of each task. Project costs are often contingent on equipment and staff specifications as well as the speed with which projects must be completed. McLeod and Smith (1996, p. 100) show, based on empirical data, that IT project costs dramatically increase as managers attempt to reduce project time: Staff effort in information technology projects is found to be proportional to the fourth power of delivery time. Thus, for example, an IT project that would cost $168,000 to be completed in 11 months would cost $690,000 to be completed in 8 months. Time is therefore usually fixed in IT cost estimates as managers avoid the high costs of speeding up IT projects. Table 9.5 shows a Cost and Responsibility Table that assigns costs and responsibilities for implementing each of the tasks identified in Table 9.5 .

Typical cost components in Costs and Responsibility (C&R) Tables include labor, overhead (such as fringe benefits, payroll taxes, and indirect costs), materials, supplies, equipment rental or depreciation, administrative costs, and surcharges. C&R Tables can be modified in two ways. First, they can show both actual unit costs as well as those billed to clients. For example, Table 9.5 shows billable costs: The time of the IT director is an actual cost, but it is not billed to clients. C&R Tables are sometimes called Project Costing Worksheets: These

TABLE 9.4 Work Breakdown Structure

Project Name: Install LAN for Client Relations Group

Activity
Number   Task Description

---

1. Client Needs and LAN Specifications
   1.1   Meet with director, client relations group.
   1.2   Conduct client needs survey with users.
   1.3   Determine technical, compatibility, and user constraints.
   1.4   Prepare alternative performance specifications.
   1.5   Estimate cost and time project specifications.
   1.6   Prepare and submit bid.

2. Preparation for LAN Implementation
   2.1   Secure personnel and technical resources.
   2.2   Prepare users for necessary disruptions.
   2.3   Acquire hardware, software, licenses, cables, routers, and hubs.
   2.4   Write user manual for LAN use.

3. Physical Infrastructure Modification
   3.1   Complete wiring.

4. LAN Installation
   4.1   Complete network connections.
   4.2   Install LAN software.
   4.3   Test network, backup devices.
   4.4   Test new software.
   4.5   Document test results.

5. User Transition
   5.1   Provide one-time staff training in LAN use.
   5.2   Demonstrate user's new software for managing client relations.
   5.3   Ensure adequate end-user support.
   5.4   Evaluate user needs and satisfaction on a daily basis (informal).

6. User Satisfaction
   6.1   Provide modification, upgrades, and support (6 months).
   6.2   Provide formal evaluation (1 month, 3 months, 6 months).

---

state all of the different cost types (labor, equipment, etc.) for each project activity but do not always include project responsibilities. Second, some C&R Tables can provide a range of cost estimates rather than a single cost. Also, some clients want alternative prices for different project specifications. Cost estimates are unreliable for large projects, and many contracts are written on a cost-reimbursable basis; the quoted price is merely a price ceiling (i.e., cost maximum).

To improve the reliability of estimates, organizations sometimes request time and cost estimates from those who are not involved in the actual project. Those

TABLE 9.5 Cost and Responsibility Table

Activity Number	Responsibility	Time: Days (FTE)	Cost Other*	Cost Labor**
1.1	IT Director	1		N/A
1.2	IT Director, Scott Adams	1		$ 500.00
1.3-1.5	Scott Adams, Grace Bonfield	2		$1,000.00
1.6	Scott Adams	2		$1,000.00
2.1	IT Director	1		$ 500.00
2.2	IT Director, Scott Adams	3		$1,500.00
2.3	Scott Adams	1	$15,000.00	$ 500.00
2.4	Scott Adams, Grace Bonfield	5	$100.00	$3,000.00
3.1	Scott Adams, Mike Lord	6	$750.00	$3,000.00
4.1-4.5	Scott Adams	3		$1,500.00
5.1-5.2	Grace Bonfield	0.5		$ 250.00
5.3-5.4	Scott Adams	3		$1,500.00
6.1	Scott Adams	10		$5,000.00
6.2	IT Director	2		N/A

NOTE: *Includes equipment, supplies.
**Includes all overhead costs (fringe benefits, payroll taxes, indirect costs, administration fees).

who are not involved in the project have less reason to be optimistic about it and provide a more unbiased opinion. While adding to the cost of proposal preparation, this practice builds estimation expertise in the organization. A second practice is to use databases of past project time and costs to control estimates. These databases gain in precision as managers record actual costs and time upon completing each project phase. Third, managers may be able to negotiate providing more detailed estimates of later project phases as earlier phases are completed. This acknowledges that early estimates are often unreliable. Fourth, different managers are asked to provide a range of estimates, specifically, "most likely," maximum, and minimum estimates. The most probable estimate is calculated as (Minimum Estimate + 4 * Likely Estimate + Maximum Estimate)/6. Statistical theory suggests that approximately two thirds of actual costs and completion times lie within a range of (Maximum-Minimum)/6 from this estimate (i.e., one standard deviation). This range is often quoted as the cost and time estimate. Approximately 99% of all costs and completion times lie within the (Maximum-Minimum)/2 range, that is, three standard deviations.

Upon completion of the C&R Table, managers need to further improve their understanding of the time management aspects of the project. They need to know (a) specific start and ending dates of project tasks; (b) the sequencing of tasks, specifically, tasks whose starting point is necessarily contingent on the successful completion of previous tasks (such prior tasks can potentially delay the entire project); (c) the amount of slack time for each task (i.e., task delays that do not cause delays or interruptions of other tasks); and (d) critical success factors for each task as well as for the overall project. Figure 9.1 shows a Program Evaluation and Review Technique (PERT) chart. This time management tool shows the necessary sequencing of tasks for part of the LAN project. It shows that the start of task 4.1 is contingent upon timely completion of tasks 3.1 and 2.2. These latter tasks have no slack (or float) time, and delays in these tasks will cause a delay for the entire project. By contrast, although task 2.1 is a necessary task for 3.1, task 2.1 has a projected completion time of about two days and an estimated slack of about three days: Thus delay in completing 2.1 may not be critical to the successful completion of the overall LAN project. Note that these are real days, whereas the days stated in the Table 9.5, the C&R Table, are FTE days that are used for cost estimation.

PERT charts are thus very different than daily lists that many managers make to ensure that tasks get done. PERT charts increase awareness of critical task interdependencies and impose a sense of realism. PERT charts build upon earlier Gantt charts, named after Henry Gantt, an industrial engineer in the early 1900s. Gantt charts show the beginning and end dates for each task. Each task occupies a separate line, and the horizontal axis is a time line similar to that shown in Figure 9.1. PERT charts were developed by the U.S. Navy for managing submarine construction and are useful when task interdependencies exist. Identifying critical tasks is also a preliminary step toward identifying critical success factors, that is, factors that may cause substantial delay or failure of projects. In practice, although many managers fail to use Gantt or PERT charts, most are aware of critical factors and deadlines that are important to the project.

The above analytical techniques help managers develop a rational project plan. However, effective implementation also requires attention to the human dimension of motivating and leading team members and involving users with project development and implementation to ensure client satisfaction. The above tools further these goals by increasing discussion and involvement. For example, PERT charts help team members understand their role in the project and, for example, why timely completion of some tasks is deemed critical. Work Break-

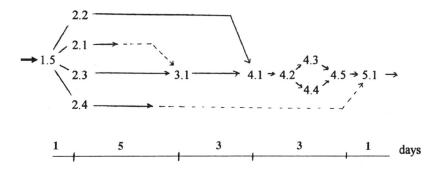

Figure 9.1. PERT Chart

down Structures are opportunities for managers to solicit employee input about the need for tasks, as well as tasks that may be missing. Clients can be extensively involved with client analysis. Providing feedback from this analysis shows clients that their input is being listened to. Sharing PERT charts with clients helps them understand necessary project steps and why, for example, the absence of IT project personnel in client facilities does not mean that the project is not being worked on.

The above tools also provide a basis for monitoring work and subsequent evaluation. Project planning tools allow managers to monitor (a) time schedules and deadlines, (b) performance accomplishments relative to standards, (c) user satisfaction, and (d) actual versus projected costs for each of these phases. For example, most IT system projects involve the following phases: initiation, requirements definition, technical design, parts acquisition and construction, installation, and testing. Each of these phases can be monitored. By comparing actual versus targeted achievements, managers identify the need for corrective actions. Such processes of change should involve employees and clients in ways that create mutual understanding and agreement about the need for modifications of the current project. The impossibility of accurately estimating complex projects implies that renegotiation frequently occurs. Drawing on a strong client-user relationship is an important asset in renegotiation.

The final project phase is termination. This usually involves a number of steps such as final testing, user training, providing clients with necessary documents such as license agreements and operating procedures, summarizing the project history including activities and consultations that were conducted, thanking employees for their contributions and providing formal acknowledgments (such as through documentation for later employee performance evaluation), completing a final report and audit and a final interview with the client, and declaring the project complete. At this time, IT project managers must also make arrangements to conduct subsequent client evaluations as well as other training or consulting services that may be part of the contract. The final audit often provides reliable information about actual project costs and time, and can be used for future projects as well as subsequent program evaluation (Puckett & Vogt, 1995).

Summary

Information technologies are widely used in public and nonprofit organizations, yet satisfaction with IT systems and service is sometimes low. The productivity of IT involves planning carefully, attending to customer relations, and resolving such critical issues as the extent of outsourcing, disaster recovery, security, and governance. Planning affects the role of IT in public and nonprofit organizations as well as the management of IT systems, data operations, and technical support for users. Customer relations are key to the success of IT. IT units must plan to meet their users' needs and should use surveys, advisory councils, and regular consultations with users to ensure satisfaction. Outsourcing, disaster recovery, and other strategic issues must be addressed as well. This chapter also discusses critical success factors in information technology project management as well as a range of project management tools, and applies these to information technology.

Notes

1. A 10% discount rate reflects the opportunity cost of money, for example, when invested in the stock market over time. For example, if total costs are $100 in year 0, $50 in year 1, and $35 in year 2, then the net present value of total discounted costs is $100 + $50/(1.10)^1 + $35/(1.10)^2 = $174.38. Likewise, total benefits are identified, discounted, and added. Assume that such three-year benefits equal $190.00. This implies that benefits exceed costs and that the return on investment (ROI) is (190.00/174.38) *100% = 8.96%. Spreadsheet analysis is used to estimate *a range* of likely ROI estimates. For example, assume that managers want to know the consequences of a 30% cost overrun and a 20% reduction of benefits due to unanticipated problems. Such calculations show the rationale for setting high ROI standards and developing strict management plans.

2. About $12.4 billion is for hardware, $13.1 billion for internal services, $6.7 billion for external services, and $2.2 billion for other services. This market is expected to grow at an annual

rate of 5.5% during the next five years. Federal information technology expenditures are about equal to state and local government expenditures.

3. As the saying goes, "People don't plan to fail, they fail to plan."

References

Ady, H. (1995). Changing role of information technology regulators. *Public Manager, 24*(3), 31-35.

Andersen, K. (1995, September 6-9). *Information technology and transitions in the public service: A comparison of Scandinavia and the United States.* Paper presented at the annual conference of the European Group of Public Administration, Rotterdam, the Netherlands.

Anderson, D., & Dawes, S. (1991). *Government information management: A primer and casebook.* Englewood Cliffs, NJ: Prentice Hall.

Bohan, G., & Beaulieu, C. (1993, July 17-21). *Redesigning government decision-making: Technology can empower groups.* Paper presented at the 54th National Training Conference of the American Society for Public Administration, San Francisco.

Buckholtz, T. (1995). *Information proficiency.* New York: Van Nostrand Reinhold.

Cats-Baril, W., & Thompson, R. (1995). Managing information technology projects in the public sector. *Public Administration Review, 55*(6), 559-566.

Cats-Baril, W., & Thompson, R. (1997). *Information technology and management.* Chicago: Irwin.

Conte, C. (1995). Teledemocracy. *Governing, 8*(6), 33-41.

Cook, M. (1996). *Building enterprise information architectures.* Upper Saddle River, NJ: Prentice Hall.

Danziger, J., Kraemer, K., Dunkle, D., & King, J. (1993). Enhancing the quality of computing service: Technology, structure and people. *Public Administration Review, 53*(2), 161-169.

Frame, J. (1994). *The new project management.* San Francisco: Jossey-Bass.

Fried, L. (1995). *Managing information technology in turbulent times.* New York: John Wiley.

Globerman, S., & Vining, A. (1996). A framework for evaluating the government contracting out decision with an application to information technology. *Public Administration Review, 56*(6), 577-586.

Gurwitt, R. (1996). The new data czars. *Governing, 9*(12), 52-58.

Guthrie, K., & Dutton, W. (1992). The politics of citizen access technology. *Policy Studies Review, 4,* 574-597.

Haynes, M. (1989). *Project management.* Menlo Park, CA: CRISP Publications.

Healey, J. (1997). The peoples' wires. *Governing, 10*(2), 34-39.

Johnson, C. (1996). Accelerating ITS deployment. *Public Management, 78*(9), 28-33.

Kearney, A. (1990). *Breaking the barriers: IT effectiveness in Great Britain and Ireland.* London: CIMA.

Kraemer, K. (1996). Managing information systems. In J. Perry (Ed.), *Handbook of public administration* (2nd ed., pp. 574-589). San Francisco: Jossey-Bass.

McCleod, G., & Smith, D. (1996). *Managing information technology projects.* Danvars, MA: Boyd & Fraser.

Moura, B. (1996). San Carlos discovers the Internet. *Public Management, 78*(1), 31-37.

Norris, D., & Kraemer, K. (1996). Mainframe and PC computing in American cities: Myths and realities. *Public Administration Review, 56*(6), 568-576.

O'Brien, J. (1996). *Management Information Systems.* Chicago: Irwin.

Pinto, J. (1994). *Successful information system implementation: The human side.* Upper Darby, PA: Project Management Institute.

Puckett, G., & Vogt, J. (1995). Use your computer to evaluate your programs. *Nonprofit World, 13*(1), 21-23.

Remenyi, D., Money, A., & Twite, A. (1993). *Measuring and managing IT benefits* (2nd ed.). Oxford, UK: Basil Blackwell.

Silk, D. (1991). *Planning IT.* Oxford, UK: Butterworth-Heinemann.

Society for Nonprofit Organizations. (1996). How nonprofits use technology: Survey results. *Nonprofit World, 14*(3), 36-39.

Stephens, C. (1995). *The nature of information technology managerial work: The work life of five chief information officers.* Westport, CT: Quorum.

Strock, B., & Atkins, D. (1989). *The municipal computer systems handbook.* Rensselaerville, NY: Rensselaerville Systems Training Center.

Swain, J., & White, J. (1992). Information technology for productivity: Maybe, maybe not: An assessment. In M. Holzer (Ed.), *Public productivity handbook* (pp. 643-666). New York: Marcel Dekker.

Thierauff, R. (1994). *Effective management and evaluation of information technology.* Westport, CT: Quorum.

Willcocks, L. (1993). *Information management: The evaluation of information systems invest-ments.* London: Chapman & Hall.

Productivity
Through People

What really matters is what you do with what you have.

Shirley Lord

People are essential to productivity.[1] Employee commitment and preparation are often critical to the success of productivity improvement strategies. When managers and workers are motivated and have adequate skills, productivity strategies such as quality management, strategic planning, and the use of information technology are readily implemented: Productivity goals are often accomplished or exceeded, and challenges are overcome. By contrast, when managers and workers are withdrawn, strategic planning becomes an exercise in futility and meaningless paperwork, and quality management often is viewed as a management fad whose success is measured in terms of getting by. The management, and especially the motivation of people, is viewed by many scholars and practitioners as vital to productivity improvement.

In addition to ensuring adequate motivation, productivity improvement also involves processes of employee feedback and empowerment. Productivity improvements require that people receive frequent feedback so that they can better gauge their performance. Frequent feedback also increases the number of opportunities for improvement. In addition, managers must sometimes also shape personal orientations that affect how people approach new challenges, acquire new skills, and deal with interpersonal relations. For example, when feedback is viewed as criticism, motivation often decreases and employees are less likely to learn new skills and try new improvements beyond those that eliminate future criticism. Most productivity improvement efforts occur through people, and the productivity of improvement efforts requires that interactions with people promote these efforts.

This chapter examines managerial strategies for increasing the commitment of managers and employees to productivity improvement. It discusses the nature of motivation and managerial strategies for ensuring motivation, as well as strategies for increasing productivity through effective training, feedback, goal-setting, and empowerment. This chapter also examines strategies for increasing productivity through teamwork, which is increasingly central to the work processes in organizations.

Motivation

Empirical data suggest a mixed view about the level of workplace motivation. In a recent survey, Berman and West (1997) find that only 29.8% of city managers in cities with populations of more than 50,000 agree or strongly agree with the statement, "Employees are highly motivated to achieve goals." Respective data from a sample of directors of large nonprofit social service organizations show that 56% agree or strongly agree that employees are motivated. These findings are consistent with studies such as that by Kanter and Mirvis (1989), who find that 41% of U.S. workers in all sectors can be classified as having generally upbeat attitudes, 16% as being wary, and 43% as having cynical attitudes about others. These data support the perspective that motivation and commitment greatly vary among employees: Some work settings are characterized by a great deal of motivation, whereas others experience varying degrees of apathy, and still others, are mixed. Individual employees within these different settings vary in their motivation too.

Many managers acknowledge the importance of motivating their employees, yet they find the topic of motivation confusing and are dissatisfied with their ability to lead and inspire workers. The above findings suggest that managers must have a broad range of strategies at their disposal for dealing with different environments. Employees vary in their needs, and managers need to know the needs of different employees if they are to inspire them. *A key principle of motivation is that people are motivated to pursue and satisfy their needs.* Some employees are motivated by the need for personal achievement, whereas others are motivated by the need to provide for their families. In addition, managers need to be aware of conditions that detract from employees' striving to meet their needs. For example, employees are not highly motivated to attempt to meet needs for which they feel fulfillment is beyond their reach.

Needs That Motivate

The idea that employees are motivated by pursuing fulfillment of their needs is well established. Five different groups of needs can be distinguished. First, people have a need for *basic security,* that is, for obtaining food and shelter. This includes current needs for food and safety as well as protection against future events that threaten food and safety. The importance of meeting current and future basic needs is widely recognized. For example, Maslow (1954) identifies physiological and safety needs as prerequisites for satisfying all other needs. According to Maslow, people do not focus on other needs until their basic needs are met. Basic needs are also recognized, albeit cynically, by managers who motivate by threatening employees with the loss of their jobs. However, these fear-based approaches are increasingly in disrepute because they produce a high level of resentment and are associated with workplace violence and low levels of employee commitment. Increasingly, managers need to look for motivators that are consistent with advancing rather than threatening employee welfare. For example, helping workers upgrade their skills increase employee commitment by helping them meet their basic safety needs. Providing job security, medical insurance, and retirement planning are examples of efforts to ensure that future needs are met.

A second group of needs focuses on receiving *acknowledgment and recognition* from others. Many employees have a need to belong and contribute to something larger than themselves. Employees who have need for acknowledgment and group belonging are motivated by the praise and acknowledgment that they receive from their supervisors and coworkers. Many employees who join nonprofit organizations have a strong need to have their commitment acknowledged and recognized by group members and to be accepted by work groups that share these commitments. Strong needs for belonging are also present among older employees who may have lost their jobs and accept pay cuts for jobs with other organizations to satisfy their needs for belonging. The need for group acceptance is very strong in many employees, and managers are therefore urged to give frequent praise that signals acceptance of individuals in their work group and organizations.

A third group involves the individual need for *accomplishment, creativity, and growth* by acquiring new knowledge or skills. These needs are caused by work itself and do not depend on how others value or otherwise acknowledge individual effort. Maslow recognized these needs as the pinnacle of human motivation following basic needs and needs of group belonging and recognition. Nadler and Lawler (1977) also acknowledge the importance of work as its own motivator, but they do not view it as being connected to these other needs. Some people have a strong need for accomplishment and creativity; such internal motivation, when it exists, is among the strongest of motivations. Employees vary greatly in their need for creative expression, and managers must be careful in terms of providing creative challenges to those who do not have this need. Employees with high achievement needs often seek out new challenges, and managers often need to do little more than ensure that employees' work provides opportunities for growth.

A fourth group of needs are those related to the acquisition, maintenance, and use of *power.* McClelland (1985) notes that employees and managers are motivated by power as well as by affiliation and achievement. Power concerns the need to influence and lead others and to be in control of one's environment. Managers in public and nonprofit organizations often have a high need for power with which to do good for others and social groups. However, some managers are motivated by the need to accumulate power to dominate and control others. This negative use of power is ego-driven, often highly abusive, and seldom benefits organizations, employees, and clients. The need for power is sometimes confused with achievement. Executives, lawyers, and politicians often have a high need for power but are only motivated to achieve to the extent that accomplishment is a prerequisite for accumulating power. Employees who are motivated by power are often motivated by material manifestations that acknowledge power, such as prestigious assignments, increases in salary, promotions, corner offices, and so forth.[2]

A fifth group are those *other needs* that are indirectly satisfied by work but not associated with work or employers. For example, a classic indirect need is to take care of one's family and help them afford a better lifestyle. Many single parents are highly committed to raising their children and are motivated to work because of the material benefits it provides them in raising their families. Many employees and managers also have ego needs that are indirectly satisfied: The need to live in an upper-class neighborhood or to purchase a luxury car signals that they have made it in the world. Work also satisfies other needs including the ability to recreate in luxurious ways such as by buying a boat, traveling to exotic locations, and so on.

In sum, employees and mangers have many different needs. Managers need to identify which needs are present in different employees. Tulgan (1995) believes that many recent entrants into the job market are motivated by a need for tangible rewards, such as money, as acknowledgment of their value to organizations that increasingly offer little job security. According to Henry (1995), research shows that employees and managers in public and nonprofit organizations have higher needs for achievement and security and somewhat lower needs for acceptance and financial rewards than those in for-profit corporations. While these are useful generalizations, managers must determine the needs of individual employees.

Conditions That Affect Motivation

It is obvious that organizations do not exist solely to satisfy employee needs. Employees and organizations engage in an exchange of efforts to satisfy mutual needs. Motivation is increased when employees feel that organizational goals are consistent with their own. Organizational goals must either support employee needs *indirectly,* by rewarding performance with means that help employees satisfy their needs (e.g., promotions that satisfy the need for power), or *directly,* which occurs when organizational goals are identical to those of employees (e.g., an environmentalist who joins the Sierra Club). When goal congruence is insufficiently present, motivation suffers and employees do not feel that the goals of organizations or managers are aligned with their own.

In addition, how organizations go about achieving their goals must be consistent with furthering employee needs. Some writers view human motivation as a function of the consequences that employees experience from their behavior. Skinner noted (1971) that behavior is affected and reinforced by its consequences, which suggests that needs are largely shaped by positive or negative feedback that individuals receive from their actions. For example, frequent negative feedback often causes some employees to reduce their own needs as a way of reducing future disappointments about unrealized needs. This reduces motivation, too. This perspective is consistent with the use of incentives to shape behavior, and mediocrity is sometimes explained by the presence of punishments for negative behavior and the absence of rewards for positive behavior and accomplishments (Werther, Ruch, & McClure, 1986). Employees need positive feedback and rewards. Although behavioralists sometimes maintain that all needs are a function of social reinforcement, an integrative perspective maintains that humans have needs that exist independent of the feedback that they receive.

Employee motivation also affected by the feasibility of goals. Expectancy theory suggests that goals that are aligned with employee needs may still not be much pursued when employees feel that they are infeasible. Research shows that performance increases as the perceived difficulty of goals increases from low to moderate to challenging, but quickly diminishes when goals are perceived as impossible; the latter causes feelings of resignation (Locke & Latham, 1990). It follows that managers should not set impossible goals and that they should support workers by suggesting strategies for realizing difficult goals. However, excessive guidance diminishes the challenge and may reduce motivation among employees who have a strong need for creativity or achievement.

Employee motivation is further affected by workplace conditions. Herzberg (1959) observes that poor company policies, supervision, salary, working conditions, and interpersonal relations with supervisors often demotivate employees. These are called "hygiene factors." Poor working conditions complicate employee efforts to satisfy their needs. For example, mediocre wages affect the ability of employees to provide a better lifestyle for their families or to satisfy their ego needs. However, Hertzberg also notes that the presence of good policies, salaries, relations with supervisors, and so on, seldom leads to high levels of motivation. Rather, motivation is more strongly increased through motivators that include opportunities for advancement, accomplishment, recognition, challenge, and responsibility. These are consistent with those identified above. *Managers must provide motivators and avoid hygiene factors.*

Many authors self-improvement books acknowledge that people often are motivated by accomplishment and opportunities for advancement. However, they note that an excessive focus on accomplishment induces feelings of meaninglessness (or emptiness). Workers have a need for lasting fulfillment and meaning, and some may be motivated to achieve that. Various authors find that emptiness is caused by (a) a lack of authentic connection with one's environment and (b) the inability to fully live in the present without being preoccupied with past or future events, accomplishments, feelings of anger, sadness and fear, or consequences for ego or professional identity (e.g., Almaas, 1990). Fulfillment in pursuit of accomplishment becomes possible when the act of accomplishing is embraced and issues of anxiety, resignation, anger, belonging, and ego are resolved. Some managers and employees are motivated by work environments that provide support dealing with these issues and opportunities for fulfillment through accomplishment.

Finally, employees need to feel that they are treated and rewarded fairly. Equity theory discusses that workers experience sharp demotivation when they perceive their rewards to be unfair (Adams, 1963; Cobb, Folger, & Wooten, 1995). Two important standards of fairness are (a) expectations about rewards for individual performance based on standards of merit, agreements with employers, or past patterns of giving rewards, and (b) rewards that are compared against those of coworkers or other referents (i.e., equity). When rewards are withheld or are perceived to be unfair, motivation plummets and workers may question the goal congruence with their employers.

A Strategy for Motivation

Employees are apt to vary with regard to what they seek from their employers and work and, as previously stated, managers must engage in conversation with workers to identify their needs. The lack of dialogue increases the possibility that managers project their own expectations onto workers. The saying "Do to others as you would like others to do to you" is misleading: Managers who have learned to moderate their needs in accordance with their position and the realities of their organization may have greatly different needs than, for example, new employees or those who have different personal situations.

Kolb, Osland, and Rubin (1995) suggest that managers and employees should engage in a process of establishing a "psychological contract" as part of their employment negotiation. A psychological contract is defined as an unwritten understanding about mutual needs, goals, expectations, and procedures (such as feedback and evaluation). Mutual needs and goals are seldom addressed in employment contracts. Topics for psychological contracts include support in dealing with child care responsibilities, the frequency and nature of managerial feedback, the possibility of training and of acquiring new skills, and so on. Psychological contracts are potentially broad in scope but usually limited to those issues that are highly valued by employees. Psychological contracts increase motivation by allowing managers to better understand the needs of individual employees, by helping to provide rewards and conditions that address individual needs, and by ensuring a high degree of clarity about roles and expectations.

Psychological contracts also provide a framework for dealing with inevitable moments of disagreement or disappointment. Unless managers wish to rely on formal grievance processes (which are time-consuming and apt to ruin the reputation of all involved), they must develop and maintain open lines of communication that address disrupted expectations. Unfulfilled expectations, stated or unstated, give rise to feelings of resentment, distrust, and betrayal. Such emotions create social distance and diminish commitment. When left to fester, these emotions may lead to actions of sabotage, passive aggression, and workplace violence.

Psychological contracts are usually entered into upon joining an organization. During the job interview and thereafter, employees have a window of opportunity to shape the expectations of their new supervisors. Existing employees must find other occasions to reshape these expectations. The process of creating mutual understanding is often entered into a process that acknowledges mutual dependency and uncertainty: Both employees and managers may be uncertain about the extent to which their needs will be met. Employees who acknowledge and address the uncertainty of their managers are often able to create an opening for expressing their own needs as well. Although many employees are rightly hesitant about making demands on managers, it is often noted that those who fail to express expectations for raises, time off, promotions, and other benefits frequently fail to get them.

Although many employees express a need for greater financial rewards, such rewards are often unavailable to managers of public and nonprofit organizations. Financial rewards are consistent with meeting many basic and indirect, non-work-related needs, as well as needs for acknowledgment and power. However, the lack of financial rewards in many public and nonprofit organizations implies that managers must use other rewards. Nonfinancial rewards must often be targeted to meet specific employee needs, unlike financial rewards, which serve a broad range of needs. For example, an employee who expresses a need for more salary to better provide for her children may be helped by a flextime schedule that gives her time off to find a second job. However, this motivator is not applicable to those who do not have this need. Financial rewards are also regarded as acknowledgment of employees' accomplishments, especially merit increases.[3] The lack of financial rewards implies that managers must seek other forms of recognition. Some nonfinancial forms of recognition include assignments to important committees and resume-building projects, which also serve power needs of employees.

Table 10.1 lists some alternative rewards that managers might consider that do not involve salary raises or promotion. These rewards are illustrative and managers should consider other rewards, according to employee needs. For example, free parking for a month might be meaningful for lower paid employees but not for executives, and job rotation is a motivator only for those who

TABLE 10.1 Alternative Rewards

Acknowledgment from supervisor	Gift certificate
Acknowledgment from team members	Guest of honor
Acknowledgment from the organization	Job rotation
Birthday card	Movie certificate
Book certificate	New computer or printer
Choice assignment	New furniture
Computer training	Office decoration
Conference travel	Personal stationary
Dinner certificate	Small cash award
Extra night's stay during travel	Team leader for a week
Flextime	Theater certificate
Free parking for a month	Training
Free transportation for a month	Use of an assistant
Friday off	

have expressed a need for new experiences. While these rewards address a wide range of employee needs, they do not substitute for providing adequate basic rewards such as salary and retirement contributions, which respond to other employee needs.

A challenge is dealing with workers who have low expectations about jobs and rewards. These employees are often downtrodden, resigned, and fearful of disclosing their real needs or preferences. Such workers appear to go by the premise that "whatever you tell your boss is sure to be used against you at some point." Such workers put in a "full day's work for a full day's pay" and no more. Although they often require little supervision, they produce very little, too. Many managers wonder how they can light a fire under such workers. The process of identifying the needs of such workers and establishing a "psychological contract" must be entered into slowly, piecemeal, and initially with limited scope. Managers must show that rewards are available to satisfy the needs of these employees in return for greater commitment. Adverse working conditions must also be addressed. Trust is reestablished in small increments. It must be shown that new commitments will be honored and that initiative is not punished. Establishing a psychological contract with downtrodden managers is even more difficult; they are likely to misunderstand such efforts as insubordination or as attempts to undermine their authority. Here, too, efforts must be undertaken in a piecemeal fashion.

Finally, psychological contracts enable managers to engage in productive, counseling-oriented discussions with employees about their performance. The key questions of counseling are as follows: What have we agreed that you would accomplish? What are your accomplishments thus far? Do you understand the consequences of not achieving your goals? What can be done to improve performance? Is the level of support that you receive reasonable? Counseling must be sharply separated from criticism that is negative and destructive in nature. Some managers feel that employee underperformance is sometimes caused by a lack of responsibility-taking. External circumstances are blamed for failures, even though many circumstances could have been avoided, foreseen, overcome, managed, or otherwise dealt with through proactive behavior (Glasser, 1994). Research shows that people who believe they can control events and consequences that significantly affect their lives exhibit greater motivation, set higher goals, and achieve higher levels of performance than those who believe that their performance is greatly affected by circumstances outside their control (Spector, 1982). Thus an outcome of counseling might be to help employees better control conditions in their environment.

Beyond Motivation: Further Strategies for Increasing Employee Productivity

Modern approaches to productivity management also use other strategies such as feedback, empowerment, and an effective training process. These strategies advance productivity improvement efforts and also affect employee motivation.

Feedback

Feedback is an integral part of motivating and ensuring productivity. Through feedback, employees obtain assessment of their performance. Feedback gives supervisors and others an opportunity to signal their approval of performance and employee behavior, and to attach rewards and punishments to such assessments. It provides information that is the basis for performance improvement. In short, feedback regulates future expectations and motivation. Feedback and communication are also essential in dealing with differences that arise from different cultural backgrounds.

Feedback is often discussed in the context of employee performance evaluation, but the frequency of annual evaluations seldom provides for sufficient feedback. Productivity requires that workers receive ongoing feedback about their performance so that they can (a) make corrections when needed and (b) enjoy frequent praise, which leads to high levels of motivation and performance.

Indeed, if performance is inadequate, why wait until the annual performance evaluation to provide feedback? If performance is adequate, why wait to provide praise and further encouragement? High-performance organizations give employees and managers frequent, almost ongoing feedback. A request from one police precinct to provide performance measures on a quarterly rather than biweekly basis was denied because doing so reduces the number of yearly improvement opportunities from 26 to only 4. Managers also mistakenly assume that workers receive feedback about their performance from other sources. A TQM adage is that few dissatisfied clients express their complaints to service providers and that they do not always do so to the employees who cause complaints. In addition, performance appraisal does not provide an environment that is conducive to problem solving. Performance appraisals have legal implications for the employment status of workers, and admitted shortcomings may be used against employees. Although efforts are made to conduct performance appraisals in a less formal atmosphere, their legal significance remains.

Workers and managers should get feedback from their supervisors, subordinates, clients, and coworkers. Each of these sources has different knowledge about the services that they receive and is able to make valuable contributions to further improvement. Fox and Klein (1996) discuss the use of such "360° feedback" in annual performance evaluation in Bismarck, North Dakota. These evaluations are weighted by supervisory evaluations (50%), anonymous evaluations of peers and subordinates (25%), and self-appraisals (25%). However, 360° feedback can also be provided more frequently. Informal exchanges between workers and managers, clients, coworkers, and subordinates provide important feedback. Such comments sometimes must be solicited. Systematic assessments through client surveys, feedback from subordinates, and compilations of client or other complaints can be solicited on a quarterly basis, thereby increasing the frequency of 360° feedback.

The specific strategy of providing feedback is straightforward: Managers should (a) provide a balanced assessment of employee performance (including both the positive and the negative), (b) emphasize the objective nature of service outcomes (some facts are indisputable), (c) establish their commitment to helping employees achieve positive results, and (d) work collaboratively with employees to develop strategies for improving performance (solutions should not be imposed). They should also (e) help employees develop the perspective that it is within their power to develop conditions for success and (f) agree on a timetable for monitoring improvement as well as (g) further strategies for support and feedback and, importantly, and (h) future rewards for improvement. This eight-step approach helps minimize the potentially demotivating effects of negative feedback by depersonalizing outcomes and providing strategies for success. Demotivation occurs when employees feel bad about themselves as professionals and fail to develop efficacious response strategies. Negative feedback is often negatively interpreted. Managers should know that they may not be fully aware of other feedback that employees have received.

A challenge is dealing with employees and managers who do not believe that feedback is important and who exhibit low levels of productivity. These latter conditions often go together. Such employees and managers must be approached carefully. Piecemeal efforts are often needed to increase awareness about the importance of feedback. These are also undertaken to introduce employees and managers to the use of frequent feedback, sometimes by suggesting that such feedback prevents more serious problems later. This is quite similar to the issue of introducing employees and managers to the concept of making psychological contracts. Strong resistance to feedback may indicate more serious employee or manager problems with control, authority, social interaction, and self-judgment.

Empowerment

In recent years, empowerment has become an important productivity improvement strategy. Empowerment involves the delegation of decision making to employees while holding them accountable for outcomes. Empowerment is consistent with productivity improvement because it allows organizations to respond more quickly, and with greater flexibility, to client concerns. In this regard, it addresses concerns that organizations, public and private, are unresponsive to their stakeholders. Empowerment also decreases unnecessary layers of decision making. It is consistent with the use of psychological contracts, because both involve the renegotiation of expectations and rewards. The diffusion of information technology further increases empowerment because it increases the amount of information that is available to employees (Berman, 1995).

Empowerment is consistent with increasing motivation through job enrichment, which actually preceded empowerment as a management strategy and was popular in the late 1970s and early 1980s. Job enrichment is defined as redesigning jobs to increase the variety of tasks and skills, autonomy in performing tasks, the extent to which work is seen as producing a final product rather than discrete pieces, and the amount of feedback that is received (Morley, 1986). In theory, job enrichment produces productivity gains by providing an enriching job experience, but job enrichment is often criticized for failing to produce evidence of productivity improvement. By contrast, empowerment is directly linked to tasks that are designed to produce these gains. Job enrichment is also criticized by workers who complain that it is tantamount to job enlargement: Workers are often asked to do more of the same without learning or applying new skills. The success of empowerment efforts depends, in part, on the ability of organizations to learn from these past mistakes.

This section addresses the empowerment of individuals, whereas the next section addresses team empowerment. The basic steps of empowerment are as follows:

- Deciding what should be delegated, and why
- Identifying who should be empowered
- Ensuring adequate resources for successfully fulfilling the new tasks and addressing changes in working conditions
- Creating a pilot effort (with participation from employees)
- Monitoring implementation and outcomes
- Making adjustments as needed

Tasks that lend themselves most to empowerment are those that involve highly differentiated or customized services, customer-intensive relations (see Chapter 7), complex technologies, and unpredictable service requests, as well as employees with high needs for self-actualization or social interaction (Bowen & Lawler, 1995). Examples of tasks that require high levels of empowerment are community-based policing, neighborhood casework, building long-term relations with funding agencies, and various business inspection and regulation activities.

Empowerment is often frustrated by unrealistic assumptions and inadequate planning. Plunkett and Fournier (1991) discuss various myths about empowerment. Although some managers believe that many workers are waiting for empowerment, in practice, many workers prefer the predictability of their current routines and expectations. Introducing empowerment can cause anxiety about uncertain demands and rewards (or punishments). Managers must overcome such fear by clearly explaining the rationale for empowerment as well as steps that are undertaken to ease implementation and ensure fair and positive consequences for employees. "Walking the talk" implies that managers should involve employees in decisions about empowerment and its implementation. Another misconception is that empowerment is tantamount to democracy. It is not. Managers retain important veto power and determine the rules of the game, even though many decisions involve more worker input. A further myth is that empowerment produces instant results or quick returns. Workers need to be given leeway to discover new approaches to achieving their goals. This is a process of trial and error that requires patience and encouragement by managers, not criticism and micromanagement.

Inadequate planning and foresight cause empowerment to fail. For empowerment to work, workers must be given decision-making authority, information, skills, and rewards that are consistent with their tasks (Bowen & Lawler, 1995). Managers must ensure these conditions *prior* to empowering employees. For example, officers involved in community-based policing must be given discretion in handling a broad range of issues. They must be provided with training opportunities to acquire needed skills, information about changes in their neighborhood, and rewards and incentives that reflect goals for community-based policing. Managers must also decide which tasks cannot be delegated, such as those that involve significant legal issues. To test whether these conditions exist, managers should ask employees whether they feel that they have adequately control over their ability to perform well in the manner by which they will be held accountable. Employees should also be asked what, if anything, management can do to help them perform better.

Empowerment is closely related to goal-setting. Employees and managers engage in a process in which new objectives and accomplishments are agreed upon. Goals should be SMART, that is, specific, measurable, achievable, realistic, and time-based. Discussions about goals require that managers and employees are aware of each other's broader needs, such as general directions in which organizations are developing and the overall career objectives of employees. Goal-setting is related to management by objectives (MBO), which gained popularity during the 1970s and emphasizes periodic meetings between managers and employees to discuses future goals and to assess progress toward current ones. However, MBO has often been criticized because it results in too much paperwork that documents progress toward goals but provides little delegation. In retrospect, it might be said that this outcome was to be expected from organizations that rely heavily on bureaucratic controls and procedures. Today, many organizations emphasize greater responsibility-taking and direct, open communication. Empowerment finds fertile ground in such organizations. Table 10.2 provides a checklist for implementing empowerment.

Training

Employees typically receive a wide range of training experiences that increase their knowledge and abilities to deal with new technologies, job tasks (i.e., productivity measurement), interpersonal relationships, client relations,

TABLE 10.2 Checklist for Empowerment

- Did I clearly explain to workers why I am asking them to do more?
- Did I clearly explain to workers what they are expected to achieve?
- Are the selected tasks appropriate for empowerment?
- Which other tasks should be targeted for empowerment?
- Do workers have adequate resources to succeed?
- Do workers feel that they have adequate resources to succeed?
- Does the organization support the empowerment effort?
- Are conflicts with other policies addressed and resolved?
- Do workers have sufficient authority to deal with events that they will encounter?
- Are workers clear about the limits of their authority?
- Do workers have access to adequate information for making the correct decisions?
- Do the empowered individuals have adequate skills and experience to succeed?
- Do workers feel comfortable with the contingency plan for unexpected obstacles?
- Do workers understand the criteria and methods of evaluation?
- Do workers feel comfortable with these criteria and methods of evaluation?
- Do workers feel that they will be learning and applying new skills?
- Do workers feel adequate control over their ability to achieve results?
- Do workers share expectations for initial progress?
- Do workers have a process for getting started?
- Is there sufficient feedback to help workers make adjustments?

laws and regulations (e.g., Americans With Disabilities Act requirements), and general trends that affect their work or industry. Training helps employees acquire requisite abilities. While some employees resist training, others embrace it because it creates opportunities for advancement. Modern training methods emphasize (a) integration between formal, classroom learning and on-the-job applications, (b) active participation by adult learners in the learning process, and (c) just-in-time delivery of training, that is, training provided as it is needed so that its relevance is readily understood and lessons are absorbed through immediate use.

Training is big business. U.S. businesses spend about $35 billion annually on employee training programs. About one third of the entire adult population is estimated to be functionally illiterate, and employers often complain about the lack of job skills of U.S. high school graduates: Only 38% of young adults can figure out the right amount of change they should receive from $3.00 if they order a 60¢ cup of soup and a $1.95 sandwich, and 80% of Motorola job applicants fail seventh-grade math and English tests (Boyett & Conn, 1991). This section focuses on two types of training directly relevant to productivity improvement: technical training for productivity measurement and the development of skills for improved interpersonal relations. In addition, stress management training is also discussed.

Many managers and employees are confused about such concepts as efficiency, effectiveness, and workload and require training in productivity measurement. The confusion is heightened by the use of different productivity measures in different units. Limitations of formal training also play a role. For example, managers with a formal business education often search for the elusive "bottom line" in productivity improvement; they must be trained to understand that public and nonprofit organizations pursue multiple objectives and that nonprofit organizations maximize service rather than profit. Managers must also be trained to use the process of productivity measurement in the development of measures. They must be assisted in the development of specific productivity measurement forms and data collection instruments. Employees must also be trained in their contribution to the measurement of productivity.

In recent years, an important barrier to achieving productivity improvement has involved the lack of an adequate orientation toward open communication the lack of emphasis on performance and accomplishment, as well as on flexibility, empathy, and understanding of the needs of others, and the ability to handle conflict through mediation. Managers and employees increasingly receive training in developing interpersonal skills that are needed for empowerment and teamwork. Although few people admit interpersonal deficits, the sources of interpersonal problems often lie in past experiences that are beyond the ability of most people to address without professional assistance (see Chapter 2). Denial of interpersonal deficits runs deep.

Self-assessments are often a first step toward increasing awareness of orientations and behaviors. Psychometric instruments provide a balanced perspective of different aspects of individuals. Two popular tests are the Myers-Briggs Type Indicator (MBTI) and the Adjective Check List (ACL). Mani (1996) describes how the U.S. Internal Revenue Service uses these instruments in its management training program. The MBTI provides an overall assessment of an individual's personality, including orientations toward creativity, empathy, obedience, and responsibility. The ACL provides an account of an individual's preferences for dominance, endurance, achievement, autonomy, deference, self-control, readiness for counseling, and other traits. Kolb et al. (1995) provide a Learning Style Inventory (LSI) that focuses on strengths and weaknesses in dealing with the world from the perspective of learning, improving, and adapting. Managers and employees usually acknowledge these tests as being largely accurate, and discussion of test results usually creates an opening for further intervention. Such interventions typically include feedback from others in the employee's direct environment.

Self-assessment instruments are also used for stress management. Stress is a major cause of illness and hence loss of productivity. Stress also causes poor judgment and, in some instances, strained interpersonal relations. Some major causes of stress include a lack of time management, inability to handle job conflict, or tensions between work and personal life (including those caused by guilt), compulsive personality disorders, and ingrained behaviors such as the need for competition, lack of relaxation, chronic needs for consistent hurry, and perfectionism. Employees and managers with such characteristics are made aware of them and are offered alternative behaviors and thought processes (e.g., "Do I really need to be in a hurry now?"). Such training reduces medical costs and increases the possibility of improved interpersonal relations that are consistent with increased productivity.[4]

Effective Work Teams

Teams of employees and managers are increasingly used in organizations and are an important productivity improvement strategy. Teams are often used to increase the speed at which things are done, to bring together diverse expertise for dealing with complex, multifaceted problems, to focus organizational resources on specific targets, to increase learning and sharing among group members (thereby increasing future productivity), and to provide a single point of contact for outside stakeholders, as described in Chapter 7 (Parker, 1994). Teams vary in their nature and scope and include (a) production teams that involve an ongoing collaboration among employees and managers with operational responsibilities (such as hospital case management teams), (b) project teams of collective efforts for a limited duration (such as SWOT teams), (c) advisory and decision-making teams such as quality circles or grievance and award committees that provide input, coordination, and decision making, but no implementation, and (d) coordinating teams of senior managers or interorganizational staff that vary in their degree of implementation responsibilities.

The productivity challenge is to ensure that teams produce the above outcomes. However, some team members get lost in unproductive meetings and there may be interpersonal rivalry; a paucity of cooperation, contribution, and effort from individuals; and a lack of support from other parts of the organization on which teams may depend. The potential for these problems is present in most team efforts, and the management of people is therefore critical to the success of work teams. Some specific problems are as follows:

- Confusion about the team's authority and activities
- Inability to generate consensus and support for team goals
- Inadequate support from managers or organizations outside the team
- Confusion about the team roles of individuals (e.g., Who is the leader? What is expected from this person?)
- Inadequate vision or expertise among team members or team leaders
- Concerns about performance appraisal
- Team goals or rewards not aligned with the needs of team members
- Inability of leaders to arrest interpersonal rivalry or immaturity of team members
- Inadequate resources and mandates to accomplish team mission

Effective team-building requires competencies in the following areas, which are sometimes addressed through the following questions (Adair, 1986; Clark, 1994; Schein, 1988):

1. Effective group problem-solving skills to achieve *tasks*
   What is the group to do? How, when, by what means, and under what conditions is it to accomplish this?
2. Generating and maintaining *group cohesion*
   What are the rules and norms of working together? How are these maintained?
3. The development of *individual behavior and motivation* that support group problem-solving and group-building
   What roles should individuals play? How can unproductive behavior be arrested? Are individuals adequately motivated? Are their needs sufficiently being attended to?

In recent years, the term *high-performance team* has been used to refer to groups that have effectively developed these aspects. Specifically, high-performance teams are characterized by the following:

- A strong sense of shared ownership and commitment to team goals
- Participative and empowering leadership
- A high degree of open and fearless communication
- Trust among team members
- Emphasis on developing, using, and evaluating new approaches

■ Time, quality, and task focus

The next sections discuss strategies for achieving productive task, group, and individual behaviors.

Task Behaviors

Authority, responsibility, accountability. Effective teams are goal oriented. However, to accomplish goals, teams require a clear understanding about which goals are being pursued, the authority for defining goals and mobilizing resources, and responsibility and accountability toward accomplishments (Chapter 2). Such clarity furthers consensus-building and allows teams to focus their efforts. This need for clarity about authority, responsibility, and accountability occurs at two levels: (a) between organizations and teams and (b) among team members. Teams must have a clear understanding of what organizations are expecting from them, as must individuals as well. They must know the scope of their authority and its limits. The lack of clarity about authority, responsibility, and accountability creates ambiguity that undermines effective task definition and accomplishment.

These problems are sometimes encountered by quality circles, which are teams of employees who meet to study problems of quality (Chapter 7). Managers often use such teams to recommend process improvements because front-line employees often have detailed and unique knowledge of both problems and production processes. An important lesson from the use of quality circles is the need to establish realistic expectations and meaningful mandates. When quality circles are given open-ended commitments, team members often make recommendations that their managers cannot implement without authorization from higher managers, which may not be forthcoming. When recommendations are asked for but are not acted upon, employees are demotivated and often unwilling to participate in future problem-solving efforts. Thus quality circles should be given clear mandates and managers must demarcate their scope of responsibility, for example, the realm within which they have advisory rather than operating responsibilities.

In addition, some managers experience problems in deciding how much authority or responsibility should be given to teams. Whereas some teams are only empowered to provide advice, others have decision-making responsibilities, including those of implementation. Some teams with operating responsibilities are limited in their choice of methods and goals, whereas other teams are given wide latitude. In recent years, "self-managed teams" have been advocated also. These are teams with far-reaching power over goals and methods, as well as oversight, evaluation, and responsibilities that come from exercising such oversight. Self-managed teams often evaluate their own effectiveness and that of team members, and some determine which problems they choose to work on. They also develop their own leadership style.

The extent of responsibility depends in large measure on how the following questions are answered: Do the tasks require extensive autonomy? Do employees have adequate knowledge and experience to make wise decisions? Are employees adequately aligned with the goals of the organization? Do work teams have adequate task and group management skills to handle increased responsibilities? Is empowerment a necessity for managers? (They can't do everything themselves.) Are work teams are willing and legally able to handle increased accountability for their actions? Affirmative answers suggest greater responsibility. In addition, the culture of organizations, and the role that managers wish to play regarding specific tasks, are also important considerations. Regardless of how much responsibility is transferred from managers to teams, they must work within a clear understanding of their responsibilities to achieve their goals.[5]

Problem solving. Goal accomplishment often involves successfully completing the following tasks:

- Gaining a normative appreciation of problems
- Understanding problems in ways that invite meaningful responses
- Developing goals and objectives
- Formulating action strategies
- Valuing and taking into account legal, ethical, policy, and other constraints in the development of action strategies
- Assigning tasks
- Implementing tasks
- Dealing with unintended obstacles and nevertheless achieving goals

The leadership challenge is to ensure that each of these tasks is completed in ways that generate commitment and consensus. Team members should be selected whose knowledge and capabilities are relevant to the problem at hand. Each task is characterized by (a) brainstorming and the contribution of perspectives and information, (b) clarification and assessment of these perspectives, and (c) decision making that allows teams to conclude tasks and move on to the next tasks. Leaders engage in "positive politics," that is, trying to find commonality, support, and objective assessment of ideas. Goals maintain consensus. Group members should be invited to share what's on their minds and to elaborate and explain what they intend to say. An important challenge is the lack of expertise. Leaders must recognize this problem and offer to obtain the necessary expertise for a subsequent meeting.

An important strategy is to invite outsiders to meetings whose support or future involvement as allies is likely to be important. Their participation is likely to increase their support, and it increases the scope of available information for decision making. Outsiders also help deal with the problem of "groupthink," that is, excessive cohesion among group members. This can cause intolerance for unorthodox ideas and new facts, and thus decisions that are poorly tested and may be wrong (Kayser, 1994). Groupthink can be avoided by inviting outsiders to participate or appointing one or more persons to be critics.

The ability to lead effective meetings is critical. Meetings should have agendas so that purposes are clear and effort can be focused on meeting these purposes. Effective work teams typically follow the following code of conduct (Charney, 1995):

- People listen to each other.
- Each person has the opportunity to express his or her opinions.
- Decisions are made by consensus.
- People are asked to stick to the topic.
- Everybody is involved; no one dominates the agenda.
- Meetings stay on track and on time.

These guidelines help address such challenges as dealing with contributions that are irrelevant or sidetrack the discussion, or statements that are aimed at putting other members down.

Group and Individual Behaviors

Building cohesive groups requires ongoing efforts to (a) reconcile differences among team members, (b) maintain open communication channels, (c) help individuals to modify their views in the interest of group cohesion, (d) ensure that individual needs are met, and (e) address dysfunctional individual behaviors such as domination, withdrawal, passive aggressiveness, not listening, and coalition forming, which threaten team goals.

Participation in teams often causes individuals to raise the following questions (Clark, 1994):

BOX 10.1.
Using Quality Improvement Teams

The use of quality teams is now an enduring accomplishment of past efforts. Quality teams (also known as quality circles) are found in most organizations. For example, the State of Wisconsin, Division of Motor Vehicles, formed more than 30 quality improvement teams to deal with such issues as improving the accuracy of documents, reducing customer wait time, upgrading technology, and benchmarking. The Oregon Department of Transportation formed quality teams with its vendors to improve contracting and the ability to adapt to new requirements. The Michigan Department of Corrections used quality improvement teams to reduce the amount of paperwork. Whereas such activities were novel in the early 1990s, by the mid-1990s they are increasingly commonplace.

Quality teams are problem-solving teams. They are used when a gap exists between what is happening and what organizations want to happen, or when organizations want to move from vague dissatisfaction to a solvable, clearly defined problem. Team facilitators help teams move forward, although today many employees have sufficient experience that facilitators are not always used. Quality team training emphasizes effective task and people skills. Effective task skills include training in quality techniques (Chapter 7) and the development of problem-solving strategies that enable the team to move forward within its defined realm of responsibilities. Effective people skills usually emphasize openness, mutual support, personal initiative, and a positive style that is energizing and confident yet open to contribution and acknowledging the value of other contributions. People are also taught to accept responsibility and accountability, acknowledge others, and reject patterns of blaming and victimization.

In the early 1990s, there was some concern about the use of quality teams during downsizing. Some scholars feared that quality initiatives would be scaled back as a result of downsizing. In fact, organizations greatly varied in their responses. Some organizations scaled back their efforts but increased the use of quality improvement teams to restructure their activities and produce cost savings. What is remarkable today is that quality improvement teams are now so widespread that they barely receive special notice. Managers go by the new adage: Have a problem, empower a team to fix it.

- What is my role in this effort? Is it consistent with my goals?
- Who is trying to dominate me, and why?
- Are team goals and actions supporting my needs?
- Am I being accepted by the group? Will what I say lead to rejection?

Unsatisfactory answers to these questions may result in very strong feelings of frustration, anxiety, and insecurity: Individuals may even have these feelings without full awareness of these questions. In addition, as previously mentioned, organizational politics and dysfunctional behaviors induce individuals to engage in activities that are designed to produce disagreement among team members and are not necessarily aligned with task-oriented behaviors. Group maintenance activities are often much needed when teams are involved in activities of goal formulation, but the need for such activities may erupt at any time.

Maintenance tasks. One strategy to maintain group cohesion is encouraging individuals to clarify their needs so that group leaders can help provide adequate motivators and incentives to make participation worthwhile. Although teams are unlikely to satisfy all of an individual's needs, they may satisfy some and managers may suggest other ways through which individuals can meet their other needs. Of course, a problem occurs with individuals who for reasons of organizational politics or dysfunctional behavior refuse to express their real needs.

A second strategy of group maintenance is standard testing. The above code of conduct for meetings provides essential strategies for building and maintaining group cohesion as well as the basis for holding individual team members accountable. Ground rules provide members an opportunity to steer conversation back on track as well as to arrest domineering behavior and political infighting. Groups in their initial stages of formation often spend substantial time and effort formulating ground rules for action, and even established groups frequently go back to formulating new rules for dealing with problems that they had not anticipated.

Third, group members must feel that they are treated in ways that are commensurate with the roles they have agreed to play. Consistency and transparency of managerial actions are important. For example, if a team is to make all essential decisions on the basis of consensus, it follows that each team member's opinion must be solicited and that discussion must continue until consensus is reached. It also follows that information must be widely shared. For example, memos and other information received between meetings must be made available to all. E-mail greatly facilitates such exchanges, and groupware furthers this process by creating a central depository of contributions.

Other strategies include using humor, maintaining open communication, and using tactics for dealing with inappropriate behavior. It is often useful to balance seriousness with humor. Humor is a great equalizer that brings out the human characteristics of people. It eases tensions and enables transitions between phases of task accomplishments, such as from information collection to assessment and decision making. Humor can also be used to facilitate compromising, although managers must be careful not to brush aside objections of team members or to use humor to diminish the self-worth of others.

Although open communication usually results from undertaking the above activities and adhering to acceptable standards of conduct, managers must deal with the following problems as well. Increased workplace diversity means dealing with people for whom English is a second language and having an awareness that some phrases may be interpreted differently, even among native speakers. People should express themselves clearly. Another problem is dealing with hearsay and rumor. Managers should address the source of rumors and deal with them immediately and directly with openness and candor.

A final problem is dealing with domineering and passive-aggressive behavior, both of which are obvious challenges to group cohesiveness. Many authors agree that the best way to deal with such problematic behaviors is by exposing them. In group settings, people can express that they feel intimidated by domineering behavior or are disappointed by withholding or sly actions that frequently accompany passive-aggressive behavior. Others can then agree that such behaviors are inconsistent with the established codes of conduct for the group. At issue is the behavior, not the intentions or personality of individuals. Individuals who exhibit problem behavior should be asked to change such behavior.

Self-appraisal and development. As teams become more common so too do expectations about their ability to perform and improve. Self-managed teams are increasingly expected to evaluate themselves, and managers rely on these self-appraisals in varying degrees as part of their assessment of team functioning and accomplishment. However, *self-appraisal is an important developmental strategy* too. Self-appraisal encourages teams to develop processes for better managing their internal dynamics. Members receive 360° degree feedback about their functioning and are made responsible for obtaining improvement. Teams are also sometimes responsible for distributing rewards for individual accomplishment and effort. As self-contained units, they encompass mechanisms for setting expectations and evaluating past performance (Klagge, 1995). These processes may also improve the ability of teams to deal with dynamic environments.

Self-managed teams invite concerns about fairness and effectiveness. For example, employees worry about whether they will be treated fairly by their colleagues, and managers worry about whether they will get high performance rather than underachieving mediocrity. These concerns are typically addressed (and, ideally, allayed) during the formation process for such teams. Members may request appeal procedures, and managers often demand oversight, accountability, and procedures for abandonment. Such safeguards are reasonable and can be agreed upon. Initial teams rules often resemble those with which members are familiar. Procedures for determining leadership and responsibility must be discussed. However, as teams experience good functioning, managers can relax initial limitations and safeguards in periodic assessment of team functioning. Thus the degree of self-management is usually increased over time.

Summary

This chapter discusses strategies for increasing productivity through individuals and teams. It discusses motivation, which is essential to individual productivity, and multiple needs are suggested that motivate employees and managers. Because managers cannot know by which needs employees are motivated, they need to engage in conversation with employees. The objective of managing productivity is to align individual motivation with the needs of organizations. In addition, feedback, empowerment, and training are discussed as approaches to individual productivity. This chapter also examines the use of teams and strategies for increasing team productivity. The three essential challenges of team management involve task orientation, group processes, and individual behaviors.

Notes

1. The title for this chapter is borrowed from Werther et al. (1986).

2. Different needs may be related to career choices: For example, politicians often have a high need for power, research scientists usually have a high need for accomplishment, marketing personnel often have a high need for affiliation, and managers can be driven by different needs. Individuals tend toward careers and activities that allow them to meet their needs, and, perhaps because they eventually acquire facility in these areas, they tend to excel in these careers, too.

3. Salary increases are increasingly tied to merit-based pay schemes. According to Gabris (1992), the problem with merit pay is that although the level of merit pay is often minimal, it drives a wedge between employees and many believe that the allocation of merit pay is unfair.

4. The development of awareness and self-improvement is, of course, insufficient to increase productivity in the absence of other strategies that are mentioned in this book.

5. Vroom and Jago (1988) provide a detailed framework for determining the extent of consultation in decision making based on many of these factors.

References

Adair, J. (1986). *Effective teambuilding.* London: Gower.

Adams, J. (1963).Toward an understanding of equity. *Journal of Abnormal and Social Psychology, 68*(11), 422-436.

Almaas, A. (1990). *Diamond Heart III: Being and the meaning of life.* Berkeley, CA: Diamond.

Berman, E. (1995). Empowering employees in state agencies: A survey of recent progress. *International Journal of Public Administration, 18*(5), 833-850.

Berman, E., & West, J. (1997). [Survey of productivity in local government]. Unpublished raw data.

Bowen, D., & Lawler, E., III. (1995). Empowering service employees. *Sloan Management Review, 37*(2), 73-83.

Boyett, J., & Conn, H. (1991). *Workplace 2000.* New York: Dutton.

Charney, C. (1995). *The manager's took kit.* New York: AMACOM.

Clark, N. (1994). *Team building.* New York: McGraw-Hill.

Cobb, A., Folger, R., & Wooten, K. (1995). The role justice plays in organizational change. *Public Administration Quarterly, 19*(2), 135-151.

Fox, J., & Klein, C. (1996). The 360-degree evaluation. *Public Management, 78*(11), 20-22.

Gabris, G. (1992). *Monetary incentives and performance.* In M. Holzer (Ed.), *Public productivity handbook* (pp. 443-461). New York: Marcel Dekker.

Glasser, W. (1994). *The control theory manager.* New York: Harper Business.

Henry, N. (1995). *Public administration and public affairs.* Englewood Cliffs, NJ: Prentice Hall.

Herzberg, F. (1959). *The motivation to work.* New York: John Wiley.

Kanter, D., & Mirvis, P. (1989). *The cynical Americans: Living and working in an age of discontent and disillusion.* San Francisco: Jossey-Bass.

Kayser, T. (1994). *Building team power.* New York: Irwin.

Kolb, D., Osland, J., & Rubin, I. (1995). *Organizational behavior* (6th ed.). Englewood Cliffs, NJ: Prentice Hall.

Locke, E., & Latham, G. (1990). *A theory of goal setting and task performance.* Englewood Cliffs, NJ: Prentice Hall.

Mani, B. (1996). TQM management development in public agencies using the Myers-Briggs type indicator and the adjective check list. *Review of Public Personnel Administration, 16*(4), 79-96.

Maslow, A. (1954). *Motivation and personality.* New York: Harper & Row.

McClelland, D. (1985). *Human motivation.* Glenview, IL: Scott, Foresman.

Morley, E. (1986). *A practitioner's guide to public sector productivity.* New York: Van Nostrand Reinhold.

Nadler, D., & Lawler, E. (1977). Motivation: A diagnostic approach. In J. Hackman & L. Lawler (Eds.), *Perspectives on behavior in organizations.* New York: McGraw-Hill.

Parker, G. (1994). *Cross-functional teams: Working with allies, enemies and other strangers.* San Francisco: Jossey-Bass.

Plunkett, L., & Fournier, R. (1991). *Participative management: Implementing empowerment.* New York: John Wiley

Schein, E. (1988). *Process consultation.* New York: Addison-Wesley.

Skinner, B. (1971). *Beyond freedom and dignity.* New York: Bantam.

Spector, P. (1982). Behavior in organizations as a function of employees' locus of control. *Psychological Bulletin, 78*(5), 482-497.

Tulgan, B. (1995). *Managing generation X.* Santa Monica, CA: Merritt.

Vroom, V., & Jago, A. (1988). *Participation in organizations.* Englewood Cliffs, NJ: Prentice Hall.

Werther, W., Ruch, W., & McClure, L. (1986). *Productivity through people.* St. Paul, MN: West.

Conclusions

11

The Future of
Productivity
Improvement

━━━ This book makes the case that productivity matters. The use of productivity improvement strategies is increasingly important as public and nonprofit organizations face rapidly changing environments that require new goal-setting, constrained budgets that require heightened efficiency and effectiveness, increased demands from customers, and a diverse workforce that requires a wide range of motivational strategies. This book assists in addressing these challenges. It discusses strategic planning, which helps organizations and managers set new goals and achieve consensus. It also examines strategies for effectively managing partnerships, as well as ways to achieve efficient service delivery, quality improvement, innovation, the use of information technology, and outcome measurement. In addition, implementation strategies are discussed, for example, through effective project management, wholesale organizational change, and the effective management of people and work teams.

This chapter discusses the current state of the field of productivity and productivity improvement. It examines the quality paradigm as a driver of future efforts, the relevance of recent lessons, and the effect of productivity improvement strategies on the careers of managers and employees. It identifies various strategic issues that are likely to determine future directions of productivity improvement.

Where Things Stand

Human endeavors can be assessed from many different perspectives. Two key dimensions for assessing fields such as productivity are the relevance of their *ideas* to current challenges and the extent to which they attract adequate *people and resources* to their causes. A "healthy" field is one that is full of useful ideas for addressing current problems and that attracts an increasing number of practitioners and resources; by contrast, a "dying" field is often characterized by a dearth of relevant new ideas and a declining interest among potential practitioners.

The Quality Paradigm: A Driving Idea

The single greatest influence on productivity improvement in recent years has been the quality paradigm. As discussed in Chapter 7, the quality paradigm is viewed as a management philosophy that consists of five distinct strategies: customer service, reengineering, continuous improvement, empowerment, and benchmarking. The quality paradigm took hold in the federal government in the late 1980s, and since then it has increasingly been used in other public as well as nonprofit organizations. The core idea is to provide services that meet the needs of customers, clients, and citizens. This involves not only the elimination of waste and delay but also the implementation of new service objectives. Such efforts cannot be considered radically new. Quality management fundamentally differs from past productivity efforts by putting customers, clients, and citizens in the driver's seat: It gives them ultimate responsibility for identifying needs and working with public and nonprofit organizations in partnership for meeting their needs. Citizens and clients get choices and tailored solutions, and the above strategies serve the purpose of client empowerment. Quality management also requires public organizations to make the case that their contributions are worthy of the support of citizens. Performance measurement helps provide the data for such efforts (Gaster, 1995; Milakovich, 1995; Seidle, 1995).

The above quality strategies reflect key interest topics at recent annual conferences of the American Society for Public Administration and the International City/County Management Association. The tenets of quality find increasing acceptance, and many public and nonprofit organizations are now thought to be at the beginning or middle stages of strategies that implement the quality paradigm. Quality continues to be a driving paradigm because it helps organizations address their challenges and improve stakeholder relations and trust. However, it is very difficult to predict which quality theme will emerge as the next key strategy du jour, because the salience of topics and strategies depends on the entrepreneurship of individual managers, consultants, and academics. Benchmarking, customer service, continuous improvement, reengineering, and empowerment have been emphasized in the recent past; no doubt, other quality strategies will be identified in the near future, including the use of information technology and heightened individual and group accountability.

The quality paradigm includes ideas about making implementation more effective. A concern of many past efforts is that implementation challenges foul up good intentions and productive outcomes. Such challenges often involve overcoming resistance to change from employees and managers (Chapter 1). Important "lessons" about effective change include the need to start small (e.g., though pilot projects), produce in short-term results, ensure leadership from top and senior managers, provide consistent policies (including rewards and incentives for performance), and create a supportive environment that encourages learning and trial by error and that is committed to results and outcomes (rather than efforts and compliance). There is consensus that many productivity improvement efforts fail in the absence of these conditions (Rosen, 1993).

Although the quality paradigm drives new developments in productivity improvement, productivity draws on different disciplines: From industrial engineering, concepts of time-motion and demand analysis are used to rationalize work processes; from organizational behavior, processes of organizational change and development are used; from economics, cost-benefit analysis is used; from computer science and operations research, tools of linear programming and queuing are used to increase efficiency. Old ideas continue to find productive use, even as they are applied to new challenges. For example, process flowcharting finds increased use in the context of process reengineering, and strategic planning becomes community-based strategic planning as public organizations aim to meet increased demands in an environment of constrained resources and the increased competence of other organizations. Thus productivity as a field includes a vast array of strategies that address many problems that public and nonprofit organizations face today.

Table 11.1 shows the use of various ideas in practice. Specifically, it shows the application of productivity improvement strategies in cities with more than

TABLE 11.1 Use of Productivity Improvement Strategies

Strategies	Cities	Social Services	Museums*
Public-private partnerships	3.32	2.63	3.27
Strategic planning	3.25	4.32	3.69
Performance measurement related to budgeting	3.13	3.30	2.41
Contracting for service delivery	3.13	2.66	2.07
Reorganization	3.00	2.54	2.46
Interpersonal skill development for managers	2.90	2.65	2.21
Empowerment	2.86	3.06	2.35
Multiunit work teams	2.84	3.26	2.89
Citizen surveys	2.83	1.41	2.78
Customer surveys	2.72	3.06	3.12
Customer/client service improvement effort	2.74	2.84	2.02
Community-based strategic planning	2.47	1.72	1.43
Performance measurement separate from budgeting	2.35	2.98	3.18
Management by objectives	2.23	3.11	1.93
Benchmarking	2.21	2.17	1.24
Program evaluation by external consultants	2.09	2.49	2.42
Process reengineering	2.07	1.85	1.27
Downsizing	2.06	1.20	0.90
Continuous improvement (data based)	2.03	2.23	1.64

NOTE: *Scale: 0 = did not use; 1 = had some discussion or activity, but little or no follow-through; 2 = undertook a pilot project; 3 = ongoing applications were conducted in one or more departments; 4 = at least one department uses the strategy departmentwide; 5 = all departments use the strategy agencywide.

50,000 in population and large social service organizations and museums.[1] It is found that strategic planning and public-private partnerships are among the most popular strategies. The results also show some differences among these organizations: Social service organizations are less likely to use public-private partnerships, museums are less likely to use performance measurement related to budgeting, and cities are less likely to use citizen surveys. These differences reflect the different missions of these organizations. Further analysis shows that cities use an average 11.4 of the 19 strategies as ongoing, department- or agencywide applications (scale response greater than three; see Table 11.1). Social services and museums use 10.9 and 9.8 strategies in this manner. Thus it is found that, on average, public and nonprofit organizations do not vary much in their use of productivity improvement strategies.

Table 11.1 also shows the use of strategies associated with quality management: customer service, reengineering, continuous improvement, empowerment, and benchmarking. The relatively lower use of these strategies is consistent with their recent introduction in many organizations. In a separate question, respondents report relative low use of TQM as a strategy, and subsequent interviews confirm that mangers now regard it as a philosophy that encompasses discrete strategies (Chapter 7). Subsequent analysis shows that customer service efforts are used as ongoing, department- or agencywide applications (scale response greater than three) by 61% of cities, 68% of social service organizations, and 45% of museums. Process reengineering is used in similar manner by 46% of cities, 38% of social service organizations, and 45% of museums. While these data show that quality management applications occur in public and nonprofit organizations, they are not always widely used. For example, only 8% of local governments use process reengineering agencywide. Such use by social service organizations and museums is, respectively, 3% and 11%. Low agencywide use rates are replicated for other quality management strategies as well. This suggests that while the ideas of quality management find application in public and nonprofit organizations, much more could be done.[2]

Although the successful application of many quality strategies demonstrates their usefulness, many organizations and managers only have a limited commitment to new efforts (e.g., Berman & West, 1995). Small-scale efforts often reflect experimentation, misguided implementation, and tokenism. Experimentation may reflect appropriate trial and error or awareness-enhancing efforts that, in time, find greater use throughout organizations (Chapter 4). Other efforts are small because they are undertaken with no intention of achieving success: Tokenism is a self-serving management behavior that aims to further individual careers by giving the appearance of professionalism. Misguided and token efforts harm stakeholder relations by raising false expectations. New efforts are often only marginally used except by a few exemplary organizations and managers. Studies of older productivity improvement strategies show that many strategies, such as strategic planning, eventually find widespread use (Chapter 1). In the interim, strategies are needed to help employees and managers distinguish between token and earnest levels of commitment and also to assist managers and their organizations to move toward widespread use.

People and Resources: Link With Professionalism

Productivity attracts many outstanding managers, but not all managers view productivity improvement with great enthusiasm. Some managers consider productivity improvement to be a hallmark of professionalism and essential to career advancement, whereas others have only a limited commitment to it. For example, in the above survey, 46% of municipal respondents agreed with the statement that implementing productivity improvement strategies is a hallmark of professionalism, whereas 33% only somewhat agreed with this statement and 21% disagreed or didn't know. The respective responses of respondents from social service organizations are 55%, 36%, and 9%, and those of museums are 45%, 20%, and 35%, suggesting a similar pattern. Across all cities, social service organizations, and museums, those who view productivity improvement as a hallmark of professionalism are also more likely to view it as a useful vehicle for creating change in their organizations.

In an earlier survey, city managers indicated a high level of familiarity with productivity improvement strategies, and such familiarity is associated with career advancement.[3] This is consistent with findings from the 1997 survey, which shows that those who associate productivity improvement with professionalism are also more likely to attend professional development seminars, undertake a broader range of productivity improvement strategies in their organizations, and have a graduate degree. This finding is consistent among cities and social service organizations, although less so for museums. For example, whereas 51% of municipal respondents with graduate degrees agree with the statement that implementing productivity improvement is a hallmark of professionalism, only 32% of respondents with an undergraduate degree agree with this statement. This suggests that appreciation and use of productivity improvement is, in part, a function of the professionalism that increasingly characterizes management in many public and nonprofit organizations. Of course, managers need not have an advanced degree to be professional.

Productivity improvement requires the investment of time and resources. Most productivity improvement efforts require substantial employee training, and many require additional investments as well. For example, customer service improvements often require facility changes such as updated interiors or customer service windows. Productivity through information technology requires obvious investments in hardware and software as well as additional technical personnel to service new equipment and applications. Information technology sometimes requires expansion of telecommunication capabilities. The ability to attract resources is a sine qua non for using productivity improvement strategies. In this regard, 88% of municipal respondents agree that their organizations provide adequate resources to improve productivity or otherwise provide resources to test new ideas, as do 90% of respondents in social services organizations and 75% of museum respondents. This suggest that in a majority of organizations, managers who make productivity improvement a priority often are able to mobilize necessary resources. It is not surprising that those who believe that their organization has adequate resources for productivity improvement also undertake more productivity improvement efforts than those who state that their organization has inadequate resources.

Professionalism and resources are not the only determinants of the use of productivity improvement strategies. In a detailed statistical analysis, West and Berman (1997) show that organizational culture matters also. Cultures of "revitalization" promote the use of productivity improvement efforts and are characterized by openness, empowerment, and rewards for innovation and accomplishment. By contrast, cultures of fear and lethargy are viewed as impediments to undertaking activities that foster productivity improvement, such as bringing managers together to discuss new ideas or identifying citizen and community needs. Such cultures often have policies that inhibit innovation as well as employee and managerial behaviors that promote secrecy, detachment, and self-serving advancement strategies. Good managers in constraining environments are less productive than those who are supportive and proactive (Bardwick, 1995).[4]

Shaping the culture of organizations and increasing the readiness of managers and employees to use new productivity improvement strategies is a characteristic of many successful managers. It is also the perennial challenge of productivity, as organizations must adapt strategies that are used elsewhere to their own unique problems and constraints. The process of adaptation requires strong change-management skills in managers as well as commitment to making a positive difference in their organizations and for their stakeholders. Both requirements are linked to professionalism in management: Management education instills advanced understanding of productivity, productivity improvement, and the importance of both as well as the need for ethical conduct. The latter is increasingly recognized in public and nonprofit administration. However, while change management skills are increasingly emphasized and understood to be a hallmark of professionalism (for example, Chapter 4), incorporating ethics into productivity improvement is still in the developmental stage.

Strategic Issues

Bringing Ethics Into Productivity

The importance of ethics increases as productivity emphases shift from program efficiency to increasing the effectiveness of services according to customer-defined standards and using empowered employees for that purpose. For example, the Code of Ethics of the American Society for Public Administration includes such aspirations as "involving citizens in policy decision-making," and "exercising discretionary authority to promote the public interest," as well as "promoting ethical organizations," "taking responsibility for one's own errors," and "striving for professional excellence," all of which are requirements for quality management strategies. Ethical cultures emphasize integrity, openness, accountability, and service to others. These values are also addressed by Jeavons (1994) in his discussion of ethics in nonprofit organizations. For example, cultures of openness allow employees to discuss opportunities for improvement and to readily share information about workplace challenges and solutions. Integrity creates constancy and transparency, which furthers open communication. The values of a citizen orientation guide managers to search for strategies to better serve citizens and their customers, and keep them searching until improvements are found.

Ethics has become increasingly associated with rather narrowly defined rules and regulations that aim to prevent legal wrongdoing, such as those dealing with financial disclosure and conflicts of interest. Transgressions of these laws are "ethics violations." However, the increased development and emphasis of such laws does a disservice to ethics. Rather, ethics is more appropriately defined as a set of normative, moral principles and values that guide people. *Ethics* in this broader sense enables people to rise above their own self-interest and that of others, and allows people to examine existing practices for being insufficiently open, supportive, accountable, or focused on stakeholder needs. It is astounding that self-serving managers and organizations are labeled "ethical" when they merely comply with ethics laws or rules. Guidance by strong ethical values, such as the aspirations mentioned above, also helps managers avoid the pitfalls of blind entrepreneurship. For example, the Orange County, California, financial debacle involved the county treasurer taking unacceptable risks trying to maximize market returns on a pool of public resources with insufficient concern for stakeholder interests. Greater attention to the values of protecting the public interest would have led these officials toward a more conservative course of action (Cohen & Eimicke, 1996).

An increasing body of anecdotal and systematic research shows that high-performance organizations often have ethical cultures and policies, and that these organizations routinely introduce and improve productivity improvement strategies. In the above research, municipal respondents who identify ethics as a priority in their organizations also use more productivity improvement strategies than those who do not rate ethics in this way. They also associate ethics with implementing productivity improvement as a hallmark of professionalism. Berman and West (1997) report from other surveys that efforts to increase awareness of ethical conduct are also associated with implementing productivity improvement strategies and increasing employee and citizen trust.

A frontier challenge for many organizations and managers is to increase the alignment of ethics and productivity improvement. Effective productivity improvement requires ethical behavior, ethical attitudes, ethical dialogue, and organizational policies and practices that are consistent with furthering ethics. An effective starting point often is for managers to emphasize integrity, accountability, and a customer orientation by personal example (without being self-righteous, of course). Ethics is about leadership. Managers should also treat their employees as customers. Leaders with a passionate commitment to these principles will positively affect the behavior and conduct of many managers and employees at lower organizational levels. Incorporating ethics into personal conduct furthers the development and maintenance of "revitalized" environments in which productivity improvement efforts are often more effective.

Effective Change Management

Productivity improvement requires knowledge of productivity strategies as well as effective change management. The latter is increasingly important and requires creative abilities to (a) identify and pursue strategic goals and values, some of which require a long-term focus, and (b) foresee, plan, and overcome obstacles and challenges that threaten to derail improvement efforts without losing sight of long-term goals or creating new problems or resistance in the process. Such abilities require a degree of abstract thinking and belief in the power of ideas that must often be nurtured and developed. Managers frequently have orientations that reflect strong preferences for responsibility and thoughtfulness as well as decision making by rules and procedures that provide specific guidance and rely on empirical facts. While such orientations support a broad range of daily activities, few managers can be described as visionary, and most are impatient in the presence of abstract principles and goals.[5]

Many recent productivity improvement strategies by nature involve an emphasis on fundamental changes that require abstract thinking. Osborne and Plastrick (1997) refer to the need to fundamentally change the way that public organizations function as changing their DNA, that is, the coded instructions that employees and managers follow. To increase accountability, managers should give customers greater choice and ensure that customer satisfaction has consequences for employees. In Chapter 5, it is argued that public organizations should take responsibility for helping communities achieve strategic goals that require collaboration among diverse organizations. These goals are truly strategic and somewhat abstract. Productivity requires that managers increase their ability to formulate and attain such goals. A danger exists that managers implement strategies while insufficiently emphasizing or even ignoring the fundamental, strategic goals that these strategies aim to achieve. Goals make strategies more effective. Process facilitators further the effectiveness of strategic planning by keeping participants focused on the purpose of each step and the relationship of each step to final goals. The need for focus also exists in the implementation process, which is made complex by the need for involving employees and managers in the efforts and dealing with a wide range of anticipated and unanticipated barriers and challenges to change.

The success of productivity improvement requires that managers increase their ability to deal with abstract goals. Increasingly, they must be able to develop road maps that support the strategic pursuits of their organizations. No longer can they rely on consultants for this purpose. In this regard, managers need to increase their creative capacities and those of others. One strategy is to create processes of creativity through which new ideas are generated and accepted by organizations. Processes of creativity are built on group efforts whereby managers bring together other managers or employees to discuss problems, evaluate different solutions, and reach consensus about initial implementation. Such processes often draw out alternative perspectives and help clarify abstract or strategic purposes. They also support goals of openness and empowerment as well. A useful mental tool to overcome the hurdle of abstract thinking is the development of milestones that relate concrete efforts to ultimate, strategic goals. Milestones further goal attainment by focusing seemingly disparate efforts toward a unified purpose and providing a tool for communicating strategic efforts to others. Milestones operationalize abstract ends. The future of productivity improvement will likely involve the development and use of tools that help managers to work with abstract goals and multifaceted activities.[6]

Individual accountability has also become increasingly necessary for effective change management. When groups of managers are made responsible for achieving goals, they often increase their willingness to work through the vagueness of abstract goals and reach consensus about specific strategies that can be used to achieve goals. Accountability makes goals real and urgent, and it also increases tolerance for pain and discomfort. In this regard, managers and employees sometimes experience creativity and abstract thinking as painful. Individual accountability also causes managers to focus on outcomes rather than activity, effort, or compliance with requests or processes. Responsibility encourages reasons for failure to be explored as well as strategies for overcoming barriers to success. Individual accountability is essential to successful implementation, and managers do well to hold themselves and others accountable for pursuing effective strategies and achieving results.[7]

Increased Appreciation
for Analytical Techniques

Managers sometimes seek out managerial work because it is less analytical, conceptual, or quantitative than other activities. Some become public or non-profit managers because they have good people skills and want to address important social problems. Although good communication and values remain important, conceptual and analytical abilities are increasingly crucial as a qualification for professional management. This expectation is likely to increase as more and more senior managers have graduate degrees. Managers are increasingly expected to use analytical techniques in addressing such problems as staffing, fund-raising, outcome measurement, effective communication, strategic planning, resource allocation, and time management. Managers who lack adequate analytical skills are also unable to take advantage of information that is presented in quantitative form or, equally deplorable, they must rely on employees, staff analysts, and consultants whose work they are unable to assess critically (Brudney, 1997).

The increased use of analytical techniques is the result of the growing application of quality management strategies and survey research as well as the diffusion of user-friendly statistical and spreadsheet software. Tools such as demand analysis, process flowcharting, and staffing analysis are straightforward, and even operations research is increasingly performed on user-friendly software. Managers who are familiar with these skills are better able to meet the above expectations as well as integrate the skills into productivity improvement efforts. For example, managers who are proficient at survey research often involve potential users of results in the development of survey questions; by doing so, they can better "sell" surveys to others in their organization. They also involve their employees in the data collection process, thereby increasing awareness about department priorities and possible changes.

The growing application of analytical techniques also increases the need for familiarity with issues pertaining to their use in public and nonprofit organizations. For example, with regard to surveys, managers frequently make the argument that surveys are necessary because they are the only valid (and cost-effective) way to assess customer and citizen satisfaction. They will have to address a broad range of concerns that relate to the reporting and use of survey results (Kraut, 1995). Although surveys are used to identify new needs and to assess improvement, managers may be concerned that survey results will reflect poorly on their programs and that upper managers will use such results to justify budget cuts. Managers must address such concerns, for example, by explaining that budget allocations take into account multiple criteria and organizational needs and that program improvements should be continuous and use survey data as one of several sources of feedback. Managers must also address concerns of employees about the fairness of questions and assessment methodologies.

Effective analytical skills are strategic assets to managers and their organizations. They help organizations justify their accomplishments and improve their activities. The future of productivity improvement depends, in part, on ensuring that managers have adequate analytical skills.

Linking Productivity to New Challenges

The history of productivity improvement is one of addressing new challenges. The present challenges of customer and client satisfaction, and meeting increasing demands with constrained resources, are likely to be replaced by new challenges tomorrow that are largely unknown today. It is true that many public and nonprofit organizations are still struggling to meet their customers' needs, and that many employees and managers are not wholly persuaded of these goals. Still other organizations, and certainly some departments within organizations, have yet to take quality seriously. Nonetheless, it is necessary for all organizations to remain alert to changes in their environments so that they do not become obsolete in their strategies.

The current concerns about program effectiveness are already being accompanied by new concerns that are decidedly fundamental and strategic. Public and nonprofit organizations need to repeatedly justify their existence in the face of continuing concerns about their effectiveness to improve the quality of their communities. Many citizens and clients also have high levels of distrust toward these organizations and the professionals who work in them. Yet, at the same time, there is public understanding that public organizations must protect the well-being of citizens in the face of disease, unscrupulous businesses, terrorism, and so on. Nonprofit organizations are expected to step up and fill the welfare void that is left by for-profit service providers.

Understanding and addressing the *trust deficit* is a prima facie example of the abstract and strategic problems described above. Meeting the trust challenge requires (a) that public and nonprofit organizations take the lead in addressing the needs of communities through collective leadership and (b) that they interact with citizens and clients in new ways that increase their trust in public and nonprofit organizations. The former requires community-based strategic planning as described in Chapter 5 as well as, perhaps, innovative ways of financing new efforts in the face of ongoing taxpayer revolts. The latter requires rethinking how governments relate to the public. Many citizens feel disconnected from the organizations that serve them. Analysis suggests that many citizens develop negative attitudes toward public organizations because they are seldom aware of the long-term benefits of government action (environmental protection, health research, effective national defense, etc.) but are often well aware of its costs, for example, through taxation and regulation. Berman (1997) suggests that governments need to explain to citizens what they do, how government furthers the interests of the citizens, and how citizens can affect public decisions in meaningful ways through authentic participation. Cities that undertake a range of strategies in these areas are found to have less cynical public attitudes.

Other challenges deal with increased employee diversity and the lack of motivation that comes from disappointment over wages. In any event, public and nonprofit organizations periodically need to develop new strategies that effectively address new human resource and performance challenges. This creates ongoing opportunities for managers and employees to contribute to processes of increasing organizational productivity.

Advantages for You

The use of productivity improvement strategies often advances the careers of managers and employees. Organizations need managers and employees who produce results and make resources stretch further. Productivity improvement strategies are designed to produce these outcomes, and managers who use these strategies in effective ways increase their value to organizations.

Many managers find it advantageous to manage their rewards from their efforts. By and large, positive accomplishments are usually noted and rewarded in some way. However, some good deeds do go unnoticed, and others may attempt to take credit for work they have not done. Worse, rivals discredit the good efforts of others by selectively emphasizing adverse results and purposefully ignoring positive achievements. Managers need to make certain that they receive the rewards they deserve. Advantageous use of career advancement strategies increases the likelihood of rewards. Such self-promotion and marketing are an integral part of managing individual careers: As the saying goes, "If you can't sell yourself, who can?"

Despite different contributions that employees and managers make, the principles for ensuring rewards are much the same. These principles are to (a) negotiate rewards for special accomplishments as part of any prior agreement for undertaking them; (b) ask others such as influential program clients to recognize your accomplishments and bring them to the attention of those who affect your career; (c) plan a minor campaign to increase your visibility in those aspects, and to those clienteles, that are beneficial to you, and plan to minimize visibility in areas that might hurt you; (d) speak out in other forums about your accomplishments and the types of problems that you can solve because gaining appreciation from other organizations makes you more attractive to your current employer; and (e) avoid making enemies but acknowledge the presence of rivals and deal with them and their criticism effectively. These principles help promote careers.

Senior Managers

Many productivity improvement strategies are ideally suited to address the challenges of senior and top managers. These challenges include positioning their organizations or departments for future growth, ensuring client and citizen support for their missions and program achievements, and ensuring that policies are adopted and resources are available for increasing productivity. Strategies such as strategic planning, community-based strategic planning, partnering, privatization, reengineering, and the use of alternative revenue sources support these purposes. Senior managers also promote productivity improvement by supporting quality management and information technology strategies that assist lower managers. Senior managers benefit from using productivity improvement strategies by increasing their reputation for accomplishment among key stakeholders, peers, and other organizations. Speaking out at conferences and symposia furthers their reputations as well.

The advantages of productivity improvement efforts are reflected in the self-assessments that are shown in Tables 11.2 through 11.4. Almost 48% of municipal respondents agree or strongly agree that using productivity improvement strategies makes them more attractive to *other* employers, and an additional 27% "somewhat agree" with this statement. Almost 42% agree or strongly agree that these strategies makes them more attractive to their *present* employers, and 31% somewhat agree with this statement. More than half of the respondents agree to varying degrees that using productivity has helped them get a job (59.5%), which is significant, because getting a job depends on a wide range of factors. In addition, 39% agree or strongly agree that using productivity im-

TABLE 11.2 Career Impacts of Productivity Improvement: Municipal Respondents

Statements	Agree/Strongly Agree (%)	Somewhat Agree(%)*
Positive:		
"Using productivity improvement strategies . . ."		
makes me more attractive to other employers	47.7	27.1
makes me more attractive to my current employer	41.7	30.7
has helped my career	38.5	29.9
has helped me get a job in the past	27.9	17.2
Negative:		
"Using productivity improvement strategies . . ."		
has sometimes hurt my career	5.5	8.7
is a risky way of advancing one's career	5.0	10.1
creates resistance that has hurt my position	4.5	14.1

NOTE: *Percentage of respondents who agree, strongly agree, or somewhat agree with the statement (based on a seven-point scale, strongly disagree to strongly agree).

provement strategies has helped their careers. These findings are quite similar for respondents of social service organizations and museums. For example, 49% of social service respondents agree or strongly agree that using productivity improvement has helped their careers, as have 35% of museum respondents. On average, museum respondents indicate somewhat lower benefits from using

TABLE 11.3 Career Impacts of Productivity Improvement: Social Service Organization Respondents

Statements	Agree/Strongly Agree (%)	Somewhat Agree (%)*
Positive:		
"Using productivity improvement strategies . . ."		
has helped my career	49.1	25.5
makes me more attractive to other employers	40.0	18.2
makes me more attractive to my current employer	38.2	32.7
has helped me get a job in the past	32.8	14.8
Negative:		
"Using productivity improvement strategies . . ."		
has sometimes hurt my career	3.6	5.5
is a risky way of advancing one's career	1.8	5.5
creates resistance that has hurt my position	1.8	16.4

NOTE: *Percentage of respondents who agree, strongly agree, or somewhat agree with the statement (based on a seven-point scale, strongly disagree to strongly agree).

TABLE 11.4 Career Impacts of Productivity Improvement: Museum Respondents

Statements	Agree/Strongly Agree (%)	Somewhat Agree (%)*
Positive:		
"Using productivity improvement strategies . . ."		
makes me more attractive to other employers	40.0	27.5
has helped my career	35.0	35.0
makes me more attractive to my current employer	32.5	40.0
has helped me get a job in the past	23.1	20.5
Negative:		
"Using productivity improvement strategies . . ."		
creates resistance that has hurt my position	7.5	7.5
is a risky way of advancing one's career	2.6	5.1
has sometimes hurt my career	2.5	5.0

NOTE: *Percentage of respondents who agree, strongly agree, or somewhat agree with the statement (based on a seven-point scale, strongly disagree to strongly agree).

productivity improvement strategies, and this is consistent with the somewhat lower use of productivity improvement strategies in museums, as shown in Table 11.1. By and large, these ratings support my experience that productivity improvement efforts confer positive outcomes on managers.

The results presented in these tables also show assessments of possible negative impacts. A small minority of municipal respondents agree or strongly agree that productivity improvement creates resistance that has hurt their positions (4.5%), that it is a risky way of advancing one's career (5.0%) and has sometimes hurt their career (5.5%). An additional 8% to 14% "somewhat agree" with these statements. These negative ratings are, on average, somewhat less for social service and museum respondents. The negative consequences of productivity improvement occur as a result of faulty implementation or inappropriate use. For example, strategic planning sometimes backfires in the face of managerial resistance, and adverse publicity also damages the reputation of senior managers. These adverse outcomes imply the need for effective implementation. Respondents with positive assessments of productivity improvement outnumber those with negative ones by a margin of about eight to one.[8]

Middle and Supervisory Managers

Middle managers and supervisors also benefit from productivity improvement efforts. They are often responsible for efforts that affect their departments or work teams rather than the strategic objectives of the organizations for which they work. For example, middle managers and supervisors often use productivity improvement strategies such as customer surveys, quality improvement efforts, process flow analysis, demand analysis, as well as the implementation of new information technologies. They also use motivational strategies for their work teams. In addition, although they are seldom responsible for strategic planning efforts, they can also support senior management productivity improvement efforts by providing coordination, facilitation, and analytical support such as by conducting surveys or performance measurement.

Middle managers and supervisors increase their rewards from productivity improvement efforts by (a) getting prior agreement or approval from senior managers for undertaking productivity improvement, (b) negotiating rewards for undertaking productivity improvements as part of setting annual performance expectations, (c) clarifying support and resources from senior managers for implementing productivity improvement strategies, and (d) developing final reports and other materials that promote their accomplishments and distributing these widely among senior managers.

Many productivity improvement strategies require approval or consent because they change the way that operations are undertaken. Informing upper managers of intended efforts also sets the stage for maximizing returns from such efforts. It places middle managers and supervisors in a position to state and clarify the importance of their actions, to demonstrate commitment to their employer, and to show that they are able to relate their department's objectives to that of broader strategic issues facing the organization. In so doing, it is natural to identify the risks and payoffs of the intended efforts, and to link them to their own performance evaluations.

An important benefit from seeking prior consent is that it may alert middle managers and supervisors to issues or constraints of which they may not be aware. Involving senior managers also helps to secure resources and support. For example, some lower managers or employees may test their manager's resolve by raising concerns or complaints to senior managers about the proposed changes. Getting consent from higher managers prepares the way for them to provide support. Managers may seek agreement about dealing with opposition if it arises, which is easier in cultures of openness rather than fear. The tactic of seeking higher support is also used by senior managers and directors who seek support from their boards or elected bodies. Such statements from senior managers endorse the efforts of managers to implement new productivity improvement strategies. Securing required resources and support helps minimize negative outcomes.

Middle managers and supervisors also build on the outcomes of their efforts to ensure rewards. For example, they make presentations about their efforts at senior managers' meetings or otherwise get reports into the hands of influential managers. They also include reports about their accomplishments in annual performance evaluation activities. Sometimes program clients are asked to speak to senior managers about the accomplishments of lower managers. Middle managers also gain attention by speaking at national or regional conferences about their accomplishments. These activities underscore the accomplishments and abilities of managers, their contribution to the organizations, and the justification of rewards.

Recent Graduates, Generation X-ers

New entrants into organizations often have insufficient authority or responsibility to effect much change. Although sometimes new employees and managers who "hit the ground running" are valued for doing so, in many organizations the culture is such that those who are active or inquisitive or who demonstrate advanced thinking are viewed as "troublemakers" or as "making waves." New employees and managers need to earn their stripes. Productivity improvement can help. Rather than using these strategies to make organizations better—which may be viewed as a little presumptuous as well as dangerous because of a lack of allies—new entrants should support those who are using productivity improvement. Recent graduates contribute to productivity improvement efforts by providing analytical capabilities, such as implementing surveys, analyzing data, assisting in designing performance measures, developing new information technology applications, or assisting those in the use of process flow or demand analysis. Such skills are needed and are often lacking in organizations.

However, some employees fail to seek out opportunities that help promote their competencies. This is a catch-22 situation, in which both employees and organizations withdraw from being proactive in trying to help each other. Organizations underappreciate employees' abilities. This situation is furthered by stereotypes of Generation X-ers, who are recent entrants into the job market. These entrants often give the appearance of being downbeat and apathetic—hardly model employees. The reason for apparent lethargy is disbelief in the possibility of advancement through subsequent promotions. This appearance is unfortunate, because, despite outward appearances, many are hardworking and committed to making a difference. They are also highly technically competent (Tulgan, 1995).

Generation X-ers are apt to want to negotiate their rewards for efforts, but they are also skeptical that organizations have any real rewards to give. Other entrants may question the wisdom of negotiating their rewards—they don't want to antagonize their supervisors. But unless employees speak up about what they want, others will not know what it is that they seek. Managers might, quite reasonably, mistake the absence of complaints for employee satisfaction. The key is timing and approach. New employees need to establish the confidence of their superiors before they can negotiate specific rewards. That confidence is based on establishing attributes such as reliability, technical proficiency, the ability to get along with people, and the ability to see the broader picture of things. Very new employees should communicate their long-term career hopes as well as their desire to learn new skills and the broader picture. Getting involved in productivity improvement strategies is a certain way to demonstrate one's worth and the ability to get along with other employees and managers. Productivity is a good foundation on which to build one's reputation and career.

Summary

This chapter examines the state of productivity improvement and charts future directions. Many productivity improvement strategies are widely in use. Managers believe that productivity improvement enhances their careers and makes them more attractive to their current and other employers. Those who use productivity improvement strategies associate it with professionalism. This chapter discusses future directions in productivity improvement that include a heightened appreciation for ethics, analytical techniques, and the ability to grapple with abstract goals and strategies. This chapter concludes with suggestions for improving the career rewards that managers and employees receive from productivity improvement.

Notes

1. The sample of museums was drawn from the *Official Museum Directory* (1994) and the *Charitable Organizations of the U.S.* (Gale Research, 1992). The sampling frame of museums includes those that employ more than 50 people, and the sampling frame of social service organizations, those that have more than $1.5 million revenue (FY1990) and more than 50 employees (1996), excluding organizations that are funded by these organizations but under separate ownership. The lists of museums and social service organizations include mostly well-known, large organizations in these fields. The respective sample sizes are 148 (museums) and

241 (social service organizations). The median size of museums and social service organizations of respondents are, respectively, 125 and 235 full-time equivalent employees. The mean sizes are, respectively, 212 and 382 employees, which includes a few organizations with more than 1,000 employees. The response rates are 41% and 30%, or 61 and 73 completed surveys. The sample of all cities of more than 50,000 consists of 544 jurisdictions; 232 cities responded for a response rate of 43%. All samples were examined for nonresponse bias. The surveys were sent to the city managers and directors of these nonprofit organizations. About two thirds were completed by the addressee, and the remainder by his or her designee, who invariably holds a senior title. The survey of cities was undertaken in collaboration with J. West.

2. Further analysis also shows that the productivity improvement strategies listed in Table 11.1 are used only somewhat more by larger organizations.

3. See Table 1.2 in Chapter 1. This 1995 survey was only conducted among city managers; no respective data are available for museums and social services.

4. Their analysis also shows that budgetary surpluses are not associated with productivity improvement. Other studies suggest that client complaints and the use of innovations by nearby or affiliated organizations may also spur the use of new productivity improvement strategies. Further barriers are discussed in Chapter 1 and in Ammons (1992).

5. This is based on results from the Myers-Briggs test as used in Keirsey and Bates (1984, pp. 139, 145) on more than 120 MPA students, of whom 85% are practicing managers. More than 80% of these students are found to have an "SJ" temperament, which is more than double that of the general population which is associated with values mentioned in the text. Only four students score as "NT," which is associated with visionary leadership, pursuit of ideas, and being an architect of change.

6. Milestones are also linked to the need for short-term results in implementation by staggering them in such a way that their attainment produces a pattern of frequent accomplishments. They also provide performance measures for change efforts.

7. This does not imply that managers should give "impossible" tasks to managers and employees.

8. Across all three groups, agreement with the statements that productivity improvement has helped careers and makes one more attractive to present employers is positively correlated with using more productivity improvement strategies. For cities, using more strategies is negatively associated with each of the three negative items. These correlations are significant at the 1% level.

References

Ammons, D. (1992). Productivity barriers in the public sector. In M. Holzer (Ed.), *Public productivity handbook* (pp.117-138). New York: Marcel Dekker.

Bardwick, J. (1995). *Danger in the comfort zone.* New York: AMACOM.

Berman, E. (1997). Dealing with cynical citizens. *Public Administration Review, 57*(2), 105-112.

Berman, E., & West, J. (1995). Municipal commitment to Total Quality Management. *Public Administration Review, 55*(1), 57-66.

Berman, E., & West, J. (1997). Managing ethics to improve performance and build trust. *Public Integrity Annual, 2*(1), 21-29.

Brudney, J. (1997). Public administration you can count on . . . *PA Times, 20*(2), 1.

Cohen, S., & Eimicke, W. (1996). Is public entrepreneurship ethical? *Public Integrity Annual, 1*(1), 3-12.

Gale Research. (1992). *Charitable organizations of the U.S.* Detroit, MI: Author.

Gaster, L. (1995). *Quality in public services.* Philadelphia, PA: Open University Press.

Jeavons, T. (1994). Ethics in non-profit management: Creating a culture of integrity. In R. Harman (Ed.), *Handbook of nonprofit leadership and management* (pp. 184-207). San Francisco: Jossey-Bass.

Keirsey, D., & Bates, M. (1984). *Please understand me.* Del Mar, CA: Prometheus Nemisis.

Kraut, A. (1995). *Organizational surveys: Tools for assessment and change.* San Francisco: Jossey-Bass.

Milakovich, M. (1995). *Improving service quality.* Delray Beach, FL: St. Lucie Press.

Official museum directory. (1994). New Providence, RI: Bowker.

Osborne, D., & Plastrick, P. (1997). *Banishing bureaucracy.* Reading, MA: Addison-Wesley.

Rosen, E. (1993). *Improving public sector productivity.* Newbury Park, CA: Sage.

Seidle, L. (1995). *Rethinking the delivery of public services to citizens.* Montreal: Institute for Research on Public Policy.

Tulgan, B. (1995). *Managing Generation X.* Santa Monica, CA: Merritt.

West, J., & Berman, E. (1997). Administrative creativity in local government. *Public Productivity and Management Review, 20*(4), 446-458.

Index